CONCEPTS IN

Strategic Management

SIXTH EDITION

CONCEPTS IN

Strategic Management

SIXTH EDITION

C. Patrick Woodcock
School of Management
University of Ottawa

Paul W. Beamish
Associate Dean, Research
Richard Ivey School of Business
The University of Western Ontario

 **McGraw-Hill Ryerson**

Toronto   Montréal   Boston   Burr Ridge IL   Dubuque IA   Madison WI   New York   San Francisco
St Louis   Bangkok   Bogatá   Caracas   Kuala Lumpur   Lisbon   London   Madrid   Mexico City
Milan   New Delhi   Santiago   Seoul   Singapore   Sydney   Taipei

McGraw-Hill
Ryerson Limited

A Subsidiary of The **McGraw·Hill** Companies

Concepts in Strategic Management
Sixth Edition

ISBN: 0-07-091719-1

1 2 3 4 5 6 7 8 9 10 TR 1 0 9 8 7 6 5 4 3

Printed and bound in Canada

Care has been taken to trace ownership of copyright material contained in this text; however, the publisher will welcome any information that enables them to rectify any reference or credit for subsequent editions.

VICE PRESIDENT, EDITORIAL AND MEDIA TECHNOLOGY: Pat Ferrier
SPONSORING EDITOR: Lenore Gray Spence
MANAGING EDITOR, DEVELOPMENT: Kim Brewster
MARKETING MANAGER: Kelly Smyth
SUPERVISING EDITOR: Jaime Duffy
COPY EDITOR: James Gladstone
PRODUCTION COORDINATOR: Andrée Davis
COMPOSITION: Lynda Powell
COVER DESIGN: Sharon Lucas
COVER IMAGE: Ryan McVay/Photo Disc
PRINTER: Tri-Graphic Printing

National Library of Canada Cataloguing in Publication

Woodcock, C. Patrick
    Concepts in strategic management / Patrick Woodcock. — 6th ed.

Previously published under title: Strategic management.
Includes bibliographical references.
ISBN 0-07-091719-1

    1. Strategic planning—Canada. 2. Industrial management—Canada.
I. Title.

HD30.28.W655 2002   658.4'012'0971   C2002-903730-1

about the author

C. Patrick Woodcock is an assistant professor at the University of Ottawa where he teaches Strategic Management and International Business Strategy. He is the author or co-author of a number of articles, some of which have appeared in *Business Quarterly, Group Decision and Negotiations*, and the *Journal of International Business Studies*. Prior to entering the academic world, he worked for over a decade as a mergers and acquisitions analyst and consultant for a variety of companies including Steetley Plc., Holderbank Corporation, and St. Lawrence Cement. He has received business research awards from the Academy of Management in the United States, the Canadian Exporter's Association, and the Administrative Sciences Association of Canada.

contents

READINGS   188

preface

This textbook has evolved considerably since the first edition in the early 1980s. During this time, business policy and strategy has matured into an important field in the management school curriculum, and the field has developed its own set of analytical approaches. Although this textbook continues to emphasize a general manager's perspective to decision-making, it has broadened in scope to include frameworks and analytical approaches that have been developed specifically for strategic planning and implementation.

We have attempted to keep this textbook concise, yet it is almost double the size of the text portions of previous editions. This enlargement enabled us to expand most chapters in scope and depth, and to create some new chapters. Newly created chapters include topics such as high-tech and Internet strategies, corporate and international strategies, and evaluating strategic performance. Furthermore, the case portion of the textbook has been separated into a stand-alone casebook, edited by Paul Beamish, and entitled "Cases in Strategic Management". This provides greater flexibility to the professor when developing the course, and it enables the cases to be updated in a timely manner. An Online Learning Centre, located at www.mcgrawhill.ca/college/woodcock services both texts, and includes Web links, instructor supplement downloads, and a Case Analysis appendix for student use.

The primary consumer focus for this textbook continues to be the undergraduate student. Their limited work experience requires a resource that provides a straightforward presentation of strategy and its components, with many explanations and examples. This textbook explains concepts in a simple logical manner where strategic notions are broken down into their component parts and defined. This enables students to apply the resulting tools and frameworks quickly and effectively in class. In addition, examples are selected with which students can easily identify. The personal strategy of singer/songwriter, Sarah McLachlan, is one example.

Another important feature of this textbook is its focus on the Canadian business environment. Almost all of the examples used in the textbook are Canadian, such as strategies in not-for-profit entities and the development of international strategies from a relatively small market environment. Furthermore, a number of strategic issues that are important in the Canadian business environment are examined.

Finally, this textbook includes a variety of readings selected from some of the top ranked, pragmatically oriented, business journals. The readings supplement the textbook, particularly when topics are deemed very important to the strategic process and where new strategic ideas have become relevant. A few readings examine Canadian-specific business issues.

C. Patrick Woodcock

acknowledgements

A number of people were important to the successful completion of this textbook. The person most important to its ongoing success over the years is Paul Beamish. Paul wrote the inaugural editions many years ago, and has continued to be instrumental in shaping the textbook's content. He is also editor of the companion casebook that is associated with this textbook.

I would also like to thank the reviewers who spent considerable time providing very helpful suggestions and comments. We solicited and received much useful feedback on the fifth edition of Beamish/Woodcock: *Strategic Management*, as well as on the sixth editions of the newly split Beamish: *Cases in Strategic Management* and Woodcock: *Concepts in Strategic Management*. The reviewers included:

Kamal Argheyd, Concordia University
Raymond Leduc, University of Western Ontario
Alfie Morgan, University of Windsor
Allan Matadeen, Simon Fraser University
Knud Jensen, Ryerson University
David Allwright, Mount Royal College
Maureen Nummelin, Conestoga College

Finally, I would like to thank my family, Trish, Charlie, and Anna.

C. Patrick Woodcock

chapter 1 Strategic Management —an Overview

Business luck is the kind of luck that strikes only when the co-ordinated planning, arithmetic, preparation and patience of the dozens of minds in Power Corp. ... are transformed into action by opportunity.

JIM BURNS, DEPUTY CHAIRMAN OF POWER CORP.

The CityTV philosophy is galactic vision, local touch.

MOSES ZNAIMER, PRESIDENT AND EXECUTIVE PRODUCER OF CITYTV

Businesses and managers are successful for a variety of reasons. Some are the first to develop a product. Some do a very good job at one or two things, while others have developed complex skills, technologies, and systems to support their success. All of these approaches are valid and successful strategies. But how does one develop such a strategy?

The goal of this textbook is to examine the various complexities and approaches to strategy and provide the student with a formalized approach to developing a successful strategy. Strategy can be applied to personal, group, or organizational undertakings, and the tools and processes by which one applies strategies to these different levels in strategy are similar. Therefore, this text, although specializing in business strategy, does provide the student with insight into approaches to developing personal strategies, such as career management strategies.

Developing a good strategy is all about winning, whether it be a business or a personal strategy. Some people are successful because they follow a winning personal strategy in developing their career. Similarly, some top business managers consistently develop successful business plans and execute them effectively. The study of strategic management formalizes concepts and approaches that have been observed to produce business success over the long-term. These strategic approaches are not a substitute for hard work or functional skills. Rather, they are management decision tools aimed at improving a firm's long-term prosperity.

Does strategic planning result in higher performance? Many studies have examined this relationship and the majority of studies have concluded that firms having a formalized strategic planning process outperform those that do not. Furthermore, firms taking a proactive approach to strategy perform better than those that take a passive or reactive approach. This evidence suggests that it is necessary for managers to actively develop a formal, proactive strategic planning process in their firm—for both small and large firms. In this textbook, we provide students with the frameworks, tactics, and processes of strategy that have been developed in this fast developing field.

EXPLAINING STRATEGY—WHAT IS IT?

The word *strategy* derives from the ancient Greek word *strategos*, meaning "the art of the general." This root meaning is still central to the meaning of strategy, as it is the CEO or general manager who ultimately is responsible for planning and executing strategy in the firm.

From a modern day perspective, strategy has been defined in countless ways. For example, the definition of strategy in academia has evolved in a number of ways including:

- In the 1960's business strategy, or policy, was defined as the role of the general manager, where the manager must integrate and coordinate all of the various functions, such as production, marketing, sales, R&D, etc. into a harmonized approach and direction that enabled the firm to achieve a specific objective.
- During the 1980s, strategy was conceived as having two broad responsibilities and processes. These were the formulation and implementation responsibilities of strategy, where formulation involved the planning of strategy and implementation involved the execution of the planned strategy.

More recently, strategy evolved into two different academic research perspectives, each of which stresses an important aspect of strategy as it is conceived today. They are:

- Strategy is the pattern of positions that the firm seeks out or creates for itself in its competitive and market environment. This notion of strategy emphasizes the importance of the external environment of competitors and customers on the selection of an appropriate strategy.
- Strategy is the process by which managers continuously improve competitive resources and capabilities within the firm. This involves developing, acquiring, or allying with important competitive resources, capabilities, assets, knowledge, skills, etc. available to the firm. This perspective emphasizes the importance of continuously developing and improving the ability of the firm to compete effectively both now and in the future.

A broad definition that we think encapsulates many of the important perspectives in strategy and relevant to this textbook is:

- Strategy is the art and science of continuously developing new advantages for the firm so that it effectively executes and competes within its chosen position in the market place and successfully achieves top management's identified objectives, including that of creating value for all stakeholders in the firm.

This definition is helpful because it emphasizes the basic tenant that strategy is about using advantages to effectively compete in a specific market, and thereby accomplish specific objectives. In addition, this definition emphasizes a number of consequential dimensions that include planning versus executing, science versus art, and external market versus internal firm advantage approaches. Most importantly, it emphasizes value creation.

EXAMINING THE DIMENSIONS OF STRATEGY

As suggested in the previous section, strategy has a number of dimensions that provide managers with important perspectives on how to better understand and analyze strategy. These important dimensions are corporate versus business strategy, science versus art, external versus internal nature of strategy, and formulation versus implementation.

Corporate Versus Business Strategy

Strategy is broken into a number of different hierarchical levels as shown in exhibit 1-1 below. These levels, although in reality intimately linked, are studied separately for analytical purposes. The levels, illustrated in exhibit 1-1, are differentiated based upon the nature of the decisions, who makes them, and how the decisions have impact on the firm. Exhibit 1-2 further characterizes the different levels of strategy.

exhibit 1-1 Levels of Strategy

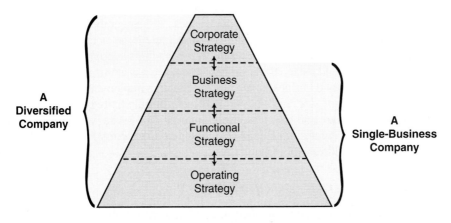

exhibit 1-2 Description of Levels of Strategy

Level of Strategy	Level of Influence	Strategy Makers	Types of Decisions
Corporate Strategy	• Corporate strategies	• Corporate managers and Board members	• Allocation of resources to businesses, and scope of business diversification
Business Strategy	• Business strategies	• Top business managers in company or business division	• Types of products/ markets to be in and the organizational and resource specific attributes required to support the product/ market focus
Functional Strategy	• R&D, finance, marketing, manufacturing, human resource strategies/functions	• Top functional within a business managers	• Types of operational techniques, approaches, and resources that best support the overall business strategy
Operational Strategy	• Plants, teams, sales groups, and individuals within functions	• Individuals within the functions that have responsibility for tasks or decision–making units	• Specific operational tactics, approaches, and resources that support the business and functional strategies

Corporate strategy focuses on decisions related to what types of business the firm should be in and which businesses should they support for growth. The types of questions posed at this level are: Should the firm enter a new business or get out of an old business? To which of its businesses should the firm allocate resources (i.e., capital, equipment, skills, etc.) in the future. This level of strategy is most important for a diversified firm (i.e., a firm owning several different types of businesses). Chapter 9 examines the issues and tools used in corporate strategy.

Business strategy focuses on decisions about how a specific business competes in its particular market for product or service emphasis. This strategy is the principal strategic concern of a manager who is in only one business or manages a single business division in a diversified firm. The business-level strategy is the primary focus of this textbook.

Functional and operational strategies occur in the functional and operational levels of the business. They provide critical input into the formulation of a business strategy and are important tools for implementing the business strategy at the functional and operational levels within the firm. These latter two strategies are not actively studied in this textbook because they are covered elsewhere in the business school curriculum. However, the student must understand these strategies because it is at this level that managers translate the corporate and business strategies for effective implementation.

Another category of strategic analysis is **international strategy**, which is important both at the corporate and business levels. International strategy is concerned with where and how firms enter and manage businesses in international locations. International strategies are addressed in Chapter 9.

The Science and Art of Strategy

Strategy is both a science and an art. The study of strategy emphasizes the science and analytical undertaking of making strategy. However, in reality strategy requires considerable creativity and seasoned wisdom to enable firms to rise above the ordinariness of the industry pack. In many ways, it can be compared to the work of an artist. Many artists have developed a proficiency at producing art using the learned skills of manipulating colour and shape. However, great artists go beyond these abilities by injecting creativity and uniqueness into the process as well as the outcome.

Strategy is very similar in that the techniques and frameworks are taught to many managers, but it is seasoned wisdom and creative talent combined that produce great strategies. An example is Magna's (the auto parts company) original strategy of keeping its auto parts plants as independently owned organizations. This enabled the organizations to foster an entrepreneurial culture that infused each plant with a highly motivated and resourceful employee attitude. This organizational strategy produced tremendous efficiency and inventiveness throughout Magna, enabling it to become the largest auto parts manufacturer in the world.

External Versus Internal Strategic Analysis

The dimension of external versus internal strategic analysis is an important dichotomy in strategy. Almost all research in strategy can be categorized on this basis. The two main strategic paradigms, resource-based and industrial organization (IO) economic theories, are the foundations upon which most strategic frameworks and analytical tools are founded. Resource-based theories examine the development of an effective set of advantages in the form of skills, assets, knowledge, and capabilities that enable a firm to successfully compete against other firms. From a management perspective, this paradigm provides managers with means in which to understand what advantages they should attempt to assemble, and how they should attain and coordinate those advantages to be most effective. These are the issues that managers must deal with on a day-to-day basis, creating and developing abilities within their organization to make it more efficient and effective.

IO economic theories focus on studying the external competitive market, since competitiveness is the single most important influence on financial performance. Managers can use IO theories to assess the competitive pressures in a market, and analyze how they may be able to influence the competitiveness through different strategic moves. These two paradigms provide the basis for the content in the first several chapters in this textbook.

Formulation Versus Implementation

The distinction of formulation versus implementation, or, in management terms, planning versus execution, describes the classical separation of the strategy process into the formulation and implementation stages, which was highlighted in the earlier definition (i.e., the planning versus executing dimension). Strategic formulation is deciding what to do, while implementation of strategy is doing it and achieving results. Some of the considerations that must be assessed within the formulation stages are what should be done and how should it be done. In the implementation stage, managers must decide who should do it, by when, and how it should be coordinated and monitored to ensure the correct results. Exhibit 1-3 provides some of the concepts, issues, and questions that tend to fall into these two process stages. The first half of this textbook focuses on the formulation process, while the latter half focuses more (although not exclusively) on the implementation process.

exhibit 1-3 Planning the Formulation and Implementation in Strategic Management

	Formulation	Implementation
Strategic Business Description	• Deciding what to do	• Doing it & achieving results
Description	• Planning a desired set of objectives, strategic position, and set of competitive advantages that are consistent with the forecasted competitive environment and management preferences as well as developing the appropriate resources, organizational systems, processes, and structure	• Planning how and when to implement the desired strategy in a logical and doable manner • Delineating who should do what by when as delegating and coordinating are vital tasks in the implementation process
Basic Questions Considered	• What business or market/product/service emphasis should the firm take, what competitive advantages or capabilities must it have to take such an emphasis, and where should it take such an emphasis?	• How and when to implement strategic positions, positions, advantages, components, and tactics? • Who should do what by when? • How is the strategy going to be monitored?
Examples of Detailed Questions	• What products should the business focus on? • What type of customer should the business focus on? • What geographic market should the business focus on? • What competitive advantages or skills, capabilities, etc. should the business develop?	• When should various aspects of the strategic change be implemented? • How will the managers overcome political resistance and get employees to embrace the change? • How should the company develop? • How should the resistance to change be handled? • How does the firm control and review strategic action?

In reality, managers do not consciously separate strategy into formulation and implementation stages. Rather, these processes are integrated into the overall strategic process. This is because formulation depends upon implementation and vice versa. A formulated strategy requires management to assess their ability to implement the strategy, and, as a strategy is implemented, uncertainties and new information tend to continuously force management to revisit and alter the formulated strategy. Therefore, in reality, these processes often must be done almost simultaneously to produce an effective overall strategy. The following section describes more appropriately what occurs in a firm's strategy development and execution process.

THE REALITY OF THE STRATEGIC PROCESS FOR MANAGEMENT

Most of this textbook is devoted to formalized strategic analysis and decision making. However, in reality, strategy is much messier than the formulation and implementation decision-making process suggests, as was indicated earlier. In fact, managers are often faced with new situations, very different from that which they had assessed during their formal strategic planning. This forces them to adjust by making decisions outside of the normal strategic planning process. Moreover, these decisions often must be made unexpectedly and quickly. For example, in high-tech industries, customer demands and technological changes may make products obsolete very quickly, requiring managers to make quick decisions on limited information so they effectively adjust strategically.

Exhibit 1-4 illustrates how the strategic process in reality evolves in a firm. As shown, management initially goes through a formal strategic planning process. Such a process usually involves scanning the market and competition as well as reviewing the available and potentially required capabilities the firm may require in the near future. Objectives are set for the upcoming operating period and projections for revenues, profits, and capital expenditures are developed and longer-term strategic tactics and procedures are planned. The result is a planned strategy. However, as managers implement this planned strategy, changes in the market environment, or other surprises, force managers to adjust their strategy. This involves discarding some of their planned strategy (discarded strategy) and adopting emergent strategies appropriate to the new developments in the firm or industry.

There are two important aspects of emergent strategies that managers and students should understand. First, emergent strategies often provide a firm with a tremendous opportunity to gain a competitive advantage because many managers in firms have trouble adjusting quickly enough to these strategic opportunities. Therefore, being able to react quickly and effectively to these opportunities is an advantage. A number of top CEOs, including Jack Welch of GE and Andrew Grove of Intel, have said that the strategic decisions that separate the winners from losers in an industry are not planned strategies but emergent strategic decisions.

The second important aspect of emergent strategies is not only the speed with which the decisions are made but the quality and effectiveness of the decisions. The planned strategic process provides managers with the required information to make these difficult emergent decisions most successfully. Therefore, a formalized planned strategic process is critical in firms because it enables them to make the appropriate emergent strategic decisions. In fact, many firms that are in highly changing environments attempt to formalize this process of emergent strategy by reconsidering and reviewing strategies on a very frequent basis.

exhibit 1-4   The Reality of the Strategic Process

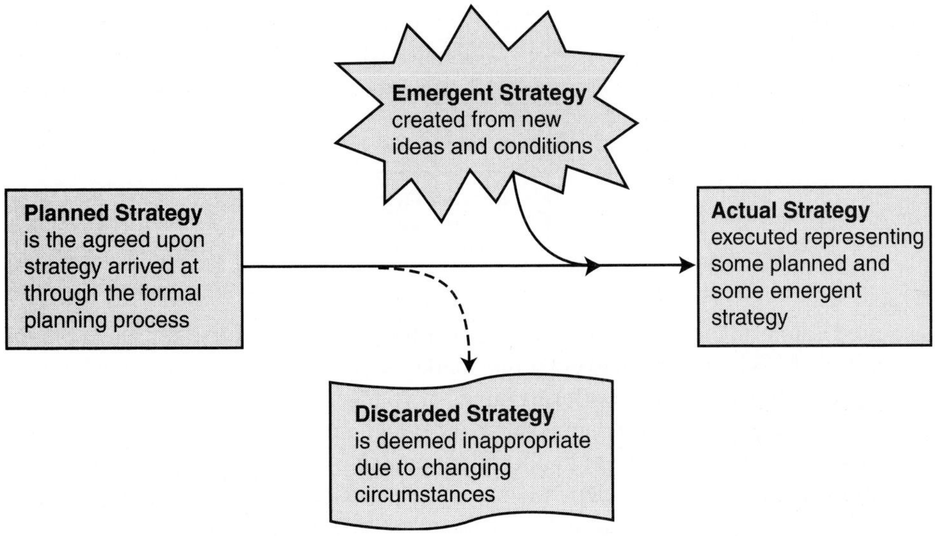

adapted from work by Henry Mintzberg

An example of where a strategy was planned and then changed drastically was the introduction of New Coke in the 1980s. For the previous decade, Coke had slowly been loosing market share to Pepsi. During this period, Pepsi had been using advertising suggesting that, in blind taste tests Pepsi was preferred over Coke. Coke's tests were inconclusive, but R&D came up with a new formula that clearly beat Pepsi in blind taste tests. Using this information, Coke replaced the old formula with a sweeter formula and called it New Coke. The strategic thinking was that the marketing campaign would further heighten the awareness of the Coke brand name, and the sweeter product would have greater customer appeal. However, loyal consumers were very upset at loosing their Classic Coke product and sales began to tank. Within days, Coke management understood they had a problem and quickly reintroduced Classic Coke into the market amid tremendous fanfare and apologies to loyal customers. The eventual strategy was quite successful because the notoriety produced an almost cult-like branding of Classic Coke and Coke actually gained market share from this convoluted strategic process.

A BASIC MODEL FOR STRATEGIC ANALYSIS

The basic underlying model for understanding a firm's strategy emphasizes the two main paradigms of strategic research: the resource-based, and io economics perspectives, illustrated in exhibit 1-5.

As illustrated in exhibit 1-5, managers select a strategy that maximizes market opportunities, minimizes external competitive pressures, and capitalizes on the internal competitive abilities of the firm. Consistently developing this match between the external market characteristics and the internal abilities in the firm is the role of strategy. A good match produces a strategy that maximizes performance.

The analysis of the external market and competitive environment is done both when a company first enters a market and on an ongoing basis. For example, Sears

exhibit 1-5   Basic Paradigm in Strategic Management

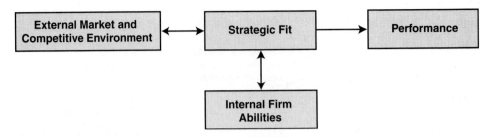

acquired Eatons to enter a new market segment for two reasons. First, it wanted to limit the ability of US competition to enter this market sector in Canada. Second, it believed that more fashionable product offering aimed at younger buyers would complement the offerings at Sears, which were aimed at an older and more staid market segment. Sears was unsuccessful because the higher fashion young buyer market was not well enough developed to support a major department chain in Canada. This example illustrates the strategic assessment of the external market and competitive environment.

Correspondingly, executives must actively manage the internal abilities of the firm so that the firm is competitively superior in its selected market. For instance, many firms are progressively developing a reputation and brand name, skills and organizational capabilities, assets, capital resources, technical innovation, industry specific knowledge, patents, and strong customer and supplier relations, all of which make these firms more efficient and effective relative to their competition. Many new high-tech companies in Canada are striving to build these internal abilities and the lack of such abilities was the downfall of countless e-commerce companies during the past several years.

This process of strategically managing the external competitive environment in conjunction with the internal firm abilities is an ongoing and dynamic challenge for management as illustrated in exhibit 1-5. These internal and external strategic perspectives are not completed independently, but must be done in a mutually coherent way so that strategic decisions and actions are specific to both the external competitive environment and this environment is exploited fully through the development of appropriate internal firm capabilities. It is this unique and dynamic fit between a good external competitive environment and the appropriate firm capabilities that make a firm's strategy attain superior performance. Furthermore, because nothing is static in the business and competitive environment, managers must continually adjust this strategic coherent fit on an ongoing basis.

THE STRATEGY FRAMEWORK

The strategy model illustrated in exhibit 1-5 can be expanded to give us a more detailed framework with which to analyze strategic formulation in companies. This framework, as illustrated in exhibit 1-6, has all of the concepts of the model in exhibit 1-5, plus a new concept called stakeholder preferences. In this framework, the external analysis perspective is the environment concept, the internal perspective is the resources and organizational concepts, and the performance and strategy concepts fill out this framework. This framework also adds the stakeholder and organizational culture preference concept, something that also directly influences strategy as will be explained further in subsequent sections.

In each of the concepts there are components that characterize important issues pertinent to strategy making. These components are the characteristics that managers must analyze in each concept if they want to understand how the concepts influence strategy and ultimately influence the performance of the firm. The various components in the strategy and performance concepts are examined in this chapter, and the components in the other concepts are examined in subsequent chapters.

Students almost always start by using this framework to assess the present strategy of a firm in a static strategic sense. This type of assessment is a useful starting point. However, it is also important to assess the possible dynamic factors of strategy using this model. For example, what would happen if competition did this or if the market did that, and how the firm could adjust its strategy dynamically to fit these new and different conditions? This dynamic assessment of strategy is much more difficult and time consuming than the static assessment, but it is where managers can develop progressive strategic tactics and be fully versed in the possible emergent strategic options they may face in the near term.

What is important to understand about the concepts and components in this framework is that they all must fit or be in accord with one another to provide a successful strategic result. By "fit," we mean that the organizational elements must be appropriate for the resource components that are in the firm, and then these must supply the appropriate competitive advantages for the firm to compete effectively in its selected

exhibit 1-6   A Strategic Management Conceptual Framework

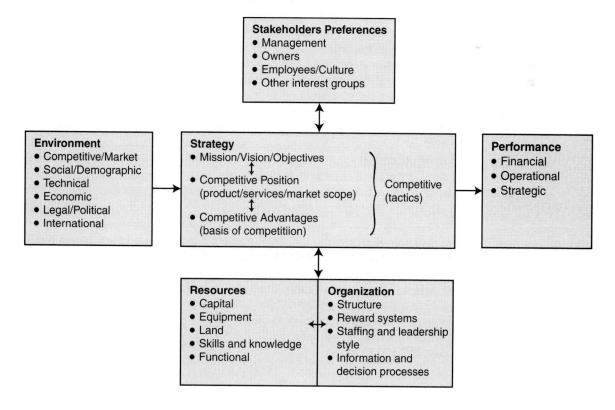

competitive position in the market. Finally, the competitive position selected by management should be in a competitive and market environment that enables the firm to grow and develop given its competitive advantages. If any one of the components does not fit with all of the others, then superior performance will not result. Therefore, when you read through the following explanations of the concepts and components of strategy, attempt to understand this notion of "fit" that is so vital to a good strategy.

COMPONENTS OF STRATEGY

There are three principal components of strategy formulation, as is shown in the strategy concept in exhibit 1-6: (1) mission/vision/objectives, (2) competitive position (i.e., market/product/service emphasis), (3) competitive advantage (i.e., basis of competition). In addition, there are competitive tactics that constitute a dynamic implementation aspect of strategy.

Each of these concepts is explained more fully in the following sections, and an example is provided that more fully clarifies the components.

Mision and Vision/Objectives

In many of the more successful organizations, there is a clear sense of "who we are and where we are going." A firm's mission answers these questions: Who are we? and What business are we in? A firm's vision is the top management's perspective of what direction the firm should take in the future. It is important that the management have a sense for both of these strategic issues, and that they communicate them clearly and effectively to the firm's other stakeholders, such as the owners, customers, and employees. It provides these stakeholders, and, in particular, workers in the organization, with a sense of urgency about competition, pride in the organization, and it motivates them to achieve on a task–by–task basis in an effort to achieve the firm's future vision.

The organization's vision or purpose can be translated into specific measurable performance targets. These objectives typically relate to profitability, growth, return on investment, market share, technological strength, and so forth. In addition, there are "soft" goals and objectives. These might include such things as benefits to society, employee welfare, and management autonomy. Knowledge of the existence of a "soft" counterpart to "hard" terms is essential if one is to have a more complete understanding of an organization

A firm's vision and objectives are intimately linked to the other strategic components because the vision and objectives describe the desired strategic results for the future. The other strategic components govern what, how, and when these various objectives are attainable. An abbreviated example of a firm's mission, vision, and objectives is described in exhibit 1-7. This example Kinnikinnick Foods Inc. is a relatively small baking products firm that specializes in gluten and lactose free foods (i.e., foods that are free from wheat and milk products). This firm was awarded the New Venture Award of Distinction by the Alberta Chamber of Commerce in 2001 and was nominated as a finalist for the 2002 Alberta Business Awards of Distinction and the 2002 Premier's Award of Distinction. In its ten years of existence, this private company has grown from a small kiosk operation in the Edmonton Farmer's market to having a retail store of 2,500 sq. ft. and a production plant of over 15,000 sq. ft.

exhibit 1-7 Kinnikinnick Foods Inc.

Mission/Vision/Objectives: Kinnikinnick's mission is to provide celiac's and people having special dietary requirements with uncontaminated, risk free food products. Management has focused on supplying the highest quality food, but that is also pleasing to the palette. Kinnikinnick's objectives for growth are to continually expand both geographically and in product scope, although, within the restrictive diet food category. Annually, management in this private company has developed specific financial and non-financial goals such as revenue growth and consumer satisfaction rates.

Competitive Position: The market and products that Kinnikinnick focuses on is the gluten and lactose free food market niche, and which includes on celiac, autistic, and food sensitive customers. The product selection consists of 120 brands of breads, cookies, bagels, muffins, mixes, cereals, cakes, soups, sauces, desserts, donuts, snack items, and so forth. Kinnikinnick further specializes in developing extremely good tasting products (something unusual to this type of food category). The prices are moderate to high and they are distributed and sold throughout all regions of North America.

Competitive Advantages: A very important competitive advantage that Kinnikinnick has is its strong and continually expanding brand and product reputation. This brand reputation was developed over the past ten years through its consistent adherence to the highest quality standards and innovative and flavourful product development. Kinnikinnick also has a modern well-organized production facility that enables it to manufacture these products efficiently and effectively. Kinnikinnick has developed a strong retail distribution network throughout the US and Canada, and sells products through mail–order and over the Internet. Kinnikinnick has also developed a technological advantage over many of its competitors; indeed, its Web site has been nominated for several awards. Other advantages include the strong relations Kinnikinnick has developed with customer groups by working with medical and sponsoring agencies on dietary solutions to specific problems. Kinnikinnick also has discussion groups on the Web and disseminates medical and dietary information for these groups. Finally, Kinnikinnick is constantly improving its recognition and reputation with these groups by sponsoring community activities, including funding a children's summer camp for celiac's and autistic children. From an organizational perspective, Kinnikinnick has created an organizational culture that cares about both its customers and products, which ensures that they receive the highest quality service and products.

Competitive Tactics: Kinnikinnick has used a number of tactics to develop its competitive position and competitive advantages. The tactic of developing alliances has been a successful tactic in its growth. Kinnikinnick has developed alliances with community groups, health food advocates, and associations representing various medical interests. In addition, it has used the tactic of growing and promoting from within to develop an organization with a strong culture and set of competitive advantages that have constantly evolved. This internal growth tactic is particularly useful when a firm has very unique competitive advantages in comparison with the tactic of acquiring competitive advantages externally.

A clear strategic mission and vision are particularly important in not-for-profit organizations because they are driven by their duty to the community and society. Thus, workers must understand this duty clearly because they are not working for the profit motive. However, in not-for-profit organizations, translating the mission and vision into a clear statement can be very messy. The lack of a clear profit motive means that many other objectives, some possibly inconsistent with each other, are pushed on the organization by the different funding and customer stakeholders. Therefore, it is vital that all employees, volunteers, donors, and customers understand and agree upon a consistent mission and vision statement, as well as objectives.

Competitive Position

A second component of strategy is a firm's competitive position, or positions if the firm is diversified into several businesses. Competitive position is defined as the firm's market/product/service emphasis, and it can be described as the location and type of customer it services, the product and service attributes that the customers it focuses upon value, and its market/product/service emphases relative to other competitors.

Competitive positions acknowledge that few companies can be everything to everybody in a market, and, in fact, research suggests that there are four generic competitive positions that tend to be profitable for firms. Exhibit 1-8 illustrates these generic competitive positions, which are produced by differing product/market scopes and product/service value. The product/market scope indicates the diversity of product markets that the firm focuses upon, and the product/service value represents the added value that the customers perceive is present in the product and service package being sold.

exhibit 1-8 Generic Competitive Positions

Product/Market Scope	Product/Service Value	
	Low Cost	**Differentiation**
Breadth	Breadth/ Low Cost	Breadth/ Differentiated
Focus	Focused or Niche/ Low Cost	Focused or Niche/ Differentiated

Explanations and examples of these dimensions follow.

A **customer focus strategy** entails having a competitive position that focuses on specific set of customers of niche. An example is a travel agency that focuses on high-risk adventures, or skin divers.

A **customer breadth strategy** is when a firm has a wide offering of products that appeal to a breadth of markets and types of customers. An example is Air Canada, which offers first class, business, and economy fares on most of its routes, but also offers discount and charter services through separate branded subsidiaries.

A **low cost strategy** naturally focuses the firm to be competitively positioned in the low cost market of the industry. An example of a low cost strategy is Wal-Mart, Costco, or Westjet Airlines.

Firms that take a **differentiation strategy** attempt to provide the customer with valued yet distinctive products or services that other competitors are not providing. Examples of this strategic approach are Holt Renfrew, Birks Jewelry Stores, and the Concorde air service between New York and London.

These competitive positions ensure that the firm directs its efforts towards a specific market segment and type of customer, and that its competitive advantages both efficiently and effectively provide its customers with the appropriate perceived value offering. These generic competitive positions are discussed further in Chapter 4.

Geographic location and scope is another important dimension of competitive position, particularly when considering international strategy. The example in exhibit 1-7, Kinnikinnick Foods, has a geographic competitive position that encompasses all of North America. Kinnikinnick's competitive position in the market place is more aptly described as high quality, specialized diet foods for celiac, autistic, and food sensitive customers. It is important to note that Kinnikinnick's selection of a competitive position in the market has significant growth and minimal competition both of which are significant to its success as an entrepreneurial company.

A firm's mission/vision/objectives and competitive position are intimately linked because managers must decide whether the firm's competitive position (i.e., market/product/service emphasis) will provide it with the desired growth and performance levels and fulfill its vision as a company. If the competitive position is not going to provide such growth, then either the objectives must be changed or the competitive position must be changed. Both the existing and the potential range and focus of market/product/service alternatives must be considered in analyzing possible competitive positions. Exhibit 1-9 delineates some of the alternative market and product/service alternatives one should examine when considering possible new competitive positions.

exhibit 1-9   Competitive Position Growth Alternatives

Product/Service Alternatives	Market Alternatives			
	Reduced Market	Existing Market	Expanded Market	New Market
Reduced Product/Services				
Existing Product/Services				
Modified Product/Services				
New Product/Services				

Competitive Advantages

The third component of strategy is the firm-specific competitive advantages that enable the company to compete effectively in a specific competitive position. These competitive advantages represent the bases upon which a firm competes in its industry and market. Clearly, the competitive advantages are important because they enable the firm to occupy a competitive position. However, these advantages also are important because they characterize how easily and quickly a firm will meet its strategic objectives. A firm with stronger competitive advantages will achieve more challenging strategic objectives than a company with relatively weak competitive advantages. In this context, competitive advantages are relative to those that competitors have. However, examples of strong competitive advantages include highly valued product patents, highly trained managers and workers, or a mix of capabilities that provide synergies that other companies have trouble duplicating. The competitive advantages in a company originate from the resources and organizational design and capabilities as is illustrated in exhibit 1-8.

The example in exhibit 1-7 describes Kinnikinnick's competitive advantages. These are principally related to attributes that provide the company with specialized skills to manufacture products, and to service its value-added niche customers. More specifically, it understands the gluten and lactose free product and market sector, it has high quality and delicious products, a recognized brand name, a large, efficient manufacturing plant, and strong relationships with its specialized customer segment and distributions channels that service these customers. These advantages enable Kinnikinnick to be both the lowest cost and recognized highest quality gluten and lactose free baker in Canada, which is its competitive position. These advantages also enable the firm to achieve its desired growth and profitability objectives.

Some of the questions related to the various levels of strategic decision-making at the corporate, business, and international levels are described in exhibit 1-10. These questions attempt to illustrate the practical decision-making emphasis both from a firm competitive position(s) and competitive advantages perspective at these various levels.

Competitive Tactics and Implementation

Another component of strategy is the competitive tactics that enable the managers to execute the strategy. Competitive tactics are the means by which management accomplishes various strategic objectives. For example, if the objective is to expand one's competitive position, then a variety of competitive tactics could be used, including growing internally into a new geographic region or acquiring a competitor having a broader product scope. Also, management can use a variety of tactics to obtain additional competitive advantages, such as training present employees on new techniques, or hiring experts from competitors. Thus, tactics are important methods and courses of actions for altering strategic direction or initiating strategic change.

exhibit 1-10   The Relationship Between Strategic Component Variables and Strategic Hierarchical Level

Level of Strategy	Questions Related to Competitive Position	Questions Related to Competitive Advantages
Corporate Strategy	• Is the firm's competitive position(s) good from an investment perspective? • Will the firm's portfolio of competitive positions satisfy the corporate objectives? • Should the firm consider either investing or divesting in a business?	• Do the competitive advantages in the various businesses that the firm holds provide synergy to one another? • Can the firm provide corporate level competitive advantages such as financial acumen to the individual businesses?
Business Strategy	• Would the business's performance be enhanced if the competitive position was changed? • Does the business's competitive position satisfy the firms objectives?	• Do the competitive advantages support the business's competitive position? • Can the firm improve its business competitive advantages?
International Strategy	• When entering a new country, what competitive position should the firm seek? • Does the new international competitive position satisfy the firm's objectives?	• Does the firm have adequate home-based competitive advantages to move into international markets? • Does the firm have enough international competitive advantages, such as organizational control capabilities and market and cultural knowledge, to enter an international market?

Competitive advantages and tactics are intimately linked because a firm's competitive advantages often provide it with the ability to effectively carry out tactics, yet these tactics then enable the firm to obtain more and better competitive advantages. For example, some companies, such as Cisco, have become very good at acquiring other firms, a competitive tactic. Yet it is the knowledge, experience and skill of the managers, a competitive advantage that enables the firm to be an effective acquirer and obtain more competitive advantages. Competitive tactics are discussed throughout this textbook.

EVALUATING STRATEGIC PERFORMANCE

The ultimate evaluation of a firm's strategy is its performance over the long-term. This is illustrated in exhibit 1-7. When assessing a firm's strategy, performance outcomes should be examined because they provide evidence of the quality of a strategy—both the formulation and implementation.

There are three basic types of performance indicators: financial, operational, and other strategic indicators. Exhibit 1-11 describes these various performance indicators. Financial indicators are broad performance measures that provide one with an indication of how the firm is doing financially. Operational performance indicators enable the analyst to focus on evaluating and comparing specific operational aspects of the firm that are relevant to its competitive advantage. For example, a service firm depends upon the efficiency and effectiveness of its people. Therefore, sales per employee may be an important operational indicator to examine. Furthermore, it is critical to look at both static comparative indicators as well as their trends over time. Other strategic (non-numerical) indicators involve subjective examination of information provided to the manager. This information could be in the form of dissatisfied customers, unhappy employees, or strategic changes or misalignments. This information usually requires subjective assessment, yet it is useful because it is often a precursor to financial or operational performance deterioration.

exhibit 1-11   Performance Indicators

Type of Performance Indicator	Measurement Tools
Financial Indicators	• Financial values and ratios based on standards or competitive comparisons *Examples:* Debt to equity ratio, profitability ratios, (see Appendix: Case Analysis for more)
Operational Indicators	• Operational measures are values and ratios that indicate the operational efficiency and effectiveness of the firm. These measures are often used to measure comparatively the firm's key operational competitive advantages relative to its prime competitors *Examples:* Sales to employee, sales to assets, R&D expenses to sales, market share (see Appendix: Case Analysis for more)
Other Strategic Indicators	• Strategic measures and non-numerical measures are more abstract and subtle in nature. They involve such things as the perceived strategic fit between the various components by various experts in the field, the enthusiasm of employees or employee complaints, supplier or customer complaints, etc.

A relatively new performance evaluation tool is benchmarking. Benchmarking is a technique that is used by companies to evaluate their functional and operational level efficiencies and effectiveness relative to the best in the world. Establishing a benchmarking program involves comparing your operations to firms deemed to have the best of the different types of operations being assessed. For example, if a firm wants to benchmark its purchasing function, it would find firms having world class purchasing operations and assess the differences between its operations and the deemed best operations. This type of program not only enables the firm to compare its performance with other's, but it also enables the firm to observe and learn about how possible improvements can be implemented.

Some other key questions to ask as part of the process of reviewing and evaluating a strategy are:

- Is there internal consistency between the components of the strategy (i.e., do the goals/objectives, product/market scope, and basis of competition all fit together)?
- Is the strategy appropriate in light of threats and opportunities in the environment?
- Is the strategy appropriate in light of the available resources?
- To what extent does the strategy satisfy managerial preferences and values?
- What are the key tasks arising out of the strategy and has the organization been designed so that these tasks are performed?

Further discussion on business performance is provided in Chapter 11.

EXAMPLES OF SUCCESSFUL STRATEGIES

Two examples of successful strategies follow: the first is the strategy of an individual developing a career strategy; the second is a corporate strategy. These examples demonstrate how people and firms actively manage their competitive position and competitive advantages over time to enable them to become successful. You will note that both of these examples involve evidence of conscious planning (i.e., intended strategy) as well as an evolutionary approach to developing a strategic position and specific competitive advantages to support that position (i.e., emergent strategy).

exhibit 1-12   A Personal Strategic Example—Sarah McLachlan

Sarah McLachlan, born on January 28, 1968 in Halifax, Nova Scotia, began her music career inauspiciously as a young ukulele player. Her first career success came at a local Kiwanis Music & Singing Festival where she won for her rendition of "Where the Bee Sucks, There Lurk I." She broadened her musical talents during these early years by studying some classical guitar, piano, and voice at the Nova Scotia Conservatory of Music.

At age 17, she joined a new-wave band called October Game and almost immediately a recording company offered her a contract after noticing her lyrical voice. Two years later, she accepted a contract with Nettwerk Productions and moved to Vancouver where Nettwerk is based. Both she and Nettwerk recognized her raw musical talent, but they also realized she had no distinct musical style and no song writing experience. Therefore, the "Sarah project" was started, which paired Sarah with several highly talented musical score and lyric writers. The musical style that evolved was a blend of Nova Scotian Celtic with a more contemporary pop and folk sound.

Her musical talent continued to evolve during the late 1980s and early 1990s, a period in which she determinedly upgraded her team including band members, support staff, and musical creative collaborators. She produced three albums and they garnered moderate success, although almost all in Canada. Over the next decade, she refined her distinct musical style to reflect a more modern pop flair resembling a cross between Sinead O'Connor and Joni Mitchell. The resulting sound was distinctive, but tapped into a mainstream market segment of young listeners, particularly young women.

Her perseverance and evolving talent began to pay off in the mid 1990s. In 1993, she and her manager carefully targeted a North American tour aimed at her young fans across the US. She followed this with the recording of a song for a Hollywood film in 1995. The song provided her with her first North American hit single. This target marketing approach was the beginning of her successful development of a highly loyal fan base calling themselves the "Fumblers."

This early success left Sarah in "a writing rut," and rather than stagnate she came up with a vision: she would tour with other female artists and the profits would go toward women's charities. Her managers and producers disagreed, explaining that a concert having multiple female bands would not lead to a successful tour. However, Sarah stuck with her vision, and in 1996, Lilith Fair, an all women's concert tour was kicked off. This tour became the most successful concert tour in the history of music, grossing over US $60 million and raising in excess of $1.5 million for women's shelters and domestic violence. Sarah's strategy of differentiating herself as a women's advocate and providing a venue for top women artists to push their music, made her a bona fide pop star.

Sarah went on to win two Grammies in 2000, numerous Junos, and a variety of other artistic awards. She has also become an officer of the Order of Canada and has won numerous business awards. In her nomination as Pacific Canada Entrepreneur of the Year Award, she was described as a successful businessperson for two reasons. "One, she has a valuable and unique product – her undeniable talent as a musician and singer, plus the distinct style that she has developed provide her with this valuable unique product. ... Two, despite the fact she did not start out as a businessperson, she has had the wherewithal to surround herself with qualified people and school herself in the ramifications of profit and loss." A third reason is her ability to combine marketing and other promotional attributes enabling her to focus so effectively on the young women's market segment.

McLachlan's corporate empire consists of three components: Never Get off the Boat Touring Inc, which manages tours; Amp Merchandising, which looks after merchandising (in 1998 alone, merchandising raked in an estimated $48 million); and the McLachlan Foundation, which manages philanthropy, most of which are grants to struggling musicians and artists.

In 2000, Sarah decided to take some time off to start a family, and her fans wait patiently for her to make a return to the stage.

The example in exhibit 1-12 describes how Sarah McLachlan evolved her strategy for many years. She developed musical talents at a very early age and continued to expand these talents throughout her career. Her style of music, or her competitive position in music, changed to accommodate her musical talents (i.e., her competitive advantages). This competitive position, a position called "chick pop music" by Rolling Stone magazine, had limited competition because no other musicians had focused exclusively on this customer group. The competitive advantages that she brought to this genre were a complex mixture of singing talent, youthful good looks, a strong backup band, creative talent, evolving entrepreneurial abilities, and a wonderful ability to understand the market. Her understanding of this market enabled her to create Lilith Fair, even when her most trusted advisors said, "don't do it"—largely because nobody had done it before. She also built up her brand image by establishing herself as the leader of Lilith Fair and focusing on music specific to her female audience. To even further enhance this image, she contributed generously to local female charities, such as breast cancer and shelters for single mothers. Other advantages that she brought to her business were her natural entrepreneurial abilities, employees that aided her with management details, marketing help for her ancillary products (e.g., hats, shirts, etc.) where much of her money is made, and technical expertise that enabled her to develop a Web site that has won numerous awards. In conclusion, Sarah evolved her competitive advantages to the point where they were focused very effectively on a market that was primed for growth and particularly appropriate to her competitive advantages.

Exhibit 1-12 is not a complete picture of Sarah McLachlan's strategic approach. She has not revealed some personal aspects of her strategy, such as her mission, vision, and objectives. However, we can summarize her strategy in general terms:

Mission/Vision/Objectives

Sarah has not clearly stated her career aspirations and goals. However, she appears to have a vision of herself as a leader in the women's music sector, and a mission to aid women through her music. Her career objective, ultimately, appears to be to want recognition as an internationally renowned singer.

Competitive Position

Sarah has positioned herself in a genre of music that is fundamentally rock and roll, but it also has overtones of Celtic and folk roots. Her music is focused on a female audience, although a large audience has embraced it in retail sales.

Competitive Advantages

Sarah has a variety of advantages: a unique singing voice, production and music writing supporting talent, backup band, an understanding of the women's music market, an understanding of the trends in music, a motivation to become better at singing and business, etc.

Competitive Tactics

Sarah has used a number of competitive tactics, but probably one of the most important is her ability to ally with other people that assist her with the necessary skills, abilities, recognition, etc. She has done this by using backup people, such as writers and producers, and, through Lilith Fair, she has aligned herself with other major female singers, which has aided her tremendously in developing a brand recognition around the world. This is an unusual tactic, but one that has pushed her to the top extraordinarily fast.

exhibit 1-13   A Corporate Strategic Perspective—Bombardier Inc.

Bombardier was founded in 1942 by Armand Bombardier, an auto mechanic who worked out of his rural garage. For the first decade, he custom manufactured snow vehicles for resource exploration. As designs evolved, he developed the personal ski mobile, and sold the first Ski–Doo in 1959. Throughout the 1960s and early 1970s, Bombardier focused on growing this niche-based business. However, by the 1970s, intense competition had developed and the weather uncertainties made the industry highly cyclical. Several difficult years almost forced Bombardier into bankruptcy during this period.

From this difficulty, Bombardier realized expansion was imperative. The first opportunity for expansion came unexpectedly from the City of Montreal, which needed rolling stock for its new subway. Bombardier bid and won the contract, despite having a higher bid than the competition. This was the beginning of Bombardier's development of an important competitive advantage, the ability to effectively work with, negotiate, and influence government agencies. In Quebec, working with the government is extremely important because it influences policy and financial decisions through their ownership of La Société général de financement du Québec and Caisse de depot et placement du Québec, both of which are among the largest financial institutions in Canada. Later, these financial institutions were important investors in some of the acquisitions made by Bombardier. Bombardier also developed strong federal government relations with a series of Quebec-based prime ministers and a predominantly French-speaking civil service.

Bombardier then purchased MLW-Worthington, a Montreal based locomotive and light rail manufacturer. Bombardier then went on to win a number of light rail contracts throughout North America based on their marketing prowess and manufacturing effectiveness. Bombardier's marketing prowess was based on studying and asking the buyers (i.e., governments) what they wanted rather than attempting to sell a specific solution that encompassed its technology. In reality, Bombardier did not have a technology because they lacked research and development. But, this deficit provided them with the advantage of being able to explore any technical solution, while its competitors were often married to "their solutions." Bombardier then licensed the necessary technology.

Other opportunities for diversification presented themselves throughout the next decade including shipbuilding. However, in 1986, they purchased Canadair a troubled, relatively small Canadian airplane manufacturing firm. Over the next decade and a half, they completed almost 20 acquisitions in the rail and aerospace industries. Rail related acquisitions were made in France, Belgium, United States, Germany, Mexico, Canada, and Britain; and aerospace acquisitions were made in Northern Ireland, Canada, and United States. Of the more than a dozen acquisitions and many more joint ventures completed, almost all involved negotiations with local governments either for additional financing, ownership, or marketing related benefits.

Bombardier's ability to develop strong government relations became a core competitive advantage in both of these businesses. Not only were government relations important during the purchase of these entities, but export financing is required for almost all sales deals. In the rail industry, and often in the aerospace industry, the buyer is a government owned entity, and often financing is required for technical and operational related developments to help moderate the risks in these high investment, cyclical businesses. Clearly, having an ability to work with governments and having strong relationships to people high up in many different government bodies around the world became a very important competitive advantage for Bombardier. Bombardier also benefited from a strategy that specialized in marketing effectiveness and manufacturing efficiency, but which outsources research and development. This strategy provided it with unique flexibility when all of the other companies in these industries focused on research and development competitive advantages. Finally, Bombardier evolved into specialized niches within the rail and aerospace industry, both of which had high growth, and at least initially, little competition. Bombardier's niche within the rail industry was light transit systems and within the aerospace industry it became short and medium haul jets.

Bombardier united these businesses with a lean and aggressive corporate management group that continuously demanded improvements in competitive advantages through tactics, such as Economic Value Assessment, Six Sigma quality control, and continuous new product development in every business. Therefore, through a process of trial and error, knowledge and effort, Bombardier learned how to put together a winning strategy involving unique competitive positions and matching competitive advantages.

The result of this unique strategic evolution is a multi-billion dollar globe-spanning corporation that has provided returns to its investors in excess of 20 percent annually over the last two decades. Bombardier revenues more than doubled during the period from 1998 to 2001, and, in 2001, were in excess of $16 billion. Profitability has similarly doubled over this four-year period of time. The company has plants in all continents, serving every region. Clearly, it has become one of Canada's premier business success stories.

Exhibit 1-13 illustrates how a corporate strategy involves pursuing a unique competitive position that enables the firm to have competitive advantages that support all of the positions focused upon by the firm. Bombardier carefully crafted its competitive positions in unique and relatively uncompetitive ways, at least at first (i.e., at first there was little competition in its selected competitive positions), niche positions, the recreational vehicle, train, and aerospace business niches. Bombardier simultaneously developed unique sustainable competitive advantages in government relations, technical flexibility, marketing effectiveness, and manufacturing efficiency. In particular, its ability to influence and work with governments was and continues to be extraordinary. This advantage was developed over time by hiring people with strong government knowledge and relations, as well as continually trying to enhance these relationships throughout the world. Bombardier also developed a unique marketing and technical advantage, which is that it has never developed the fundamental technologies required in its train and aerospace businesses. Rather, Bombardier purchased or licensed these technologies as it needed them, which provided it with a number of advantages including: learning what the customer wants and then getting the technology, which ensures that the product best suits the customer's needs; it does not have to spend on technology prior to its use in an actual customer sale; and it has minimal risk associated with developing technologies that are not going to work. Bombardier also built up complementary competitive advantages in marketing, brand reputation, and manufacturing and service management. Therefore, the overall set of competitive advantages provides advantages to each of its businesses, enabling it to focus on developing specific competitive advantages while simultaneously being in several different businesses.

The examples of Sarah McLachlan and Bombardier also demonstrate how strategy is about continually evolving and improving competitive positions and advantages on an ongoing basis because that is what competitors are doing.

A PRIMARY ANALYSIS TOOL FOR ASSESSING STRATEGIES

A basic tool for analyzing a firm's competitive position and advantages is called SWOT analysis, which is an abbreviation for Strengths, Weaknesses, Opportunities, and Threats analysis. The OT portion of the analysis assesses impinging opportunities and threats on the firm's competitive position that exist in the firm's competitive industry and market environment. The ST portion of the analysis assesses the strengths and weaknesses of the firm's competitive advantages, which is discussed more fully in Chapter 3. Generally speaking, the OT is done prior to the SW because the competitive advantage strengths and weaknesses are examined in relation to the opportunities and threats that are present in the firm's competitive environment. This is a relatively simple analysis tool compared to the many more sophisticated tools discussed in Chapter 2. However, the expedience with which managers can apply it make SWOT an important preliminary analysis tool for many companies. Exhibit 1-14 illustrates some of the issues considered within a SWOT analysis.

Numerous firms initiate the analysis of strategic issues and decisions using SWOT analysis. For example, Wal-Mart examines all of its decisions using SWOT analysis. Wal-Mart uses it only as an initial analysis tool to see whether an acquisition, new location, or other operational change may provide it with an opportunity, or the ability to thwart a threat, or the adroitness to upgrade its internal competitive advantages (i.e., strengths and weaknesses).

exhibit 1-14 Examples of Questions for SWOT Analysis

External Competitive Opportunities for a Company	External Competitive Threats Against a Company
• Competition is divesting out of the firm's competitive position • Substitutes have had to refocus their marketing strategy because they can not compete in your competitive position • New technology has been developed that is particularly suited for your product or process • The market for your product is growing because of greater acceptance of your product • Customers' needs are changing that is particularly appropriate to the products and services that you offer • Key suppliers are becoming much more prolific and capable	• Competitors entering an industry • A new substitute product is developed that may threaten your product • New technology has negatively altered the effectiveness and/or value of your product to the consumer • Customers' tastes have changed and your product is declining in market share • International competitors are moving into your geographic region • Suppliers have decided to discontinue the products and services that are necessary to build your product • The economy has turned bad and interest rates have skyrocketed upward

Internal Competitive Strengths of a Company	Internal Competitive Weaknesses of a Company
• The company has considerable financial strength • The company's location is advantageous • The products have a strong brand reputation • The managers in the firm are particularly able • The firm has a strong distribution system • The company has very strong R&D abilities & good patents • The sales force is adept & has excellent customer relations • The firm has an excellent production process. • The labourers in the firm are particularly skilled and experienced	• The company is weak financially • The product & service of the company is not well regarded, or does not have any brand reputation • The firm does not have many skilled managers • The production & product technology is not proprietary • The firm's locationis distant from the key market and suppliers • The distribution of the firm is poor • The firm does not have enough skilled or experienced labourers

THE STRATEGIC MANAGEMENT PROCESS

Exhibit 1-6 graphically illustrated how the various notions of strategy are linked. Another way of examining these notions of strategy is in the context of the linear decision-making process that managers broadly take when they develop their firm's strategy. Exhibit 1-15 illustrates how the various components in the previous framework (exhibit 1-6) are processed in a logical decision-making approach. What is important to note about these components is that they must all fit or match the other components for the overall strategy to be successful, just as was described in the prior framework. Fit is an important aspect of a good strategy and without it performance suffers.

Note that the process illustrated in exhibit 1-15, is a classic prescriptive approach to developing strategy. Managers and organizations clearly have different strategic processes that interface with other processes, such as budgeting, marketing research, and so on. This means that the below process can be very different from firm to firm. Furthermore, the below process suggests an orderly and neat strategic process. However, as we saw in the case of Coke, strategy is often a nonlinear task where several stages of the process are done simultaneously and feedback to previous

exhibit 1-15   The Strategic Management Process Framework

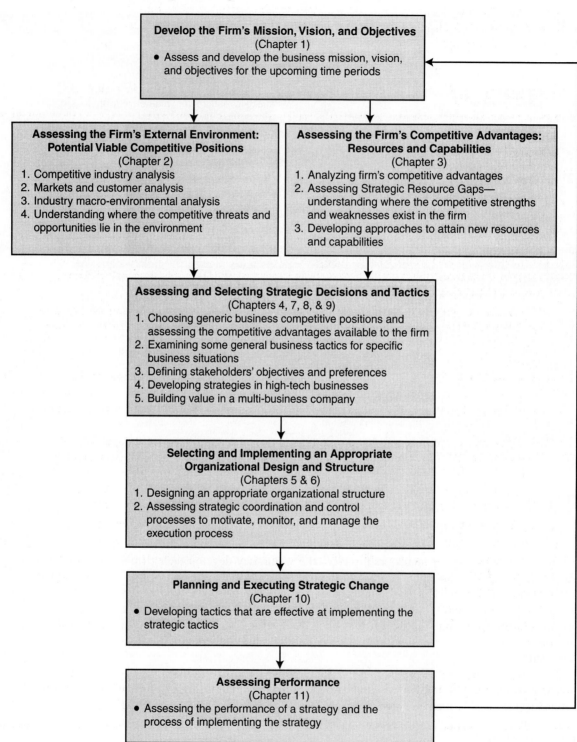

stages can occur at any point. This suggests that managers must be organized, yet flexible and probe alternative processes and approaches when developing strategy. Finally, the strategic process must be open and candid to ensure that the information being assessed is done so in an unbiased manner.

Summary of The Strategy Framework and Process

Dimensions of Strategy

- Corporate versus business
- Science versus art
- External versus internal
- Formulation versus implementation

Elements of Strategy

1. **External Competitive and Market Environment**—the setting within which the firm does business. It is made up factors such as competition, market and customers, technology, economics, and demographics

2. **Firm's Stakeholders' Preferences**—is the interested parties' preferences with respect to the firm and its strategy. Some important stakeholders are top management, owners, and labour unions

3. **Strategy**
   - Mission, Vision, and Objectives—sets the firm's direction for all of the stakeholders who are involved in the strategic process
   - Competitive Position(s)—the product and market focus of the company as perceived by its customers
   - Competitive Advantages—aspects of superiority that a firm has developed over its competition, which enables the firm to compete successfully in its chosen competitive position
   - Competitive Tactics—the ploys and actions taken that effectively enable a firm to upgrade its competitive advantages or change its competitive position

4. **Firm's Resources and Capabilities**—represent the skills, knowledge, asset, capital, brand name, patents, etc., that enable a firm to develop competitive advantages

5. **Organizational Structure and Coordination Processes**—structure is the division of the firm into efficient units; coordination is the control and integration of the different tasks to ensure effectiveness and efficiency. Resources and capabilities must be organized properly to be potent competitive advantages.

6. **Firm Performance**—assess the three types of performance (financial, operational and strategic). Performance is used as the metric upon which strategy is assessed.

SWOT Analysis—primary tool for examining strategic issues involving strengths and weaknesses in the firm's competitive advantages and opportunities and threats that exist in the industry environment given the firm's competitive position

Additional Notes and Recommended Readings

Abell, Derek F., *Defining a Business: The Starting Point of Strategic Planning* (Englewood Cliffs, N.J.: Prentice Hall, 1980), p. 169.

Adkam, J.D.; and S.S. Cowen. "Strategic Planning for Increased Profit in the Small Business." *Long Range Planning*, December 1990, pp. 63-79.

Burgleman, R.A. *Strategy is Destiny*. The Free Press, 2000.

Chandler, Alfred D., *Strategy and Structure* (Cambridge, Mass.: MIT Press, 1962).

Clausewitz, Carl von, *On War*, originally published in 1832. Translation published by Routledge and Kegan Paul, Ltd., 1908 (Middlesex, England: Pelican [Penguin] Books, 1968).

Collins, James C., "Good to Great," Harperbusiness, 2001.

Collins, James C., and Jerry Porras, "Built to Last: Successful Habits of Visionary Companies," Harperbusiness, 1997.

Curry, William, "A Condensed Version of Business Policy," mimeographed (Waterloo, Ont.: Wilfrid Laurier University, 1980).

Galbraith, Jay R., and Robert K. Kazanjian, *Strategy Implementation: Structure, Systems and Process*; 2nd ed. (St. Paul, Minn.: West Publishing, 1986), p. 3

Hahn, D.; "Strategic Management - Tasks and Challenges in the 1990s." *Long Range Planning*, February 1991, pp. 26-39

Hitt, M.A.; R.E. Hoskisson, and J.S. Harrison. "Strategic Competitiveness in the 1990s: Challenges and Opportunities for U.S. Executives." *Academy of Management Executive*, May 1991, pp. 7-22.

Hofer, Charles W., consulting ed., West Series in Strategic Management (St. Paul, Minn.: West Publishing, 1986), Common Foreword, p. xi.

Kamis, Michael, *Strategic Planning for Changing Times* (Dayton, Ohio): Cassette Recording Co., 1984).

Kaplan, Robert S., and David Norton, *The Balanced Scorecard: Translating Strategy into Action*, Harvard Business School Press, 1996.

Kaplan, Robert S., and David P. Norton, Linking the balanced scorecard to strategy *California Management Review*, Vol: 39 Iss: 1 Date: Fall 1996 p: 53-79

Markides C.C. "A Dynamic View of Strategy" *Sloan Management Review* 40 no. 3, 1999.

McMillan, lan C., and Patricia E. Jones, *Strategy Formulation: Power and Politics*, 2nd ed. (St. Paul, Minn.: West Publishing, 1986).

Mintzberg, Henry, *The Nature of Managerial Work* (New York: Harper & Row, 1973), pp. 91-93.

Mintzberg, Henry. *The Rise and Fall of Strategic Planning*. New York, The Free Press, 1994

Porter, M.E., "What Is Strategy" *Harvard Business Review* 74 no. 6, 1996.

Porter, Michael E., *Competitive Strategy: Techniques for Analyzing Industries and Competitors*. New York: Free Press, 1980.

Tenaglia, Mason, and Alistair Davidson. "A Directory of Strategic Management Software Tools." *Planning Review*, July-August 1993, pp. 38-94.

Tilles, Seymour, "How to Evaluate Corporate Strategy," *Harvard Business Review*, July-August 1963.

Watson. Gregory H., "How Process Benchmarking Supports Corporate Strategy." *Planning Review*, January-February 1993, pp. 12-15.

chapter 2 Industry and Competitive Strategic Analysis

After a small period of organized order in the telecommunications industry, we are now in a period you could almost call chaos.

JEAN MONTY, PRESIDENT AND CEO OF BCE

It's only the second inning and this is a world that can change overnight ...... I'm not going to let you sneak up on me like we snuck up on Compuserve or Prodigy.

STEVE CASE, CEO OF AMERICA ONLINE

It is very important for a manager to fully understand the market and competitive environment that his or her firm operates within and how these environments influence profits. Good managers attempt to come to terms with a number of key questions including the following: Is the competitive environment going to be particularly intense? Are the buying habits of the customers going to change? Are technologies going to alter the way business is done in the industry? Are certain competitors aggressively defending certain aspects of their business?

In this chapter, we examine some of the issues in a firm's market and competitive environment that influence profitability and, ultimately, dictate the strategy selected by the firms. To do this, managers must answer a number of different questions:

- What are the competitive characteristics in the industry and how do they influence the value or profitability of firms in the industry?
- How does cooperation influence value in the industry?
- Are there strategic sectors or competitive groups in the industry and what key success factors create value in these sectors or groups?
- Given the competitive characteristics of other firms in the industry, how might they competitively behave in the future?
- What are the drivers of change in the future for value in this industry?

Ultimately, managers attempt to direct their firm's competitive position to the most profitable and highest growth position in their industry. This requires that managers understand all the nuances of the competitive environment that presently exist in an industry, and that they have an ability to anticipate what the competitive environment will be in the future. This chapter provides students with the fundamental tools that managers use to assess their firm's present and future possibilities.

THE VALUE INFLUENCES OF COMPETITION AND COOPERATION

Exhibit 2-1 illustrates the average financial return for major industry categories in Canada over a 17-year period. As shown, the financial performance varies between industries despite the fact that they all operated in relatively similar economic conditions. The questions that we will consider in this section is why do industries have different levels of performance and how can managers use this information to aid their strategic decision-making plans?

The disparity in performance between industries, shown in exhibit 2-1, can be attributed mostly to market and competitive effects in each industry. For example, when one looks at the telephone and utilities industry, performance is substandard due to an increase in competition created by deregulation, a plethora of new substitutes (including cell phones, pagers, etc.), and market maturity. The metals and minerals industry has performed poorly because of increased global competition particularly from underdeveloped and developing nations, which have cost advantages. In contrast, the auto parts industry has enjoyed excellent performance because

exhibit 2-1   The Return in Different Industries in Canada*

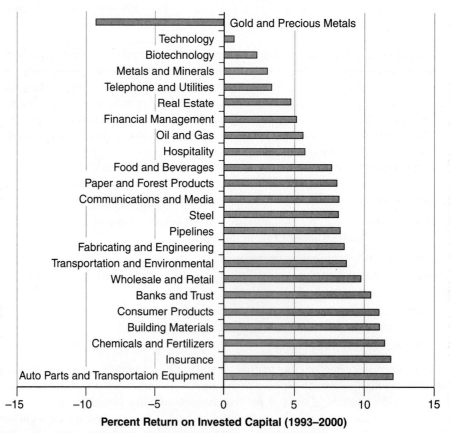

Percent Return on Invested Capital (1993–2000)

* Notes
From the Financial Post Corporate Reports 2001
RIC was calculated s an average for the years 1993 to 2000

consolidation and rapid growth in demand has decreased competitive pressures, while a favourable exchange rate has increased margins in this export driven industry. Thus, market, economic, and competitive characteristics of an industry are critical to profitability and managers must be constantly seeking credible means of creating value in their chosen industry.

Managers strategically attempt to maximize the financial performance of their company by increasing the difference between the cost of supplying products (and/or services) and the price of selling the products. This difference is graphically illustrated in exhibit 2-2. The value to the customer represents the maximum price the customer is willing to pay. And although this price is the maximum price the customer is willing to pay, it is not necessarily the price at which firms sell the product in the market place. Most firms share some value with the customer to ensure continued growth in demand and to raise the customer's perception of the firm's brand and product reputation. Strategically, a manager attempts to create value by simultaneously maximizing the worth to the customer while minimizing the cost of inputs. The dynamic trade-off between these two value-creating decisions is in reality a very difficult and complex problem for managers.

The ability of the firm to create value is a function of the firm's internal capabilities (examined in Chapter 3) and the characteristics of its market and competitive environment because both of these factors influence the worth to the buyer and costs of inputs to the firm. In this section, we explore some environmental factors that influence the intrinsic value of an industry.

Many competitive factors influence the value creation available in an industry. For example, the value to the customer is influenced by the availability of other competitive products and substitutes, and the growth in demand for the product because demand outstrips the competitive supply. The costs of inputs depends upon the competition for the supplies of inputs necessary to the production process including such things as labour, raw materials, electricity, technology knowledge, capital, etc. In fact, research has shown that a firm's ability to be profitable is more related to the competitive dynamics in an industry than the inherent abilities of a firm to create value internally.

exhibit 2-2 The Potential Strategic Profit for a Firm in an Industry

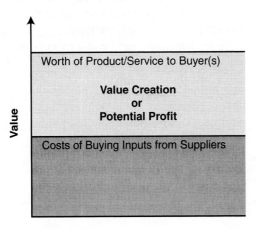

Competition

Most people think competition is comprised of a firm's direct competition. Indeed, the field of economics differentiates the competitiveness of an industry based upon the number of companies in an industry. Exhibit 2-3 describes the archetypal industry types based on the concentration of firms in the industry. There are four types of competition and they are differentiated by the number of direct competitors. The most competitive, pure competition, tends to have low profits, while the least competitive, a monopoly and oligopoly, have the highest profitability. The competitive nature of these archetypes also tends to produce characteristic market and competitive characteristics as is indicated in exhibit 2-3. This in turn makes for different competitive characteristics.

exhibit 2-3   Different Types of Competitive Industries

Type of Industry	Number of Competitors	Nature of Market	Nature of Competition	Competitive Requirements	Industry Examples
Pure Competition	• Many competitors	• Products and services are commodities that have standardized	• Competition is characteristics intense based largely on financial cost	• Relatively easy to enter this type of industry	• Milk, wheat, etc., farming, laundromats, low priced restaurants, and renovation contractors
Differentiated Competition	• Quite a few competitors but they are able to differentiate themselves into different market segments to moderate competition	• Products and services are differentiated and buyers are diversified in their desires creating different segments	• Competition varies depending upon the differentiation • It is somewhat price based, but product and service qualities and reputation are also important competitive considerations	• The costs related to entering these industries involve developing a way to differentiate as well as costs of setting up business	• Clothing designers and retailers, very high priced restaurants, and business consulting companies
Oligopoly	• Few competitors who know and understand each other well	• Products and services can be differentiated slightly	• Competition is moderated and is often based on non-price tactics	• Significant costs of entry including branding, distribution, manufacturing, etc.	• Petroleum refining, banking, auto manufacturers, and steel manufacturing
Monopoly	• One competitor	• Few products and services and customers have little choice	• No direct competition • Company must work with government	• Government regulation and control for entry	• Electricity, fire department, and regular mail

Note: In some regions, electricity is becoming deregulated and thus, competition will begin to appear. Many government services and crown corporations are essentially monopolies.

Competition and Assessing the Degree of Competition

Competition in modern strategy is conceived of as any person or entity that attempts to extract some of the firm's profits for itself. This expands the notion of competition to include other parties, including suppliers of inputs, customers, and any other influences that may alter the worth of the product or the cost of the inputs, as exhibit 2-2 suggests.

Taking a comprehensive approach to competitive analysis is vitally important to developing an effective strategy in an industry. A key tool for assessing competitive intensity in an industry is Porter's Five Forces Model, shown in exhibit 2-4. This model describes the competitive forces that influence an industry and ultimately a firm's profitability. It is a very useful tool to assess the attractiveness of an industry from the profitability standpoint.

The five competitive forces are: (1) the threat of new entrants, (2) the threat of substitutes, (3) the pressure buyers exert on prices, (4) the pressure suppliers exert on costs, and (5) the internal industry competition and rivalry. The financial performance in an industry is influenced by each one of these factors. For instance, the pressure suppliers apply on input costs to an industry directly influences the ability of firms in the industry to attain attractive profit levels. The other four factors influence the value that the customers are willing to pay for the product/services. Thus, competitive analysis is critical to understanding the latent value in an industry.

This competitive analysis tool is also helpful in reminding managers that competition originates from a variety of sources. Companies that just focus on direct competition selling similar products in the same region may be missing competitive elements that are important to their strategic decisions.

Finally, strategic research has found evidence of all of these forces being present in some industries. However, certain influences appear more pervasive than others. Exhibit 2-4 illustrates the sub-factors that contribute to the competitive factors. Sub-factors that are most pervasive to competition in almost all industries are delineated in bold.

Factors Influencing Internal Competitive Rivalry in an Industry

The factors that influence the degree of internal competitive rivalry in an industry are:

Industry growth lowers the competition because there is growing demand, which lowers price based competition for new customers.

Industry concentration (fewer firms in an industry) lowers competition because when there are fewer firms, they mutually understand that price wars hurt everybody. However, in industries with a large number of competitors, price or other aggressive competitive methods will be carried out by one firm and then every firm has to follow suit to ensure that they do not loose business.

Fixed costs value added increases competition because firms often make decisions in the short-term based upon variable costs, and, if the price is above the variable cost, then the firm is maximizing its financial position. However, it is also an incentive to lower prices when variable costs are low.

exhibit 2-4   A Tool to Analyze Industry Competitiveness Porter's Five Forces

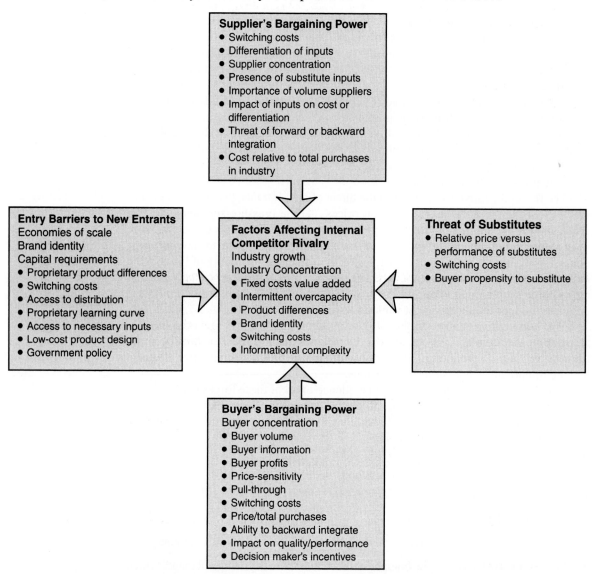

Note: The factors in bold are those that have consistently been related to competitive pressure in an industry where they are present.
The other factors must be assessed more carefully if they are present in an industry. This diagram is adapted from work by Michael Porter.

Intermittent overcapacity increases competition because firm's whose businesses experience overcapacity (i.e., demand falls below supply) have a tendency to lower prices to maintain unit sales volume.

Product differences decrease competition because the products are seen as different and, therefore, are not directly competing against one another. Commodities do not enjoy this competitive respite.

Brand identity decreases competition for firms that have brands because it enables them to separate themselves from the competitors because their products enjoy a customer loyalty.

Switching costs lower competition because it becomes difficult for buyers to switch between alternative products. These costs may be associated with ancillary services, warranties, retooling, etc.

Informational complexity decreases the competition in an industry because customers have difficulty comparing products and services.

Corporate stakes increase competition because firms that rely on specific businesses or product lines are not willing to give up market share and will fight very hard to maintain their competitiveness in an industry.

Exit barriers increase competition particularly when the industry is in the maturing or declining stages because it is difficult or costly for firms to exit the industry. Therefore, they remain for extended periods of time producing excess competition and lower profits.

Factors Influencing Entry Barriers Restricting New Entrants

The factors that influence the degree to which new entrants can enter an industry are called entry barriers. They include the following factors:

Economies of scale lowers entry because firm's entering an industry must quickly attain a certain relatively large size to be competitive either because of marketing costs, production facility economies of scale, distribution economies of scale, etc.

Brand identity lowers entry because developing a brand name requires lots of advertising and many years of marketing.

Capital requirements lower entry similar to how economies of scale make it more difficult to enter an industry.

Proprietary product differences lower entry because proprietary products, such as patents, cannot be copied easily and, therefore, present considerable barriers to entry.

Switching costs lower entry because customers may not want to incur the costs of switching to the product of a new entrant.

Access to distribution lowers entry when it is difficult to find a viable way to distribute your products. Distribution is both expensive and is built on relationships both of which provide some degree of an obstacle for a new entrant.

Proprietary learning curve decreases entry because the firms in the industry have learned how to produce, design, etc. and a new entrant does not have easy access to this knowledge.

Access to necessary inputs decreases entry as a firm must have the appropriate inputs. For example, diamonds are rare and, therefore, diamond mining is an industry with a lower competitiveness than normal mining.

Government policy decreases entry when the government restricts entry. This occurs in medicine, banking, and some other industries in Canada.

Expected retaliation, if done aggressively, can deter new entrants from entering because they think that incumbent firms will aggressively attempt to limit the new business's prospects.

Factors Determining the Threat of Substitutes

Substitutes increase the competitiveness in an industry by effectively attracting customers away from the products or services produced in an industry. This forces the companies in the industry to be more competitive to ensure that they maintain their market shares. The factors that determine the threat of substitutes are:

Relative price versus performance of substitutes can influence the competitiveness depending upon whether the customers perceive the benefits to costs of the substitute to be more or less than the comparative benefits to cost of the product in question.

Switching costs can reduce the competitive effectiveness of a substitute on an industry because customers do not want to incur the switching costs of changing to the substitute product. These switching costs may be training, installation, conversion, etc. costs that are ancillary to the main product.

Factors Influencing the Bargaining Power of Buyers

The factors that influence the degree of bargaining power a buyer has over the producer are:

Buyer size and concentration is probably the most important influence on competition because if the buyer is large and powerful, then they can demand price concessions from the producer.

Buyer volume influences competition because when buyers purchase in volume they can demand lower prices and thus generate competitive pressure through lower prices.

Buyer information is important to competition because information enables the buyer to shop comparatively and thus, increase competition in the producer's industry.

Buyer profits (and price-sensitivity) affect competition because buyers that have high profits are price insensitive and thus will not cause competitive pressure by demanding lower prices, but buyers having low profits are price sensitive and will cause competitive pressure by demanding lower prices.

Pull-through decreases competition because the products are demanded by the customers, while in push-through the producer must use incentives (that have a cost) to induce sales and consequently creates competitive pressure in the producer's industry.

Switching costs lower competition for the producers because buyers do not want to change suppliers based on lower prices due to the switching costs.

Ability to backward integrate can influence competitiveness by the buyer threatening to integrate backward and competing with the producer (makes it more competitive in the producer's industry).

Impact on quality/performance for an industrial buyer the impact of the producer's product or service on the buyer's product or service influences the competitiveness because, if it is very important to the buyer, then they are less price sensitive.

Decision maker's incentives can change the willingness of the buyer to demand lower prices. An example of this is provincial health plans or auto insurance. In these situations, price is not a factor in the decision to use a specific service because a third party is paying for the service.

Factors Influencing the Bargaining Power of Suppliers

Supplier's power is the mirror image of buyer's power, which was reviewed above. The factors that influence the degree of bargaining power a supplier has over the producer are:

Switching costs increase the ability of the supplier to compete for money in an industry because the producer does not want to incur extra switching costs.

Differentiation of inputs increases the competitiveness because the producer requires a specific type (e.g., quality, characteristics, etc.) of supply to enable him to produce the desired output.

Supplier concentration (fewer suppliers) increases the ability of the supplier to compete for higher supply prices because there are fewer options available to the producer to buy supplies and other suppliers may be reticent to sell to an un-loyal customer.

Presence of substitute inputs decreases the competitive influence of the supplier because the producer can utilize a substitute product if ones supplies become too expensive.

Importance of volume suppliers if a supplier supplies large volumes of input to an industry they may have more control over the price of the supplied inputs and therefore increase the competitive pressure on the industry.

Impact of inputs on cost or differentiation is important to competitiveness of an industry because, if inputs are important to the producer's product price, quality, etc., then the supplier can exert competitive pressure on the industry.

Threat of forward or backward integration can influence competitiveness by the supplier threatening to integrate forward and compete with the producer (makes it more competitive in the producer's industry) or the producer's ability to integrate backward (makes it less competitive in the producer's industry).

Cost relative to total purchases in industry can affect competitiveness because, if the supplier's input is a major cost to a producer, the producer will more aggressively look for other inputs, thus reducing the competitive pressure.

When analyzing the competitive nature of an industry, it is important to think dynamically. Most students analyze an industry's competitive disposition from a static perspective; that is, they look at industry as it presently can be characterized. However, important strategic questions are: How will the industry evolve in the future?

Which competitive factors are going to turn negative and which might turn positive? This enables the company to predict competitive changes in an industry and managers can anticipate and adjust their strategy as necessary.

Another important issue when analyzing the competitiveness in an industry is that, sometimes, different sectors in an industry have very different degrees of competitiveness. For example, in the grocery business there are the national chains, such as Loblaws, Provigo, IGA, and so on, and there are independent corner stores. These companies are in the same industry, but are in very different competitive situations, and, if one were to apply the competitive analysis model described earlier, the national grocery chain segment would be moderately competitive while the independent corner store segment would be highly competitive. Therefore, it is important to consider the competitiveness of different segments of an industry when testing for competitiveness. This exercise also enables a manager to understand what segments, or competitive positions, are more profitable than others in an industry.

Cooperation and Value Adding Structural Elements in the Industry

In some industries there is a cooperative structural force present in the industry that adds value (see exhibit 2-5). Such a force is a complementor and it is important for managers to recognize the significance of complementors and potential complementors so that they can position their firms to take maximum advantage of the value provided by a complementor. A complementor is not a buyer or supplier, but is a firm or entity that enhances the desirability of a product because of the complementary nature of its product to the industry's product. Examples of complementary relationships are abundant. The NBA is a complementor to the running shoe industry because it makes running shoes more valuable in the eyes of customers and, therefore, many buyers are willing to pay enhanced prices for basketball shoes. Nike takes advantage of this complementary relationship by signing up the top athletes in the NBA so that buyers preferentially attach this value to their shoes.

The other type of complementary relationship is between a complementor and supplier of an industry as is shown in exhibit 2-5. In this situation, the supplier is

exhibit 2-5   Complementor's Influence on Product Value

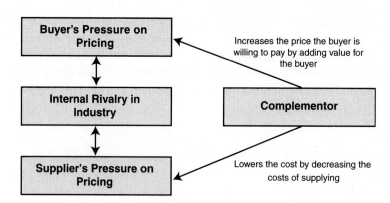

willing to supply the input to an industry at a reduced price because of the complementary relationship. For example, asphalt is the waste product derived from the processing of crude oil, with the lighter gas and oil products being the high margin primary products. Therefore, the gas and oil businesses that buy these lighter products are complementors to the asphalt paving business because they provide the paving companies with lower priced asphalt relative to what the product actually costs to produce if it were produced alone.

Sometimes complementors provide value to only one company in an industry, particularly in industries where there are network externalities and standards, such as technical or operating standards. There are a number of famous examples including game developers, such as Nintendo, which does not buy or sell games, but it is the value of these games that actually sells Nintendo machines. Microsoft and Intel are compelementors also because their products (i.e., Windows operating system and Intel based computers) complement the value provided to customers, yet separately these products would be nearly worthless to the customer.

Some examples of complementor relationships are listed below. They are of two types, as is indicated in exhibit 2-5:

1. **Increases the value of the product or service purchased by the buyer:**
   NHL hockey is a complementor to beer because customers love (i.e., added value) to sit down and drink beer while watching hockey. Labatt has taken advantage of this by sponsoring Labatt's Hockey Night in Canada every Saturday night in the winter.

   Intel is a complementor for Microsoft because, to get value out of Microsoft programs, most people use an Intel based computer. Therefore, Intel provides a tremendous amount of complementor value to Microsoft (and vice versa).

   Often complementor products come bundled together. Examples are computer hardware and software, cellular phone service and the phone itself.

2. **Lowers the cost at which the supplier is willing to sell the product or service:**
   In many situations, where there are by-products from a manufacturing process sold to different industries, the different industries provide complementor purchasing value to each other. For example, auto gasoline retail business is a complementor to hardware stores' camping kerosene sales. Since both kerosene and auto gas are different by-products of the oil refining process, the selling of auto gas to auto gas retailers enables the oil refineries to sell kerosene to hardware stores for a much more reasonable price.

   Another example is when shipping has unbalanced volumes directionally. For example, food distributors have to truck food goods up to communities in the northern parts of most provinces. However, coming back, many of these trucks have to return partially empty. A business that can take advantage of this reverse haul shipping will be able to get very good shipping rates (i.e., value). This makes the food retail industry a complementor industry to the businesses or industries that are able to use reverse hauls.

   Managers must be aware of complementor relationships and actively strategize in an attempt to capture the value that a complementor offers through their suppliers or buyers. Some companies manage to contract or build relationships with organizations producing complementor value, and thus, derive the majority of the value for themselves.

ASSESSING COMPETITIVE POSITIONS AND STRATEGIC GROUPS OR CLUSTERS

Assessing competitive and cooperative forces in an industry often requires managers to separate the industry into relevant sectors where competitors have similar competitive positions. The reason is that most industries have several viable sectors or competitive positions in the industry, and competitive forces often vary dramatically among these positions.

To begin such an assessment, managers initially should understand the customers' buying habits and, ultimately, what they value. Different buying perceptions define the relevant market segments in an industry and provide an understanding of what the viable competitive positions might be in an industry. For example, the Canadian grocery market can be divided into four types of buyers: value-oriented buyers, convenience driven buyers, buyers of great breadth of products and services, and buyers looking for the best and most exotic products available, as is shown in exhibit 2-6. Understanding what the customer values both now and in the future is essential to a good business strategy.

exhibit 2-6   Defining Market Segments in Food Grocery Business

Market Segments	Purchasing Criteria	Example of Shops Focusing on such Buyers
Convenience Buyer	• Buyer wants convenient location or service, such as home delivery	• Corner stores, gas bar stores
Low Cost/Volume Buyer	• Buyer wants many different types of grocery products at the lowest cost possible	• Costco, Wal-Mart
Wide Variety/Volume Buyer	• Buyer wants a wide variety of products (e.g., specialty and commodities) and is buying in significant volumes	• Loblaws, IGA, Provigo, Loeb
Specialty Item Buyer	• Buyer wants something unique and of high quality	• Butcher shop, bakery, fish store, specialty shops

Competitive Positions and Strategic Clusters

A strategic cluster is formed when a number of competitors have similar competitive positions in an industry and their competitive advantages are also comparable. In other words, companies in a strategic cluster provide customers with similar value propositions for their products. Defining a strategic cluster is important because it enables a manager to more effectively assess the competitive factors that are and will influence their business. More specifically, it defines who a company most directly competes with in a market. It also defines companies that have taken other similar strategies in an industry, thus enabling the manager to assess whether a change in the firm's strategy may lead to higher profitability.

An example of strategic clusters in the grocery industry is illustrated in exhibit 2-7. As is shown, there are a number of strategic clusters, some of which are more competitive than others. It is also important to realize that all of the previous assessment that one has done for the industry should be applied to the strategic clusters because competitive and cooperative forces may be quite different for each of the strategic clusters. For example, it is remarkably easy to enter the corner store industry, and this produces intense competitive pressure in this sector. However, entering the large grocery chain sector is much more difficult, and, thus, competitive forces are reduced and profits are higher. This illustrates the necessity of separating industries into their relevant sectors or strategic clusters prior to detailed competitive and market assessment taking place.

exhibit 2-7   Strategic Clusters in the Grocery Business

Name of Strategic Cluster	Examples of Companies Competing in this Cluster	Competitive Advantages of Strategic Cluster
Grocery Chains	• Loblaws, Dominion, A&P, Leob, etc.	• Broad selection of food products • Pleasant shopping environment • Relatively close to customers • Prices are moderately competitive
Specialty Food Stores	• Local butchers, bakeries, etc.	• Have high quality and specialized products • Can get customized service and products
Large Box Stores	• National Grocers, Costco, etc.	• Has low costs because industrial location, which often makes it less convenient • Costs are also minimized by stocking only high turnover products • Other products are available
Corner Stores and Gas Bars	• Local corner stores, and gas bars that have mini stores in them	• Locational convenience • Often have relatively high prices due to location and lack of economies of scale • Carries products in small quantity sizes and only conveniently required items

How does one identify strategic clusters in an industry? Sometimes strategic clusters correspond to the market segmentation in a market, although this is not always the case. The most effective way of defining strategic clusters in an industry is to identify the types of competitors in an industry and then classify them based upon their competitive positions in the market. An examination of the competitive advantages that make firms successful may also help in the delineation of strategic clusters in an industry. There are a variety of ways in which one can use competitive position to assess strategic clusters in an industry. Two of the most common techniques are the competitive position matrix and the strategic cluster map or analysis.

The competitive position matrix compares the competitors in an industry, highlighting each firm's key competitive characteristics. To develop a matrix, we must first discern what the important competitive dimensions are that provide value to customers. These dimensions could be price, product/service characteristics, product/service scope, or geographic scope. In addition, many managers also consider competitive advantages that differentiate the competitors. These competitive advantage dimensions are used to further differentiate the firms in the industry. Exhibit 2-8 provides an example of a competitive position matrix for part of the Canadian airlines industry. As is seen, the airlines shown actually have all attempted to define their own distinct competitive position. There used to be a national airlines strategic cluster made up of Canada 3000, Canadian Pacific, and Air Canada. However, the competitive nature of having three competitors in a relatively restricted market, Canada, forced two of these companies out of business. It is also interesting to note that Air Canada created

exhibit 2-8   Competitive Position Matrix: A Sample of the Canadian Airlines Industry in 2002

Airline	Geographic Scope	Pricing	Planes and Services	Customer Focus
Air Canada	• Worldwide – landing rights in major airports	• High	• Large & medium sized jets • Full Service including Aeroplan and many ancillary services, such as duty free and in-flight shopping	• Broad focus on international and customers looking for full service
WestJet	• Canadian west • Some routes into Ontario – landing rights in many secondary airports	• Low	• Medium sized Boeing jets • Minimal in-flight services	• Focused on the customer looking for no frills, but reliable air transportation
Pacific Coastal	• Regional along the BC Coast – landing rights in tertiary airports	• Moderate to high	• Small turbo-prop planes • Minimal in-flight services	• Tourists and locals who have to travel throughout this region
First Air	• Regional throughout Canada's north – landing rights in secondary and tertiary airports	• Moderate to high	• Small turbo-prop planes • Minimal in-flight services • Has a charter service available, corporate services, and Aeroplan member	• Tourists, business persons, and locals who have to travel throughout this region
Bearskin	• Northern Ontario – landing rights in tertiary airports and lakes	• Moderate to high	• Small turbo-prop planes • Minimal in-flight services • Has a charter service available and Aeroplan member	• Tourists and locals who have to travel throughout this region

Tango airlines, which is a low priced, national airline that operates out of secondary airports. This strategy is aimed at competitively confronting WestJet's rapid growth as well as a repositioning of some of Air Canada's assets so that they are competitively positioned in the fastest growing market sector.

When an industry has many similar firms, it is often more useful to combine the firms into strategic groups or clusters that share similar competitive positions. An industry that requires this approach is the restaurant industry where there are fast food, family, road houses, restaurant bars, and specialty food restaurants. An example of strategic clusters in the Canadian Furniture Retail industry is shown in exhibit 2-9. This approach, called the strategic cluster map, serves the same purpose as the competitive position matrix, but it graphically illustrates the clusters. The strategic cluster map tends to emphasize competitive dimensions that are barriers to entry between the various clusters.

One constraint of the strategic cluster map is that only two dimensions can be represented simultaneously. This limits the descriptive capacity of this approach and it

exhibit 2-9 Illustrative Strategic Cluster Map of Competitors in
Canadian Furniture Retail Business

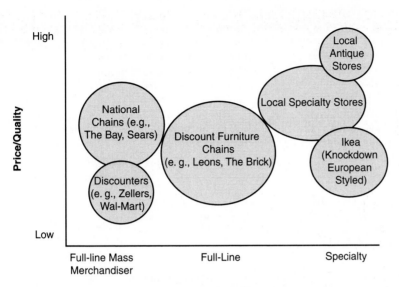

means the analyst must carefully select the dimensions in the map to represent the key
strategic dimensions in the industry. The competitive dimensions that were deemed to
be important in the Canadian furniture retail business were price/quality and prod-
uct/service scope or mix.

Once a manager defines the competitive position of the firm, they should delineate
some of the fundamental characteristics of the customers being served in that competitive position. Some of the important characteristics are the size of the market, the
firm's market share, the market growth, and the buying characteristics and desires of
the customers being serviced in that competitive position. The manager may also want
to look at some of the characteristics of "nearby" competitive positions to see if a
movement in some direction might improve their performance.

After having described the competitive position of the firm and its competitors, we
should have a good understanding of the business/market focus of the firm and its competitors. It is important to have this understanding before moving on to analyzing the
competitive influences and pressures in the industry.

AN EXAMPLE OF COMPETITIVE POSITION MANAGEMENT IN AN INDUSTRY

Loblaws is an example of how managers effectively used industry analysis to improve
their competitive position and their historic strategic evolution in the food retail industry.

Historically, the food retail business has been split into four strategic clusters as
was illustrated in exhibit 2-7. Exhibit 2-10 describes some of the key competitive
forces that impinge on these clusters and concludes as to the overall competitiveness in
the cluster. In general, this is a competitive industry simply due to the large number and
wide variety of competitors in food retailing.

exhibit 2-10   Key Competitive Forces Food Retail Clusters

Clusters	Competition and New Entry Threats	Supplier Cost and Product Clout	Conclusions
Local Corner Stores	• Highly competitive because it is relatively easy to enter this business and there are many stores competing in an undifferentiated manner	• Some suppliers are large multinationals that demand higher prices, and, at times, exclusive product supply contracts	• Highly competitive
Specialty Stores	• Competition is mixed and depends solely on the firm's ability to establish a differentiated product and service reputation • The skills and resources required are also specialized	• Smaller stores or chains have price pressure from the large suppliers	• Moderately competitive
Grocery Stores	• Relatively competitive because although there are only about a dozen companies there are many stores and most are not differentiated	• Suppliers and grocery chains are equally powerful	• Quite competitive
Large Box Stores	• Competitive because they attempt to differentiate themselves from the grocery stores by having greater product breadth • Very few in this category because it is costly and complex to enter	• Stores are large enough to demand the best prices, products, and service from suppliers	• Moderately competitive

The local corner store cluster is highly competitive because of the number of competitors, the ease of entry, and the price pressure suppliers exert. Over the years many of these stores have evolved into chains or franchises of small stores, which tend to lower the competitive pressures. However, this cluster is still an extremely competitive cluster. Clearly this is a cluster that Loblaws wanted to avoid because of the competitive pressures.

The specialty store cluster encompasses a wide variety of retailers, including butchers, cultural food shops, bakeries, and fresh fish and vegetable retailers; and although there are large numbers of specialty retailers, they have minimized competitive pressures by differentiating themselves through specialty services and products and locating in unique place. Furthermore, these stores attempt to build strong local brand reputations based upon their specialty food product and service abilities. Stores that have successfully differentiated themselves in this cluster are very profitable.

The grocery store cluster is relatively competitive with more than a dozen major players across Canada. And, although the number of companies in the cluster is relatively low, competition is quite strong because they compete in many different grocery stores some being franchises at the local level and with the other clusters.

The large box store cluster, which is a recent phenomenon, is only moderately competitive because these companies have developed tremendous operational efficiencies: suppliers are forced to provide low prices, high quality products, and excellent service; they have developed strong brand names based upon good value and a breadth of products; and the costs and expertise required to compete in this cluster make it very difficult for new competitors to enter.

In the early 1970s, Loblaws was an ailing grocery chain located in Ontario that was rapidly loosing market share. A McKinsey Consultant, Richard Currie, was hired to turn around the company. His team's early industry assessment indicated that a new market sector was emerging in the US that was based on upgrading stores in the grocery cluster by introducing fresh quality foods in a fashionably designed and decorated store. Currie realized that positioning Loblaws in this newly developing market sector would provide it with the ability to minimize competitive pressures by differentiating it from the grocery sector. Therefore, he redecorated key stores and consumers responded extremely well to the strategic differentiation.

The managerial team also noted that the specialty cluster was less competitive, and, therefore, more profitable. Based on this observation, they introduced in vogue and specialty items to their stores including foods from different nationalities, and boutique counters having fresh fish, herbs, and baked goods. These tactics enabled Loblaws to be further differentiated from its competitors in the grocery business.

Loblaws also developed its own product brand called "President's Choice," which became best selling products in many product categories. This enabled Loblaws to gain unprecedented power over suppliers. Now suppliers were competitively bidding for the contracts to manufacture these branded products. Loblaws also built ownership-based alliances in key supplier industries where economies of scale were important, such as baking. It also introduced company wide purchasing plans that reduced suppliers' power even further.

Strategically there was an added benefit that resulted from the innovativeness of Loblaws's new value added strategy. Other managers in the grocery store cluster were so accustomed to taking a cost efficiency strategy that they took several years to fully react to Loblaws's strategy. This provided Loblaws with a strategic lead that other competitors in the grocery cluster have never been able to close.

As Loblaws became successful, Currie acquired other grocery chains and built new stores in suburban areas to increase the firms buying power, expands its ability to higher top talent, and create a brand name across Canada that represented high quality products and a breadth of products and service that could not be found in most other stores. More recently, as the large format store cluster has developed, Loblaws has aggressively built large format stores having new products and services, including banking and fitness.

This example illustrates how a company recognized its competitive position in an industry, assessed the market and competitive clusters in the industry, and slowly evolved its competitive position into a differentiated position that proved to be very difficult for other competitors to duplicate. It has made Loblaws one of the most successful food chains in the world.

Not-for-Profit Organizational Competitive Position Analysis

Analyzing not-for-profit organizations' competitive positions is far more complex than for-profit organizations. Not-for-profit organizations have multiple principle stakeholders (e.g., service users, funders, volunteers) that demand complex and at times conflicting objectives (e.g., cost constraint, quality service, provide service to every one), while for-profit organizations have one main objective—to make a profit. However, competition is clearly present in the not-for-profit industry because different groups compete for similar funding dollars and they compete to satisfy similar customers' needs. For example, a symphony orchestra and an art gallery compete for funding and customer attendance in a community, although they often do not see themselves as competitors.

Consequently, it is necessary for not-for-profit organizations to find an exclusive and unique competitive position that their stakeholders (i.e., the community) perceive to be important. And thus, many not-for-profit organizations attempt to find a unique set of needs that they can satisfy most effectively in the community. Often, a market analysis, called a needs assessment, is completed prior to setting up a new not-for-profit organization. A needs assessment uses community focus groups, interviews, and questionnaires to evaluate the community's needs in specific areas, such as health care or social assistance. During this process, it is important to clarify where other competing organizations overlap or make redundant the expressed community needs. The managers then decide if there is a viable competitive position that has not been satisfied in the community. An alternative is for the competing organizations to cooperate and, thus, improve the delivery and content of needs provision to the community.

Competition for fundraising is also an issue for competitive analysis. Some organizations are privately funded while others are publicly funded. In addition, organizations take on different marketing approaches. Certain not-for-profit programs rely on the community members' philanthropic values for funding while other more entertainment-based organizations, such as symphonies and ballet, tend to rely on advertising and the quality of the product to get funding. Whether it is a community needs-based or product/service-based pitch, managers must clearly map out various funding sources, and attempt to position their organizations so that new sources and techniques for fundraising are successful.

COMPETITION CHARACTERISTICS AND THE PRODUCT LIFE CYCLE

The degree of growth and size of growth in an industry also influences the financial well-being of the companies in the industry. The product life cycle framework describes the different stages of growth in an industry, as shown in exhibit 2-11. The cycle has different stages that tend to cause different patterns of competition as well as revenue growth, profitability, and cash flow. The strategic concerns and competitive pressures at each stage vary considerably. For example, during the embryonic stage, the strategic concerns are the ultimate demand potential and the scale and timing of commitment, while at the decline stage, the concerns are milking resources to employ elsewhere, timing of a possible exit, and developing niche or value added strategies.

In summary, the life cycle model and its associated stages enable a manager to predict what the competitive forces in an industry are now and will be in the future. This, in turn, enables the manager to develop a strategy appropriate for impending business stages. Chapter 4 will consider this relationship between life cycle stage and competitive actions more thoroughly. It should also be noted that the characteristics and duration of stages in the product life cycle can differ markedly in different industries. A more thorough examination for the particular differences that occur in the high-tech industry is described in Chapter 8.

exhibit 2-11   Industry and Product Life Cycle

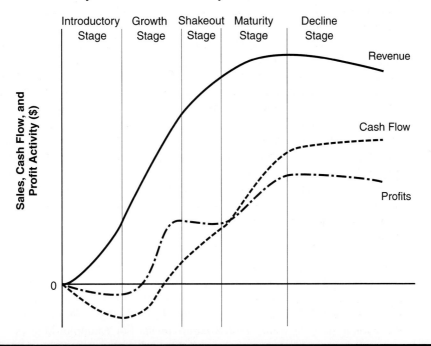

Stage	Market and Buyer Characteristics	Product/Service Features	Competitive Intensity	Strategic Focus
Introductory	• Small market of price insensitive, trial users	• Poor quality and costly	• Few competitors	• Getting financing, developing (R&D), and find a market customer group focus for your product/service
Growth	• Quickly growing market and at first often key market segments • Product shortages are a problem	• Different standards some being incompatible	• Many competitors entering the industry	• Getting more financing • Initially develop production capabilities to satisfy demand and then developing marketing and sales capabilities to improve market power
Shakeout	• Broad acceptance for the product/ services and number of segments is declining	• Product standardization occurring due to rationalization	• Rationalization is occurring in the industry	• Must be one of the leaders in the industry, if not sell-out or find a niche
Maturity	• Mainstream market acceptance and fewer market segments	• Price is important and features maybe depending upon the industry	• Competition has settled into a stable number and intensity	• Must be lowest cost • Focus on efficiency and new developing value added niches
Decline			• Some competitors going out of business • Competition can be intense prior to closures	• Continue to have low cost but also look for differen-tiation for further growth • May want to milk investment or sell if not profitable

INDUSTRY COMPETITIVE ADVANTAGES OR KEY SUCCESS FACTORS

Key success factors (KSFs) are crucial competitive advantages that firms should have in an industry in some measure if they want to be successful. For example, in the grocery store industry, "store location" has always been considered a very important KSF. For airlines, having landing rights at popular airports and efficient turn around times at the airport docks has been important to the overall success of the firms.

When managers scrutinize for KSFs, the industry must be broken into the different strategic groups because each business model in an industry may require different KSFs. Furthermore, different industry sectors and geographic regions might have somewhat different KSFs. This is because buyers may value different things and suppliers have different constraints depending upon what sector and geographic location because competitive pressures, as described in the previous section, can influence the KSFs in an industry sector and region.

How does a manager identify KSFs? Generally, KSFs are operationally critical to a business in the following ways:

- *Cost related operational requirements for the industry* For example, in the sand and gravel business, a KSF is being close to your customer because transportation costs are a critical cost to this commodity-based business.
- *Product/service value related requirements* For example, in some industries, a minimum quality is required to sell the product or service.
- *Legal or governmental requirements* For instance, banks require federal government approval to operate in Canada. Other industries require licenses or professional designations (e.g., lawyers, plumbers, bars, and hunting guide services).

One method of determining KSFs in an industry is to examine the various functional and operational aspects of the industry, such as finance, marketing, sales, manufacturing, after sales servicing, transporting, logistics, financing, etc. Then attempt to understand what elements are critical to the industry in providing value (i.e., either lower cost or superior value) to the buyer. This iterative process often identifies KSFs specific to an industry. Chapter 3 will describe firm specific competitive advantages.

INDUSTRY COMPETITIVE DRIVERS

Drivers in an industry are the forces that may change the nature of competition in an industry. It is important to analyze driving forces in an industry because it better prepares the manager and company for any potential change. Examples of driving forces are:

- Changes in long-term growth rate
- Changes in buyers' needs
- Technical innovation resulting in product or process innovation
- New methods of marketing, distributing, or in the supply chain
- Change in competitor makeup
- A change in barriers to entry

- Increases in risk and uncertainty
- Changes in government policy or societal attitudes
- New managerial techniques
- New ways of developing efficiencies or low cost
- Internationalization or globalization in an industry

The strategist should try to define what factors will be major causes of change in an industry and which will be minor causes. Then he or she can consider them in the context of the potential impacts they will have on their firm's present and future competitive position and advantages, as well as on the competitor's.

The types of competitive drivers that can influence a firm and industry are political, economic, socio-demographic, and technological. Students often remember these drivers through the acronym PEST, which are described more fully in the next few sections.

MACRO-ECONOMIC AND BUSINESS DRIVERS

The Legal and Political Considerations

The legal and political environment of Canadian business is particularly important given the scale and scope of government activity in Canada. Governments act in a wide variety of ways to create both opportunities and threats for business. Some of the most important government actions include:

- Regulation and policies, which can increase costs but also control competition or even give a competitive advantage (if firms have adapted to particularly stringent regulations in one location and are therefore better able to handle such regulations elsewhere).

- Taxation, which can reduce returns but also increase competitive advantage if a firm faces lower taxation than its competitors.

- Expenditure, which can create competitive disadvantage or advantage depending on whether government grants and subsidies received are larger than what competitors receive.

- Creation of public entities, including the creation of crown corporations, can produce an unpredictable competitor that also has deep-pockets.

- Privatization, which can increase competition but also result in a more level playing field.

- Consultation, which can become an opportunity for business to influence government policy but also provides government an opportunity to manipulate (i.e., co-opt) business by using the consultative process to justify decisions already made.

- Economic policy through debt creation or reduction can change the currency exchange rate or economic cycles, both of which will influence the economic activity in industry.

  International trade and tariff regulations can have a strong influence on industries that involve importing or exporting.

Economic Trends and Cycles

Economic cycles and trends can influence competitive pressures dramatically. For example, in a recession, many firms have to become more cost efficient due to lower levels of sales. It is important to understand short- and long-term economic cycles as well as the influence they might have on strategic plans such as raising capital or increasing plant capacity.

Different industries respond differently to economic cycles with some industries being largely immune to such cycles such as the morgue business, while others suffer considerably such as the housing industry. Furthermore, some industries are affected very quickly in an economic cycle while others are affected in the later stages of the cycle.

Long-term economic trends are just as important to strategic decision-making because firms may have to adjust their competitive position and advantages over the long-term to remain competitive. For example, in Canada, our high public debt has long-term economic implications, such as lower consumer spending, higher tax rates, and higher interest rates. These considerations may influence a firm's strategy both in Canada and internationally.

Social and Demographic Changes

Every firm should have a fundamental understanding of the demographic and social forces that it faces in the future, because these trends will influence markets and the level of competition. Examples of some social and demographic concerns are:

- **Demographics** (e.g., population growth rates and unequal distribution of population, aging work force in industrialized countries, high education requirements), which may influence competition by changing the availability of inputs, such as labour and markets by the changing nature of demands
- **Quality of life issues** (e.g., safety, health care, education, standard of living, attitudes toward work and family, etc.)
- **Moral issues** (e.g., volunteerism, pollution, attitudes towards business, charities, ecology, community needs, etc.)

Managers must actively identify and predict changes in these variables, and understand them in the context of the organization and the opportunities and concerns they may create. Strategically, it is fundamental that managers understand the demographic trends that affect their firm's markets, competitive positions, and competitive advantages in the future. Strategic decisions about possible changes in competitive positions involving new competitive advantages must be based upon a thorough analysis of these social and demographic trends. A manager must also be aware of social and moral issues that concern its other stakeholders, such as owners and employees.

Technological Trends

Technological developments have reshaped the ability of many firms to compete. The key concerns in the technological environment involve building the organizational capability to: (1) forecast and identify relevant developments—both within and beyond the industry; (2) assess the impact of these developments on existing operations; and (3) define opportunities. R&D strategy deals with choices in technology, product design and development, sources of technology, and R&D management and funding. Developing a technical strategy is one of the most uncertain aspects of strategic formulation, and it is not only critical for the internal development of competitive advantages within the firm, but to ensure that competition does not gain a technological advantage. Chapter 8 describes more fully the issues of strategy in innovative and technological industries.

International and Global Competitive Issues

A more modern driver in industry, which could be subsumed under either the political or economic titles described earlier, is the internationalization and globalization of industries around the world. This is occurring due to a number of forces, including technologies that make it easier to provide communication and transport services, information and products around the world, and political economic realities that are creating regional trading zones, one of which is the North American Free Trade Agreement (NAFTA).

International competition is often particularly difficult in countries that have small markets when the neighbouring country has large markets, as is the case with Canada and the United States. This enables the competition from the country with large markets to gain economies of scale and possibly other competitive advantages that permit them to enter and compete very effectively in the smaller country. Canadian companies should be constantly monitoring international competition for new competitive advantages and they should be striving to become internationally competitive prior to the entry of international competition into Canada.

THE PROCESS OF INDUSTRY AND COMPETITOR ASSESSMENT

Finally, the student must assess the competitive and industry issues in a meaningful and dynamic way. Competitive assessment should answer the following questions:

- How intensive is competition now and in the future?
- Will there be any preferential (or adverse) competitive positions in the industry— where are they?
- Who are the important competitors to watch, and why?
- What types of strategies could competitors take and what is their probable strategy?
- What driving forces and key success factors would dramatically alter the competitive situation in this industry and what impact would it have on your firm?
- What are the competitors' strengths, weaknesses, and preferences for strategy?
- How will competitors behave when we shift our strategy?

An approach that is being used more and more frequently to assess a firm's strategic options, given different competitive and market forces, is Scenario Planning. Scenario Planning is a dynamic approach to assessing the potential strategic options for a company. Generally, the approach examines the outcome if the firm selected one strategic option. Based on this selected strategy, how would customers and competitors tend to react? What are the potential uncontrollable risks if this strategy is selected?

Based upon the answers to these questions, managers can then select a strategy that minimizes risks and maximizes performance over the long-run. Exhibit 2-12 describes this process in more detail.

exhibit 2-12   Scenario Planning

An environmental approach used by many firms that face considerable environmental or non-controllable risks is the Scenario Planning approach. This approach was developed by Shell Oil to strategize appropriate business plans that protected them against the variety of risks they faced, including oil price changes and the uncertainty of drilling for oil.

The Scenario Planning approach involves developing different scenarios for an industry and competitive environment. The numerous scenarios developed should consider any radical change that could dramatically alter the industry or competitive environment. The previous analysis of the environmental factors should provide ample input for developing these scenarios. Once scenarios have been developed, managers then can assess how their strategy would fare if such a scenario took place and what strategies would be better. After the managers have gone through all of the scenarios, the strategy that best addresses the potential uncertainties is usually adopted.

This exercise is useful for developing strategy and for preparing a company and its managers for the potential of radical change in their environment. If such change does occur, the managers have previously considered the possible options and outcomes. This planning process also provides managers who are involved in the process with an overall appreciation of the strategic issues facing the firm, even though some of them may be outside of their responsibility.

Summary of The External Industry Analysis

Industry Economic Evaluation

- Evaluate market size, market growth, geographic scope, number and sizes of buyers and sellers, pace of technological change and innovation, scale economics, experience curve effects, capital requirements, internationalization

Analysis of Competition

- Assess competitive forces
- Analyze rivalry among competitors in industry
- Analyze threat of potential entry
- Analyze competition from substitutes
- Analyze power of suppliers
- Analyze power of buyers
- Analyze the international competitive forces

Assess Competitive Position or Strategic Groups

- Analyze the favourable and unfavourable competitive positions or strategic groups in the industry. What might change this?

Analysis of Industry

Business System Analysis

- What channels of supply and distribution are used in an industry and which are most efficient and effective?
- Are there any potential new approaches to supply or distribution that may be useful in this business?

Life Cycle

- Assess how future life cycle forces may have impact on the business and products

The Industry's Macro-Environment

- Assess the macro-environmental issues, such as economic cycles, technology, government policy, international issues (i.e., legal, taxes, duties, etc.)

Driving Forces

- Produce list of critical driving forces that may influence the industry in the future

Key Success Factors

- Develop list of critical success factors for the industry now and in the future

Industry and Competitor Assessment

Competitor Assessment

- Guess what future strategy competitors will take and assess possible impact on your firm
- Who are the strong and weak competitors (now and in the future) and why?

Industry Assessment

- Characterize the attractiveness of the industry: what major problems and opportunities will the industry face in future?
- Develop industry scenarios and assess your company's strategy against the scenarios

Additional Notes and Recommended Readings

Arthur A. Thompson, Jr., and A. J. Stickland Inc., *Strategy Formulation and Implementation*, 3rd ed. (Plato, Tex.: Business Publications, 1986), pp. 135-137.

Burgelman, R. A. and M. A. Maidique, *Strategic Management of Technology and Innovation*, (Homewood, Ill.: Richard D. Irwin, 1988).

Clarkson, Max B., "Defining, Evaluating and Managing Corporate Social Performance: The Stakeholder Management Model," Research in Corporate Social Performance and Policy, vol. 12 (Greenwich, Conn.: JAI Press, 1991)

D'Aveni, R.A., *Hypercompetition*, Free Press, 1994 (Chapters, 5 & 6)

Geringer, J. M. Paul W. Beamish, and R. da Costa, "Diversification Strategy and Internationalization: Implications for MNE Performance," *Strategic Management Journal* 10, no. 2 (March/April 1989), pp. 109-119.

Howard, T., and Pollack, T., and Gorman, P., "Global Strategic Analyses: Frameworks and Approaches." *Academy of Management Executive* 13, no 1, 1999.

Linneman, R.E., and Klein, H.E., "Using Scenarios in Strategic Decision Making." *Business Horizons*, 28, no. 4, 1995.

Mockler, Robert. "Strategic Intelligence Systems: Competitive Intelligence Systems to Support Strategic Management Decision Making." *SAM Advanced Management Journal*, Winter 1992, pp. 4-9.

Porter, Michael. *Competitive Strategy: Techniques for Analyzing Industries and Competitors* (New York: Free Press, 1980), chap. 11.

Porter, Michael. *The Competitive Advantage of Nations*, New York: Free Press, 1990.

The ins and outs of strategic cost analysis are discussed in greater length in Michael E. Porter, *Competitive Advantage: Creating and Sustaining Superior Performance* (New York: Free Press, 1985), chap. 2.

Williams, Jeffrey. " How Sustainable is Your Competitive Advantage." *California Management Review*, Spring 1992, pp 29-51.

Zahra, Shaker, and Sherry Chaples. "Blind Spots in Competitive Analysis." *Academy of Management Executive*, May 1993, pp. 7-28.

chapter 3 Analyzing Internal Strategic Resources and Capabilities

Knowledge management is critical. It's one of our core processes – sell work, do work, manage people and manage knowledge.

JOHN PATZ, CKO OF ERNST AND YOUNG

Only consider managers that you admire and trust.

WARREN BUFFET, CHAIRMAN OF BERKSHIRE CORP.

In this chapter, we examine the development of a firm's internal competitive advantages. In Chapter 2, exhibit 2-1 illustrated how the external competitive environment can influence industry sector performance. In exhibit 3-1, we examine the performance of companies in firms within a specific industry, the Canadian biotech and pharmaceutical industry. The performance differences are large, as is shown in exhibit 3-1, and this variance in firm performance is consistent in most industry sectors studied. The question that is examined in this chapter is, why is there such a variance in performance between individual firms in an industry?

The differences in performance are due to several factors. First, the firms may be in slightly different competitive positions (i.e., belong to different strategic clusters in the industry) and some positions may be more attractive than others. However, the more important difference is the disparity in competitive advantages between the various firms. Competitive advantages are abilities, assets, skills, capabilities, etc., that enable a company to compete more effectively in its industry.

In the biotech and pharmaceutical industries, illustrated in exhibit 3-1, firms that have higher return on invested capital tend to have stronger technological capabilities, including patented products and other functional competences, such as marketing and manufacturing abilities.

A comparison of the best and worst performing companies, in exhibit 3-1, illustrates how a firm's competitive advantages can influence performance. These companies, Angiotech and Biovail, have very similar competitive positions (i.e., both specialize in proprietary time-release drug technologies in the pharmaceutical industry), yet they have very different levels of performance. This performance difference is a result of the differences in each firm's competitive advantages. The poorer performing company, Angiotech, is in the early stages of drug product development—discovery and clinical trials—while Biovail is in the latter stages—clinical trials, approval, and commercialization. Therefore, all of Angiotech's efforts have been aimed at developing the necessary technical capabilities to move its products through to the approval

exhibit 3-1 Performance in the Biotech and Pharmaceutical Industry in Canada*

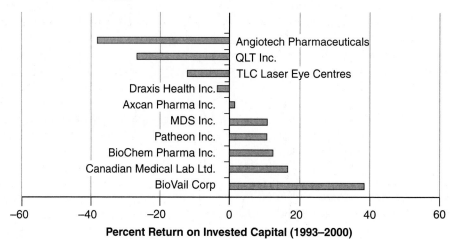

Percent Return on Invested Capital (1993–2000)

* Notes
From the Financial Post Corporate Reports 2001
RIC was calculated s an average for the years 1993 to 2000

and commercialization stages. However, Biovail has not only developed competitive advantages related to technical product development, but has also manufacturing and marketing abilities. Furthermore, Biovail's active marketing effort has created considerable brand recognition in the market place. In conclusion, Biovail's competitive advantages have produced much greater return on invested capital relative to Angiotech, which is just starting to build its competitive advantages. This example illustrates the importance of building competitive advantages continuously and in a focused manner.

TOOLS FOR ASSESSING A FIRM'S COMPETITIVE ADVANTAGES

A basic tool for analyzing a firm's competitive position and advantages is SWOT analysis, as was indicated in Chapter 1. However, before we examine the various tools for assessing competitive advantage, we should make sure we understand the concept and the different types of competitive advantages that are available to the firm.

WHAT ARE COMPETITIVE ADVANTAGES?

A firm's competitive advantages evolve from the resources available to the firm. Resources are physical assets (e.g., land, equipment, buildings, cash, etc.), intangible resources (e.g., brand name, market share, product patents, technological know-how, etc.), or capabilities (e.g., learning proficiencies, product development processes, fast delivery times, managerial abilities, etc.). Analyzing a firm's resources is an important step for a manager when formulating and implementing strategy. Strong resources must support a successful strategy, and when a strategy changes, accompanying changes in competitive advantages and, therefore, resources are usually necessary.

When formulating strategy, managers must decide what resources are necessary for a firm's strategy, and how to develop or acquire these resources overtime.

How managers evolve resources into competitive advantages and capabilities, and then eventually into sustainable competitive advantages are illustrated in exhibit 3-2. The hierarchy of development illustrates how managers select and develop specific resources available to them, then slowly shape them into competitive advantages, and sometimes competitive capabilities and sustainable competitive advantages and capabilities. The definitions of these competitive attributes are briefly described in exhibit 3-2.

Exhibit 3-2 also provides examples of the different types of resources a firm uses competitively. For example, a corner store uses its location as a competitive advantage because corner stores tend to compete on convenience. An example of a competitive capability is Microsoft's development of its brand image, something that results from a number of competitive advantages including technological, marketing, distribution as well as its ownership of the Windows operating system and the Office desktop applications. Something that provides continuous advantages competitively is

exhibit 3-2   The Hierarchy of Development of Competitive Advantages

Resources
Tangible or intangible assets, skills, abilities, etc., that enable production of products and services

Tangible Resources
- Financial resources
- Physical plant, raw materials and equipment
- Human abilities, including experience, knowledge, skill, attitude, etc.
- Organizational abilities including structure and processes

Intangible Resources
- Technological resources, including patents, trademarks, knowledge, etc.
- Innovation abilities, including facilities and employee research skills
- Reputation, including perceptions by stakeholders and brand name

Competitive Advantages
- Resources that produce value to a firm's customers
- By providing value to the customers, the resources supplement the firm's ability to compete in its selected competitive position

Competitive Capabilities
- Sets of competitive advantages that management integrates and coordinates to produce a multifaceted value-producing advantage over competitors

Sustainable Competitive Advantages and Capabilities
- Sustainable attributes that provide a firm with advantages over competition for the foreseeable future because competitors find it difficult to emulate these competitive advantages and capabilities

Core Competencies
- Sustainable competitive advantages and capabilities that a firm has relied upon as the basis for its strategy throughout all of its products and businesses over a period of time

a sustainable competitive advantage. An example of a sustainable competitive advantage is Intel's continuous ability to upgrade its product technically and market it faster than its competition. This ability to stay continuously ahead of the competition is one of the most valuable advantages a firm can have.

Very often, sustainable competitive advantages evolve into core competencies in a company. Core competencies are competitive advantages and capabilities that emerge over time as being central to a firm's overall strategy, and they are competitive advantages upon which the firm's strategy is based over time. For example, Intel's core competency is the ability to produce the fastest chip in the world. Intel has built its strategy around this core competency for the past decade. More recently, it has begun to stress efficiency in manufacturing because they realize this will become a more important strategic factor in the future as this industry matures. Multi-business firms build their businesses around a core competency and this enables them to effectively and efficiently execute their strategy in all of their businesses. An example of this is Bombardier, which has developed a core competency around its relationship building capabilities. This core competency has enabled Bombardier to market to key customers, more effectively gain financing from government, integrate acquisitions adeptly, and gain access to technology developed by other firms through alliances.

DEVELOPING RESOURCES INTO COMPETITIVE ADVANTAGES

One of the key strategic decision-making judgments managers face is deciding what resources to develop or acquire. Top managers spend an inordinate amount of time analyzing, selecting, acquiring, or developing the necessary resources to enable their firm to be competitive. These resources and competitive advantages must be constantly upgraded or altered to enable a firm to maintain its competitive advantage relative to other firms in the market.

Exhibit 3-3 illustrates the criteria that managers use to assess the quality of resources. As shown, resources must provide value to the customer (either directly or indirectly) or they are of no use to the firm. If it does not, then it should not be acquired or developed by the firm into a competitive advantage. Furthermore, a competitive

exhibit 3-3   Assessing Resource Characteristics and Quality

Quality	Explanation Question
Valuable	Is the resource or capability valuable in delivering the firm's service or product to its customer? This is a necessary resource quality.
Durable	Is the resource or capability temporal (i.e., will disappear over a period of time) in nature (e.g., a limited natural resource)?
Rare	Is the resource rare, or do many other firms have this competitive capability?
Inimitable or non-substitutable	Is the resource or capability unique to your firm relative to the competition? Can a resource or capability be substituted by another one in your business or industry?
Complex	Does a resource or capability have a breadth, scope, and complexity to make it difficult for others to both imitate and understand (e.g., organizational culture)?

advantage that should be further developed and improved is one that has the potential to be durable, rare, and so on. The more qualities the resource has, the more important it is as a competitive advantage. A competitive advantage that has characteristics of inimitability and complexity, an example being organizational culture in the advertising business, has qualities of sustainability. These latter competitive advantages and capabilities may be very effective at producing long-term competitive advantages and managers should focus considerable effort on developing them.

VALUE-CHAIN ANALYSIS

An important approach to identifying competitive advantages and capabilities in a firm is through value-chain analysis. A value chain is defined as the path upon which products or services progress along as value is added, prior to reaching the end consumer. A generic value chain is shown in exhibit 3-4. A value chain is made up of primary activities (inbound logistics, operations, outbound logistics, marketing and sales, and service) and support activities (firm infrastructure, human resource management, technology development, and procurement). Firms try to gain competitive advantage by increasing the value to customers in one or more activities relative to competitors. Value is defined as improving the worth of the product or service to the customer either through lowering the price or increasing the product or service characteristics. Managers must focus on increasing the value to the customer while attempting to minimize the costs to the firm—this maximizes total profits to the firm. These two issues are called *strategic value* and *cost analysis*.

Strategic value analysis focuses on a firm's relative value position vis-à-vis its rivals. The analytical approach must combine an analysis of the firm's total industry value chain and the firm's competitive position. The manager must appreciate the relationship between the firm's competitive position (i.e., its customers that are served by that competitive position) and the value provided to these customers by the various activities in the firm's value chain. The analysis must include value provided by assets possibly not owned and controlled by the firm, including such things as the quality of service provided by their chosen retail distribution channels, and the quality of raw materials provided by suppliers. All of these factors may influence customer value.

Strategic cost analysis focuses on a firm's relative cost position vis-à-vis its rivals. The primary analytical tool of strategic cost analysis is the construction of a total firm value chain showing the makeup of costs all the way from the inception of raw materials and components to the end price paid by ultimate customers. The activity-cost chain, thus includes more than just a firm's own internal cost structure; it includes the buildup of cost (and thus the "value" of the product) at each stage in the whole market chain of getting the product into the hands of the final user, as shown in exhibit 3-4. Constructing an integrated activity-cost chain is more revealing than restricting attention to just a firm's own internal costs. This is because a firm's overall ability to furnish end-users with its product at a competitive price easily depends on cost factors originating either backward in the suppliers' portion of the activity-cost chain or *forward* in the distribution channel portion of the chain.

It is important to note that value-chain analysis and decisions must be directed at the competitive position of the firm. In other words, increasing the value of an activity (or competitive advantage in an activity) must be related to a firm's competitive position (i.e., be valued by a company's customers). For example, if a firm is in an expensive and highly differentiated market position, customers may not want cheaper

exhibit 3-4   Generic Value Chain in an Industry

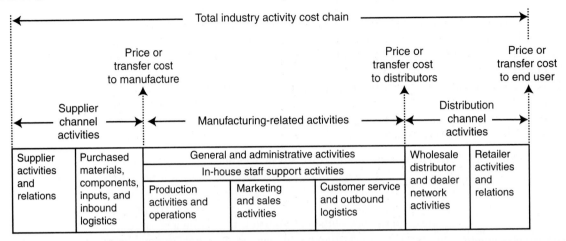

Activity	Specific Cost Activities and Cost Elements	Activity	Specific Cost Activities and Cost Elements
Supplier activities and relations	• Managing and controlling suppliers • Ingredient raw materials and component parts supplied by outsiders		• Process and product design and testing • Quality control and inspection • Inventory management • Internal materials handling • Manufacturing supervision
Purchased materials, components, inputs and inbound logistics	• Energy • Inbound shipping • Inbound materials handling • Inspection • Warehousing	**Marketing and sales activities**	• Sales force operations • Advertising and promotion • Market research • Technical literature • Travel and entertainment • Dealer/distributor relations
General and administrative activities	• Finance and accounting • Legal services • Public relations • General management • Interest on borrowed funds • Tax-related costs • Regulatory compliance	**Customer service and outbound logistics**	• Service representatives • Order processing • Service manuals and training • Spare parts • Transportation services • Other outbound logistics costs • Scheduling
In-house staff support activities	• Payroll and benefits • Recruiting and training • Internal communications • Computer services • Procurement functions • R&D • Safety and security • Supplies and equipment • Union relations	**Wholesale distributor and dealer network activities**	• Includes all of the activities, associated costs and markups of distributors, wholesale dealers, retailers, and any other forward channel allies whose efforts are utilized to get the product into the hands of end-users/customers • Outbound logistics and transportation
Production activities and operations	• Facilities and equipment • Processing, assembling, and packaging • Labour • Maintenance	**Retailer activities and relations**	• Sales support activities to retailers, including sales calls to retailers, promotions, marketing programs, etc.

continued

activities, they may in fact just want higher value products and services that more thoroughly cover their needs.

The task of constructing a complete value-chain for a firm is not easy. It requires breaking a firm's own historical cost accounting data out into several principal cost categories and developing cost estimates for the backward and forward channel portions of getting the product to the end-user as well. It also requires the manager to estimate the same cost elements for one's rivals and then estimating their overall value chains—an advanced art in competitive intelligence in itself. But despite the tedium of the task and the imprecision of some of the estimates, the payoff in exposing the cost competitiveness of one's position and the attendant strategic alternatives makes it a valuable analytical tool.

In exhibit 3-4, observe that there are three main areas in the cost chain where important differences in the *relative* costs of competing firms can occur: in the suppliers' part of the cost chain, in their own respective activity segments, or in the forward channel portion of the chain. To the extent that the reasons for a firm's lack of cost competitiveness lie either in the backward or forward sections of the cost chain, then its job of reestablishing cost competitiveness may well have to extend beyond its own in-house operations. When a firm has a cost disadvantage in the area of purchased inputs and inbound logistics, five strategic options quickly emerge for consideration:

- Negotiate more favourable prices with suppliers.
- Integrate backward to gain control over material costs.
- Try to use lower priced substitute inputs.
- Search out sources of savings in inbound shipping and materials logistics costs.
- Try to make up the difference by initiating cost savings elsewhere in the overall cost chain.

When a firm's cost disadvantage occurs in the forward end of the cost chain, there are three corrective options:

- Push for more favourable terms with distributors and other forward channel allies.
- Change to a more economical distribution strategy, including the possibility of forward integration.
- Try to make up the difference by initiating cost savings earlier in the cost chain.

It is likely, of course, that a substantial portion of any relative cost disadvantage lies within rival firms' own activity-cost structures. Here, five options for restoring cost parity emerge:

- Initiate internal budget-tightening measures aimed at using fewer inputs to generate the desired output (cost-cutting retrenchment).
- Invest in cost-saving technological improvements.
- Innovate around the troublesome cost components as new investments are made in plant and equipment.
- Redesign the product or service to achieve cost reductions.
- Try to make up the internal cost disadvantage by achieving cost savings in the backward and forward portions of the cost chain.

The construction of a value chain is a valuable tool for competitive diagnosis because of what it reveals about a firm's overall cost/value competitiveness and the relative cost/value positions of firms in the industry. Examining the makeup of one's own value chain and comparing it against the chains of important rival firms indicates who has the most efficient and/or effective activities or competitive advantages and capabilities.

Assessing Supply and Distribution Chains

A manager analyzing his or her firm's value chain must also consider potential activities external to his or her firm because competitive advantages and capabilities can be attributable to a supplier or distributor. For example, Ikea's advantage of low cost is attributable to some degree to its suppliers who provide products at extremely low costs. The suppliers are able to provide this low cost because they have minimal overhead, no labour unions, and are focused on few activities and products. Ikea has restructured its value chain to provide these suppliers with many of the activities that would otherwise make their products expensive, such as product design and engineering. Therefore, restructuring activities in a value chain and coordinating activities with external activities can provide a firm with highly valuable and complex to imitate competitive advantages and capabilities.

Another example of an firm that reinvented its business activities, making use of the supply and distribution chain, is illustrated in exhibit 3-5. The solid lines in exhibit 3-5 illustrates how office supply products, such as stationary, staples, and pens were distributed in the early 1970s. Management in a company called OfficeMax noted that medium sized customers, such as law and medical offices, purchased their supplies through retail outlets where they incurred the high costs of retailing such as retail store overhead costs, stocking fees, and so on. OfficeMax setup a catalogue delivery service, which delivered from low cost warehouses located in rural sites using contracted overnight couriers. For the medium sized businesses, this provided lower cost products, and it improved the scope of products available and lowered delivery times to within 24 hours. OfficeMax has now evolved its strategy to include large retail box stores and the ability to order products through the Internet. It is notable that many other competitors have followed OfficeMax's strategy, which uses different supply chain channels to focus on, into the lower cost, medium sized customer in this market. Therefore, it is important that all of the various channels of supply, product flow, and distribution channels be identified in an industry, as certain approaches may provide competitive advantages to companies focusing on certain types of customers.

exhibit 3-5   A Business Supply and Distribution Chain for Office Supplies

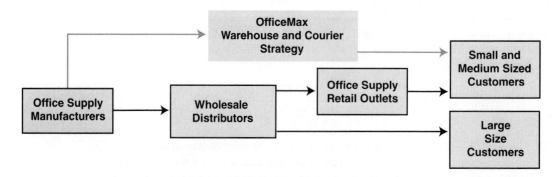

Some of the more fundamental issues to be considered when developing and examining the business system are:

- What are the various distribution and/or supply channels in the industry?
- What are the most efficient and effective channels to use in the industry?
- Are specific channels more effective and efficient for targeting specific customers (i.e., competitive positions in the market place)?
- Have any of the firms vertically integrated into different activities of the business system and will this provide an advantage or disadvantage?
- Are there any new types of channels of supply or distribution that are not being used in the industry, but might prove to be effective?

DEFINING THE "BUSINESS MODEL"

A new jargon has arisen over the last several years and it is "business model." A business model is essentially a value chain, but it also incorporates advantages provided to the firm outside of the firm itself, unlike the classic value chain that looks only at internal activities in the firm. For example, supply and distribution chains would be part of a business model. In addition, the classic value chain is essentially an accounting or financial exercise in examining value. The business model examines the value delivered to the customer from both a pecuniary and non-pecuniary perspective. Non-pecuniary value may come in the form of higher quality, more service, greater features, a wider selection of product types, more convenient location, and so on. This assessment ensures that management in a firm is assessing the complete value provided to the customer as perceived by that customer and relative to the competition. Thus, it is a more complete perspective of how much value the customer perceives the company to be providing to them.

An analysis of a business model is essentially the approach discussed above that examined the value chain and supply and distribution chains. It is important in this analysis to look not only at costs as the product and service moves through the business model activities, but also the non-pecuniary value produced by the activities and competitive advantages that the firm uses.

BENCHMARKING AND BEST PRACTICES

Benchmarking is the process of examining the value and efficiency of activities in your firm and comparing them to similar activities in other firms. Best Practices is an approach used by many good companies to better their capabilities, and ultimately their competitive advantage. The process involves identifying companies with the "best" functional activities and capabilities, and then sending in teams to study these capabilities. A team is made up of key workers and managers in the activity that will implement these "best" practice procedures in their company. The team evaluates the methods, work activities, processes, responsibilities, organizational linkages, and so on, in the company that has the "best" activity. Then they assess how and what can be implemented in their company to improve their competitive advantages in their activity.

Best Practices is usually facilitated by an outside consultant company who identifies the "best practice" companies. Normally, the firm identified is not a competitor, although some best practices companies, such as Nucor, invite its competitors into its plant as long as a reciprocal visit is possible. However, the key is getting an activity that is similar to the activity that is comparable and ultimately imitable in the target firm.

The objective of this approach is to install the best competitive advantages and capabilities into your company by copying not one firm, but by gathering the best competitive advantages from all firms both inside and outside their industry. Managers must, however, be aware that a Best Practices program is no substitute for developing one's own creative and unique competitive advantages and capabilities. The best capabilities are complex and abstruse, making them very difficult to imitate, and, therefore, poor candidates for a Best Practices program.

Finally, strategy involves developing competitive advantages built from resources and capabilities that uniquely fit the firm's competitive position. This fit must create a unique interaction and coordination between all of the parts, and selecting best practices from different firms may provide best individual capabilities that do not produce the best unified strategy.

THE PROCESS OF MANAGING THE DEVELOPMENT OF COMPETITIVE ADVANTAGES

Managing the resource identification and development process requires that managers assess what resource gaps must be filled to ensure that the firm's present strategy is competitive in the future. Now it is important to evaluate the quality of competitive advantages and capabilities required by the present and future desired strategy and competitive position. In particular, managers analyze what advantages should be focused upon to improve activities that are weak or to develop sustainable advantages or core competencies in critical activities. Therefore, the assessments of gaps and weaknesses of competitive advantages in a firm are critical to the firm's competitiveness. Exhibit 3-6 illustrates the managerial thinking during this process.

Two questions must be kept in mind when determining the specific advantages required for a strategy: Do the advantages support the firm's competitive position and core competencies, and can they be implemented effectively? Starting with advantages held, the strategist determines the unique characteristics of the firm's current advantages—those that differentiate it from its competitors. These characteristics may include competitive advantages and capabilities, core competencies, or sustainable competitive advantages and capabilities. Having established what these critical advantages are, a strategy is then developed that makes good use of them.

Advantage gaps are the differences between the advantages required and the advantages held. If most of the gaps can be reduced, then the probability of executing the strategy successfully is improved. However, if the gaps are large and cannot be reduced, the strategy probably has to be revised so that the competitive advantages of the firm conform more readily to the competitive strategic position of the firm.

It should be noted that managers often are not immediately aware of the future advantages that their company requires. However, the drivers behind development of all long-term advantages are the people in the firm. Therefore, many firms put in place programs and processes that continuously attempt to upgrade the quality and abilities of their personnel. This enables firms to continually improve the abilities of their personnel and to guide their behaviour so that they develop core competencies or sustainable competitive advantages that are specific to the firm's competitive position and strategy. These programs and processes are discussed more thoroughly in Chapter 6.

exhibit 3-6   The Relationship Between Strategy and Assessing Advantage Requirements

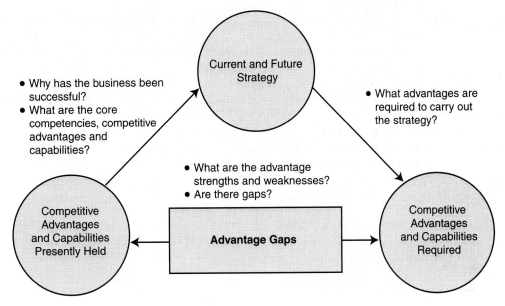

- What are the necessary changes in competitive advantages or capabilities?
- Can the necessary advantages be developed internally?
- Are the advantages within reach?
- Are some advantages precursors to the attainment of other advantages?
- Who and how will the changes be implemented?
- Does the strategy and competitive advantage need to be rethought?

EVALUATING COMPETITIVE ADVANTAGES HELD AND DETERMINING COMPETITIVE ADVANTAGES REQUIRED

Competitive advantages can be evaluated from several different perspectives. The most prevalent way of evaluating them is **by function**: finance, research and development, human resources, operations, marketing, and so forth. This really mirrors the value-chain analysis approach described earlier. Some of the important questions for such an approach are included in exhibit 3-7.

When a functional perspective is taken, the strategist also needs to consider the context within which the functions operate. The contribution of each function to the business's strategy needs to be addressed as some functions may be more important to the strategy than others. The interrelationships among the functions also need to be considered because what is done in one function may have a bearing on what can be done in another function.

A second way of evaluating resources is **by type**: financial, physical, human, and organizational. Financial resources are the funds that the company raises. They are the most basic and flexible resources of the business, and can be converted into other resources. Converting other resources into financial resources is less certain and more difficult. Physical resources are the buildings, raw material, and equipment that the company has to work with and what it can do with them. Human resources are the

exhibit 3-7   An Overview of the Functional Perspective

Function	A Partial List of Questions to Answer
Finance	• What is the apparent capacity of the firm to generate internal and external funds? • What funds are required for each strategic alternative?
Research and development	• How important is technology to the firm's processes and products? • What percentage of the firm's resources is devoted to research and development?
Human resources	• What is the ambition, depth, drive, loyalty, and skill of the managerial/administrative group in the firm?
Procurement	• What is the cost, flexibility, motivation, productivity, and skill of the work force? • How important is the procurement function to the firm?
Operations	• Does the firm have good relations with suppliers? What are the capacity, cost, and productivity of operations? • What is the age, condition, and flexibility of the plant and equipment? • What is the quality of the products produced?
Marketing	• Does the firm command a premium price, and, if so, why? • How well does the firm know its customers and its competitors?

number and type of people in the firm and what they are able to do. Organizational resources are the procedures and techniques the firm has developed that are necessary for success in the business.

A fourth way of evaluating resources is in terms of their **breadth**. A resource is essentially broad/wide when it is easily transferred to other situations and narrow/specialized when it is not. Sales staff with knowledge of many different products is an example of a broad resource, while specialized product knowledge is an example of a narrow resource. A broad resource base facilitates a business's expansion of its product, market, and industry scope, while a narrow resource base serves to limit the firm's ability to increase its scope.

A final way of evaluating resources is in terms of **location or business unit**. This is particularly useful when the firm has diverse businesses or locations. Other categorizing approaches may be useful if management in the firm identifies with the categorization methodology. Using different approaches to assessing competitive advantage gaps is useful because it forces managers to take new perspectives of their company's competitiveness.

RESOURCE GAPS

Rarely is the precise combination of resources needed to pursue a strategy in place. Furthermore, a firm is constantly trying to improve its competitive position and advantages, thus requiring new resources. This makes resource gap analysis critically important for a manager. When assessing the resources, a useful approach is to construct a table with entries down the side for the activities or functions, and with headings across the top for (1) current resources, (2) projected resources, (3) gaps between those two, and (4) how the gaps might be filled (exhibit 3-8). The body of this table is then filled in with the analytical details.

Resource gaps not only occur when a firm takes on a new strategy, but just by maintaining an ongoing strategy creates resource gaps. New resources must be developed when existing resources deteriorate, depreciate, or turn over. In addition, success with the existing strategy can create resource gaps as additional resources are required for growth. On occasion, more resources are generated than can be employed profitably in a business. Under utilization of existing resources is a negative form of resource gap analysis. Overproduction of resources can be problematic also. For example, when a firm generates more cash than it can use in the business making itself an attractive takeover target.

Identifying the Gaps

Resource gaps are identified through strength-and-weakness analysis as part of the SWOT analysis described earlier. Determination of strengths and weaknesses involves a relative comparison between those resources the company has and those it needs. In depth analysis of advantage gaps details the magnitude and type of resource needed, the availability of such a resource, methods for obtaining the advantage, and the timing or priority of need for such a resource. It should be noted that some resources may have to be sold and some acquired to meet the needs of one's competitive strategy.

Reducing the Gaps

The ability of the business to reduce advantage gaps is influenced by the magnitude and nature of the changes required, as well as the firm's ability to implement these changes. Reallocating, developing, buying, and selling advantages can reduce these gaps. Depending on how the gap is reduced, cost, ease, and timing will differ. Advantages can be acquired from the outside, but their high market cost can make it more desirable to develop them internally. Developing advantages is usually cheaper, but slower, but it can have other positive benefits, such as providing for the development of a continuous stream of advantages (e.g., managers). Moreover, development of advantages may be required if sufficient quantities or qualities are not available, either elsewhere in the business or in the marketplace. Of course, many tactical issues have to be addressed when considering how gaps might be filled.

It should also be noted that the ability to reduce an advantage gap will depend on the particular country in which the firm is located. A firm's advantage base is not simply

exhibit 3-8 Assessing Resource Gaps

Activity or Functional Area	Current Advantages	Required Advantages	Advantage Gaps	Filling the Gaps: Tactics and Risk
Finance				
R&D				
Human Resources				
Procurement				
Operations				
Marketing				

a function of its own operational regime, but a function of the location and country within which it operates. In other words, there is an interaction between firm-level and country-level sources of advantages and competitive advantage.

Changing a firm's advantages carries certain risks. These risks are associated with the number and magnitude of the advantages as well as the quality of advantages demanded by the strategic change. The manager must be careful that he or she does not make such a radical strategic so as to render the present firm advantages ineffectual and create advantage demands that are impossible for the firm to fulfill in the required time frame. It may be more acceptable for the firm to take a more incremental strategic approach to change where advantages are developed appropriate for the firm's intermediate competitive positions and associated competitive advantage.

EXAMPLE OF DEVELOPING COMPETITIVE ADVANTAGES

Loblaws developed considerable competitive advantages as it evolved into its new competitive positions, as described in Chapter 2. The following are some of the more important competitive advantages that Loblaws developed:

- Top management depth: Mr. Weston accomplished this by hiring a number managers who had MBAs from top business schools and extensive business experience in a number of different businesses. First-rate people are the underpinnings of any strong strategy because, ultimately, it is people who have to lead strategic development and execution. Most strong companies have strategically started this process by getting a first class upper management team.
- Loblaws closed store locations that were not in growth and middle to upper class residential areas. Loblaws also sold some other assets that were not key to its Canadian grocery strategy to get the capital to acquire other needed assets, such as new stores.
- The new stores were extremely well designed. They were larger than normal grocery stores and the design provided shoppers with a pleasant atmosphere. These stores improved the shopping experience immensely because they were physically pleasant, and the size allowed for a far wider product selection to be offered to the customer.
- Loblaws also began to develop a number of different types of stores that catered to different market sectors, including specialty sections in their main stores that catered to value added tastes and "no-frills" stores that sold lower cost and bulk items.
- Loblaws developed supplier relations with a far wider variety of suppliers, bringing in culturally diverse foods and a wider variety of fresh fish and vegetables. These relations enabled it to develop in-house brands of food that are manufactured to their specifications by suppliers.
- Many different types of branded foods were developed. The most prestigious was the President's Choice line of food, which was high quality food that has become the most widely recognized food brand in Canada. Loblaws also developed a "no-name" line of food that has become an economical brand despite the "no-name" title.
- Loblaws has slowly acquired competitors in regions in Canada in which it was not represented, and attempted to inject its value added, broad product scope strategy into these markets. This enabled Loblaws to become a truly across-Canada grocery chain.

The above list of advantages is a brief example of the continual development that Loblaws has developed over the past several decades. In fact, the key to its overall competitive advantage is its ability to continually innovate and become more efficient and effective.

SUMMARY

Finding an acceptable fit between the strategy and the advantages available to the business is a major step in formulating strategy. First, the firm's advantage must be examined in terms of what is available and what is needed. Advantages can be evaluated in several ways: by functional area, by type, by tangibility, by breadth, and by activity costs. Advantage gaps must be identified and evaluated to determine the likelihood of their being overcome. Whether they can be overcome depends on the gaps' size, number, and nature; the ways in which the gaps can be reduced; and the time available. When the likelihood of filling the advantage gaps poses too great a risk to be acceptable, the strategy has to be modified in order to bring its advantage requirements closer to current advantages.

Summary of The Competitive Resource and Advantage Analysis

Linking Competitive Position and Advantage

- It is critical that management examine competitive advantages relative to the demands for value by the customers in the firm's competitive position.

Analysis of Firm's Competition Resources and Advantages

- Define the characteristics of resources and advantages available to the firm, which can be categorized as one of the following:
  - Tangible or intangible resources
  - Competitive advantages
  - Competitive capabilities
  - Sustainable competitive advantages and capabilities
  - Core competencies
- Define the quality of the resources and advantages available to firm, which should be done simultaneously with the above analysis. Determine if the resources and advantages are:
  - Valuable
  - Durable
  - Rare
  - Inimitable
  - Complex

Assess the Firm's Business Model

- What are the activities in the value chain and are they quality resources to the firm as defined by the previous quality categories? It is particularly important to look at the relationship and interlinkages between activities.
- Examine the firm's supply chain both from suppliers through to the eventual buyers. How does this business model compare to other competitors' business models?

Developing New Resources and Advantages

- Benchmark similar high quality activities, advantages, and resources in other high performance companies and compare them to your own.

- Assess the resource gaps that you have as a firm. What are the resources you require to acquire, or develop, to enable you to have the competitive advantages to effectively carry out your strategy?

Additional Notes and Recommended Readings

Barney, J.P. Firm Resources; *Gaining Competitive Advantage*, 1999, Addison Wesley Publishing.

Barney, J.P. *Gaining and Sustaining Advantage*, 1997, Adddison Wesley Publishing.

Bontis, N, Gragonetti, N.C., and Roos, G., "The Knowledge Toolbox: A Review of the Tools Available to Measure and Manager Intangible Resources." *European Management Journal*, 17 no. 4, 1999.

For more discussion on the analysis of advantages, see R. B. Buchele, "How to Evaluate a Firm," *California Management Review*, Fall 1962; J. H. Grant and W. R. King, *The Logic of Strategic Planning* (Boston: Little, Brown, 1982), chaps. 4-7; M. E. Porter, *Competitive Advantage: Creating and Sustaining Superior Performance* (New York: Free Press, 1985); W. E. Rothschild, *Putting It All Together: A Guide to Strategic Thinking* (New York: AMA-COM, 1976), chap. 6; R. S. Sloma, *How to Measure Managerial Performance* (New York: Macmillan, 1980); and H. H. Stevenson, "Defining Corporate Strengths and Weaknesses," *Sloan Management Review*, Spring 1976, pp. 51-68.

George Stalk, P. Evans, and L.E. Shulman. "Competing on Capabilities: The New Rules of Corporate Strategy." *Harvard Business Review*, March -April 1992, pp. 57-69.

Joseph L. Bower, *Managing the Advantage Allocation Process*. Boston: Harvard Business School Press, 1986, p. 80

Kaplan, R.S., and Norton, D.P., "The Balanced Scorecard – Measures That Drive Performance," *Harvard Business Review*, 70, no. 1, 1992.

Lado Augustine, Nancy Boyd, and Peter Wright. "A Competency-Based Model of Sustainable Competitive Advantage: Toward a Conceptual Integration." *Journal of Management*, March 1992, pp. 77-92.

Prahalad, C.K. and Hamel, G., "The Core Competences of the Corporation." *Harvard Business Review*. 70, no 3., 1990.

See M. E. Porter, *The Competitive Advantage of Nations* (New York: The Free Press, 1990).

Teece, D., "Capturing Value from Knowledge Assets: The New Economy, Markets for Know-how and Intangible Assets.," *California Management Review* 40 no.3, 1998.

Teece, D.J., Pisano, G., and Shuen, A., "Dynamic Capabilities and Strategic Intent," *Strategic Management Journal*, 18, pg 509-33, 1997.

chapter 4 Generic Business Level Strategies and Tactics

Gambling is when you roll the dice; business is when you control the dice.

PETER MUNK, CHAIRMAN OF TRIZECHAHN

Jazz is like strategy because it allows you to approach any issue on the basis that nothing is too outrageous to consider, or too ridiculous to try. You begin with a coherent proposition, but you admit you have no idea where it's leading. In the process, you may go down blind alleys. Jazz musicians do that all the time: take off on a lick and push it to the absolute limit. That's how the best strategies are born.

IZZY ASPER, FOUNDER OF CANWEST GLOBAL

This chapter examines a variety of generic business strategies and tactics. These strategies and tactics are time-tested approaches to managing companies in specific competitive and market situations. As such, they have become important foundations, which most managers regard as starting points for developing their strategy or tactics in an industry. However, to make these strategies truly successful, managers must interpose their own originality and creativity. This is because most managers, including rivals, expect these strategies, and thus, to catch rivals unaware, a somewhat new approach must be taken. Consequently, it is necessary for managers to develop strategies having unique details and deviations from the studied approaches to obtain superior performance. Additionally, firms must continuously strive to improve their tactics as well as their competitive position and advantages, because it is only through constant improvement that one stays ahead of competitors that are both copying and improving themselves. Constant improvement, what the Japanese call Kaizen, is the only way a firm will sustain its long-term competitive advantage and success.

The generic strategies and tactics described in this chapter are specific to firms that are in particular market and competitive environments. The first section examines different types of generic strategies that are found in most industries. Then strategic tactics that are appropriate for specific industries and market situations are examined.

COMPETITIVE POSITION GENERIC STRATEGIES

There are three generic competitive strategies, or competitive positions, that researchers have found to be relatively effective. These generic competitive positions are overall cost leadership, differentiation (or value added), and market focus. Descriptions of the different competitive positions follow:

- **Overall cost leadership** is when a firm becomes the cost leader in an industry. Very often the firm is both the cost and price leader in its industry, although not always. Examples are Costco, and Wal-Mart in the retail sector.

- **Differentiation** is when management adds different features, services, and attributes valued by customers to the product, making the product distinctive from other competitors' products. A good example is Neiman Marcus; an extremely expensive department store in the U.S., where a diamond studded t-shirt sells for over US $2,000.

- **Focus** is when management designs its products and adds features and services that appeal to a distinct customer type or segment. A focused strategy zeros in on a particular type of customer or geographic area. Examples of a focused competitive position are Mr. Biggs, which sells large sized men's clothing; Air North, which focuses on providing airline services to small northern communities; and children's hospitals that exist in most major Canadian cities. There is also an implicit fourth competitive position, and this is the breadth competitive position, which is just the opposite of the focused strategy (i.e., the firm does not focus on any particular type of customer in the market). Examples of stores that use a breadth strategy are Eaton's, Sears, and the Bay.

Exhibit 4-1 illustrates the different combinations of competitive positions that can result from these three different generic competitive positions. As is seen, four actual competitive positions can be chosen based on the alternative dimensions of market scope and product/service value.

exhibit 4-1   Generic Industry Competitive Positions

Product/Market Scope	Product/Service Value	
	Low Cost	Differentiation
Breadth	Breadth/ Low Cost	Breadth/ Differentiated
Focus	Focused or Niche/ Low Cost	Focused or Niche/ Differentiated

Examples of Canadian retail clothiers that occupy these four competitive positions are:

- Breadth/Low Cost—Winners (sells seconds and out of fashion clothes)
- Breadth/Differentiated—Holt Renfrew (sells high fashion clothes and personal goods)
- Niche/Low Cost—Cotton Ginney Plus (sells low cost T-shirts etc., to oversize women)
- Niche/Differentiated—Harry Rosen (sells high fashion men's clothes)

It should be noted that these generic competitive positions tend to require specific competitive advantages. This association between competitive position and competitive advantages is consistent with the strategic framework developed in Chapter 1. A firm requires specific competitive advantages to compete in a competitive position, and very often the competitive advantages are unique to that competitive position. Therefore, firms having low cost positions require competitive advantages that promote these low cost approaches to business, while value added or differentiated companies require competitive advantages and tactics that provide the company's products with valued attributes and features. For example, a low cost auto manufacture stresses very many different competitive advantages to an auto manufacture that produces high cost luxury cars.

It should be noted that the tactical concerns related to these competitive positions often are associated with a firm's set of competitive advantages that ensure it is competitive in its position. It is vitally important that competitive advantages efficiently and effectively support the firm's competitive position. However, management also must continually look for potential changes in the market, technology, economy, customer behavior, etc., that makes a particular business model (i.e., competitive position and competitive advantage value proposition) uncompetitive. Examples of companies having these generic positions and some of their unique tactical concerns are described in the following sections.

Low Cost

An example of a low cost competitive position is Costco. This retail operation concentrates on keeping costs low. This low cost position necessitates that Costco managers concentrate on developing competitive advantages that minimize overall costs. Some competitive advantages that enable Costco to successfully compete in its low cost position are:

- Rather than locate in a typical retail store, Costco uses a warehouse facility where functionality and efficiency take precedence over aesthetics. Furthermore, this facility is normally located in an inexpensive quasi-industrial zoned location.
- Costco orders items in large volumes and items are packaged in bulk. This makes keeping inventory, ordering, and checking out much more efficient compared to other stores.
- Entrance and exits are monitored by staff to minimize theft.
- Payment must be in cash or on a pre-cleared checking account or credit card. This eliminates non-payment costs.
- Staffing needs are kept to a minimum. For example, there is no staff to help customers understand products on the floor, and there are usually long checkout lines because of the limited number of staff.
- An upfront membership fee is required (approximately $50 annually), and this helps cash flow.

Tactical concerns of companies using a low cost strategy include:

- Managers must not reduce costs to a point where the product quality is below the lowest acceptable level by customers. Companies must be aware that customers tend to have minimal acceptable quality standards, and in North America, these standards tend to be rising.
- New technologies may change the business model in an industry, making it feasible to either offer similar products at lower costs or better products at the same costs. For example, the Internet is changing how people buy airline tickets because it is both cheaper and easier for many customers compared to having to visit a travel agent.

- Managers who constantly focus on costs may eliminate a function or activity that is important to the longer-term survival. These functions can be cut to make budget over the short-term, however, they may be critical for longer-term competitiveness. For example cutting R&D advertising may save money in the short-term, but it may be strategically ill-advisable over the long-term.

- When a firm focuses on low cost buyers, managers must be cognizant of future demographic and social trends that might influence purchasers to move up market (i.e., buy products with more features or higher quality). Examples of retail companies that have made this mistake are K-Mart and Woolco, both of which have been forced into bankruptcy.

- Competition may produce a product that is not as cheap but represents a better cost/value offering. For example, K-Mart products had slightly cheaper products than Wal-Mart. However, customers felt that Wal-Mart offered better value and greater selection. Thus, firms having a low cost strategy must always be aware of the value customers perceive their products to have relative to competitors, particularly if a new competitor is entering the market or an old competitor is moving into its competitive position.

Focus

An example of a focused competitive position is Kinnikinnick Foods Inc., the specialty food producer described in Chapter 1. Kinnikinnick focuses on providing baked food products to celiac's and individuals having food sensitivities to gluten and lactose. This competitive position means that Kinnikinnick faces minimal direct competition. Kinnikinnick's advantages that support its competitive position are:

- It has extensive nutritional and cuisine knowledge of how to produce all types of baked goods without milk or flour.

- It has a strong distribution system linking it with retail outlets that specialize in providing food to customers having food sensitivities.

- It has a brand name built on its distinctive, delicious tasting unique products.

- It has a network of reliable suppliers that provide the unique organic supplies and alternatives to milk and flour inputs.

- It has built a strong organizational culture that understands, empathizes with, and has built relationships with this customer group.

- It has a mail order business and Internet Web site that has won several awards.

Tactical concerns of companies using a focused strategy include these issues:

- Managers must be aware of changing customer preferences or tastes because the strategy depends upon a certain market segment having specific needs and desires. Such a change can dissolve the market and customer segment that they have focused upon.

- Another real risk is if technology or a new substitute product is developed that provides the customers with a better value proposition.

- Another risk is that the market in which a firm is offering products merges with the broader market. This usually occurs when the broader market decides on a standard or the products offered in the broader market meet the standard of peripheral segments. This can easily occur in high-tech markets where product standards are

so important to users. An example is when Corel attempted to focus their Word-
Perfect product on the lawyer segment. This did not work because this market segment liked the standardization offered by the Microsoft Word product, a product
that had been widely adopted.

- A risk that entrepreneurial firms take when they focus on a small but growing
  market segment is that the market may become large enough to attract major competition. A firm must be cognizant of this potential because it enables it to either
  adjust its competitive position, or develop competitive advantages to compete with
  larger rivals.

- Finally, a firm taking a focused approach must be aware of both the value added
  features and cost of a product since customers are buying based on the overall offering. Sometimes companies become focused on specific attributes and forget
  about costs or vice versa. This is dangerous in a focused strategy. For example,
  Corel focused on price when it marketed to the lawyer market segment, yet this
  was probably one of the least important buying criteria for this market segment.

Differentiation

An example of a differentiated or value added competitive position is Roots clothing
stores. Roots has established itself as a strong competitor in the value added, leisure
fashion retail business. Some of the competitive advantages that support this competitive position are:

- Roots has developed a brand image of high quality, comfortable, and fashionable
  products.

- It has developed a unique fashion style, which has come to represent the "Canadian" outdoor valve added leisure look. This style has become very fashionable
  throughout North America.

- The two owners are highly capable managers. One is very proficient at marketing
  while the other is an operations oriented individual. Their combined skill and drive
  is a major reason this business has succeeded.

- Roots has a chain of stores located in fashion oriented shopping districts or malls
  across Canada and the US.

- It has developed unique, but highly effective approaches to marketing including:

  - Roots is terrific at developing event marketing programs. Their most success-
    ful event was the 2002 winter Olympics where they were the clothing suppli-
    ers for both the Canadian and US winter national teams. This was so
    successful that many products have been impossible to keep in stock during
    Olympic years.

  - Roots builds relationships throughout the fashion business and beyond by
    holding event-based parties. These parties are so enjoyable that they attract
    important political, fashion, and even Hollywood personalities who become
    important supporters of the store.

  - Roots now has upscale outdoor lodges located in several wilderness areas.
    Again, the objective is to push its image as a very high quality, casual outdoor
    "Canadian" branding reputation. Roots recently tried to enter the exclusive
    high-end air travel industry, but backed out when management realized there
    would not be a large enough market for such a service in Canada. All of these
    business tactics tend to further enhance Roots's exclusive brand image.

Tactical concerns for companies having a differentiation strategy include:

- Managers that use the differentiation strategy often focus on adding value, features, and services to their product. However, costs do matter because customers are not willing to purchase a product at any price.

- Managers must be aware of the changing tastes and preferences of customers. A change in tastes could mean that the product attribute that their differentiation is based upon becomes no longer desirable.

- Technology can marginalize a differentiation strategy if the technological change makes it inexpensive to offer such a differentiated product. For example, increasing computer chip processing speeds eliminated the need for super-computers, and all firms that specialized in super-computers no longer exist.

- Substitutes can be very damaging to differentiated products, particularly if the substitutes provide a far different, yet perceived superior set of product attributes and value to customers.

- Standardization in a market can be a challenge because it may mean that all customers want a similar type of product. This can be particularly problematic in high-tech markets as they mature. For example, in the computer database industry many firms originally attempted to differentiate their products based upon a specific set of features, and often these features were aimed at a specific type of customer. However, customers eventually realized that a standardized product would enable them to upgrade or downgrade their system, train only one set of programmers, communicate with customers, suppliers, etc., and integrate any acquisitions or new business units that were created seamlessly. Therefore, most firms now pick one of a few standard databases available.

The above examples demonstrate how competitive position, advantages, and tactics are necessarily linked. Most successful firms have to select a clear strategy that emphasizes one of the generic product/service positions (i.e., either a differentiated, or low cost strategy), and then continually work on improving their competitive position, advantages, and tactics relative to rivals. In rare cases, firms can be both a differentiator and low cost producer simultaneously. Usually, these firms dominate their industry. Examples of firms that have been able to build dual competitive positions and the associated competitive advantages include Intel, Microsoft, and Boeing.

COMPETITIVE TACTICS UNDER DIFFERENT COMPETITIVE FORCES AND MANAGING FOR SUSTAINABLE COMPETITIVE ADVANTAGE

In Chapter 2, competitive industry structure was analyzed using Porter's Five Forces. From a manager's perspective, they translate into competitive threats that must be managed actively to ensure the firm remains successful in the future. These competitive threats represent both internal and external threats to profitability in the eyes of a manager, and are illustrated in exhibit 4-2.

Managers must respond vigorously to minimize these internal and external threats, and a variety of appropriate tactical responses are described in the following sections.

exhibit 4-2   Competitive Threats on a Firm's Profitability

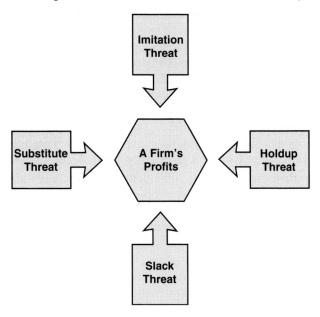

Tactical Responses to Imitation

Imitation occurs by both new entrants to and existing competitors in an industry. A good example of imitation is how Asian companies successfully imitate North American companies using their low cost competitive advantages. For instance, Intel had the majority of the computer chip memory market share. However, during the 1970s, Japanese companies successfully copied Intel's technical products and processes forcing Intel out of the computer memory chip business in the early 1980s.

It is important that managers understand and react to threats of imitation. Managers can minimize this threat using a number of tactics, which are related to building barriers to entry or imitation. Some of the more important approaches are:

- *Economies of scale and scope* should be developed by a company where possible. This does not mean just building a larger company, but tying it in with the development of specific competitive advantages, such as brand name through advertising, a broad complex distribution network, highly technical and efficient production facilities, a breadth of complementary products that use related competitive advantages, etc.

- *Learning/private information* can make it difficult because imitators do not have the necessary information to copy a business strategy. Learning enables a firm to be the forerunner competitively in an industry, while keeping information and knowledge private thwarts rivals from copying a strategy. Many service industries, such as consulting, banks, legal, and financing guard their information and learning very carefully. Learning and private information is becoming more important as the information age evolves and managers must be aware of the competitive advantage that such information provides.

- *Contracts and relationships* with key suppliers or buyers can make it difficult to imitate because imitators cannot get access to value-added buyers, large volume buyers, or quality or low cost suppliers.

- *Network externalities* are defined as markets where customers demand the same type or standard of product because they want to make sure they can interconnect either directly or indirectly with one another. An example of a network externality is telephones where phone manufacturers have come together to set a standard for phones ensuring that customers can talk to one another. Some companies have developed proprietary standards, and thus, network externalities, which make customers preferentially want to buy that company's product. For instance, Microsoft's MS Word program has become the standard for most companies because they want to be able to share and exchange word processing documents. In addition, a common standard often makes servicing and maintenance cheaper for companies. Developing a network externality can be a very valuable advantage.

- *Threats of retaliation* can minimize imitation because rivals are afraid of copying. However, the threatening firm must be able to intimidate rivals with a tactic that will punish rivals, and, that rivals know it is able to carry out. Retaliation can involve aggressive and expensive competitive actions against rivals. Retaliation tactics include legal action, aggressive pricing strategies, and other market share confrontation.

- *Time lags* can make it more difficult for imitators to catch leading firms in an industry because the leading firm can use these time lags to further their competitive advantage. Managers in a company should be aware of time lags when they are present in the industry or their strategy. An example is NutraSweet, which staggered the ending dates of the long-term contracts with their buyers. This made imitation difficult because it would take time for an imitator to aggregate enough buyers to make a plant worthwhile.

- *Strategic complexity* is an important tactic that involves developing a strategy with complex and latent competitive advantages. A complex network of advantages makes it difficult for imitators to understand and replicate a strategy. For instance, Ikea has developed a complex set of advantages, that involves designing, supplier relationships, product characteristics, services, store design and location distinctiveness. Furthermore, these advantages must be interlinked to be effective, which makes it extremely difficult for competitors to imitate.

- *Upgrading* on a continual basis can keep imitators at bay. Ultimately, upgrading is necessary in every business, but when a firm uses it as a competitive advantage, they put competitors at a disadvantage when they are trying to imitate. Corel's fast development cycle has made imitation difficult for rivals, particularly in their core product, Corel Draw.

- *Strategic Fit* is when one's competitive position is uniquely appropriate for specialized competitive advantages. This makes it difficult for rivals to imitate because they must develop or acquire competitive advantages that are only useful in this narrow competitive position, a risk that many companies may not want to take. Strategic fit is most appropriate when a firm has a focused or highly differentiated strategy and the market segment focused upon is relatively limited.

Responses to Substitution

Substitution can be one of the most dangerous competitive threats to a company. This is because substituters are often not well monitored by firms compared to direct rivals in an industry. This enables substituters to build strategic and market momentum and become formidable rivals before they become noticed. In addition, trends, including fashion, social, and technical trends, can alter customers purchasing behavior making a substitute's product suddenly more desirable and valuable. Finally, some substituters have business models that are difficult to imitate by mainstream companies. Examples of successful substitutes are desktop computers for mainframe computers, cell phones for wire-based phones, and satellite TV dishes for cable TV. As is seen, substitutes can completely take over a market sector or they may just appeal to a portion of the customers. In either case, they can do considerable damage to a firm's long-term financial prospects. The following are tactics that can be used to fight potential substituters:

- *Not responding* is an option if you think that the substitute product will not challenge the value provided by your product or service. However, substituters should be monitored, particularly how customers perceive the value of substitutes.

- *Fighting* can be useful, but it also can be expensive. Methods of fighting generally involve attempting to improve the value provided to your customer by either lowering your prices, bundling and marketing new features that improve your product or service, or instigating legal action against the substituter.

- *Switching* involves giving up your strategy and adopting the substitute's strategy and product. Switching can be done when the substituter's strategy and product are clearly superior. However, sometimes switching is difficult due to the fit issues between competitive position and advantage differences that exist between a company and their substituter.

- *Recombining* can be useful when parts of the substitute's competitive advantages can be effectively integrated into a company's business model or strategy. This is particularly useful when the recombined strategy is more value to customers.

- *Straddling* involves keeping your old business model while also adopting the substitute's strategy as a secondary business model. Straddling is an option if the manager thinks they can viably operate two business models, which often means implementing and operating two businesses. This strategy may be viable, but sometimes it is a sign of indecision by the manager who does not want to commit to either strategy.

- *Harvesting* is an option if the old business model is not viable and it would be too expensive to adopt the new substitute's strategy. Timing can be important. A manager who harvests a business prior to or early in the decline of the business may get reasonably good value for their business. Late harvesting tends to obtain less value.

Responses to Holdup

Holdup, as the name indicates, is when buyers and suppliers are "holding-up" the firm for some of their profits. Buyers and suppliers can do this if they have some type of bargaining power over the firm. These different types of powers were delineated in Chapter 2 under buyer and supplier competitive power. It is important that managers understand the negotiating power of these two parties, as well as their future power, become important considerations. Tactics that are appropriate to limit holdup are:

- *Contracting* is an option that locks the buyer or the supplier into a long-term agreement. This is particularly effective if the buyer or supplier is going to gain bargaining power sometime in the future.

- *Integrating* forward or backward into the buyer's or supplier's business is possible. However, a manager must assess the risks of integrating up or downstream versus the returns of doing so. Vertical integration tends to restrict a firm's future strategic options and may hamper the company's strategy in the future.
- *Bargaining hard* is an option that can be used in conjunction with another tactic. However, it often results in deteriorating relationships with suppliers or buyers (e.g., union negotiations). Because of this concern, it is most useful when a firm is not contemplating a long-term relationship with the supplier or buyer.
- *Reducing asset-specificity* is the action of making your company less dependent upon the supplier or buyer. Asset specificity is when the specialized assets or capabilities of the buyer or supplier are required by a firm to produce their product. This reliance gives the supplier or buyer considerable holdup power over the firm. Reducing asset-specificity is useful when these assets are either replaced or duplicated. Finally, sometimes firms can alter their business model and eliminate the need for specialized asset.
- *Building relationships* enables firms to develop mutual understanding and commitment. It reinforces the notion that firms cooperating can develop value that would otherwise not be available to them if they worked independently. The Japanese have been effective in using this advantage in some industries.
- *Developing trust* is a similar notion to the above, but this involves the act of developing a reputation for trustworthiness and fair treatment. Trust tends to increase the bargaining power of a company because suppliers and buyers want to do business with it.

Responses to Slack

Slack is the measure of unproductive behavior and the lack of motivation required to better one's advantages into the future. In a company, it represents the internal threat of not being "perfectly" efficient or effective both now and into the future. It is important for companies to continually strive to become more efficient and effective through various methods. General Electric (GE), for example, uses a variety of training programs and management control processes to improve quality and efficiencies. One quality program, called Six Sigma, is estimated to have saved GE billions of dollars. Ultimately, every individual in a company must continually improve his or her abilities and skills to ensure slack is minimized in the organization.

The following tactics should be considered when managers fight slack in their organization:

- *Gathering information* is important because it enables managers to understand where inefficiencies occur in their organization. It also allows for a better understanding of what is being done properly both within the firm and in other firms to effectively fight slack.
- *Monitoring behaviour* is similar to gathering information but it focuses on the act of watching how people act in their day-to-day roles. Are they doing their job efficiently, do they interact effectively with others in the organization, are they interacting with customers properly, and so on. This approach is useful for discovering behavioural problems that might not be revealed through other informational metrics.

- *Offering performance incentives* is a very powerful approach to motivating improved performance. However, performance incentives must be based upon measures that are controllable by the employee or group of employees being remunerated.

- *Shaping norms* can influence slack because norms or attitudes affect behaviour. Therefore, an aggressive, hard working, creative organizational culture tends to result in employees that work efficiently and effectively in an organization.

- *Changing leadership* can be helpful for two reasons. First, a new leader can be selected that aggressively supports productivity programs and stresses the elimination of slack in the organization. Second, it can be a strong signal for change, just as a change in a NHL team's coach signals to the players that the team is not playing well enough.

- *Mobilizing the organization for change* is important because it also signals to the employees that greater production is required by everybody. Types of mobilization include: changing the organizational structure (i.e., reporting structures), changing the organizational processes and remuneration schemes, and even replacing key workers, hiring or replacing groups of employees to signal the importance of change.

COMPETITIVE TACTICS OF COMPANIES IN SPECIFIC INDUSTRY ENVIRONMENTS

Highly Competitive or Fragmented Industries

Industries that have a large number of competitors are called fragmented industries because many small firms having very similar competitive positions and advantages fragment the market. Competition in these industries is intense because of the number of competitors and the inability of competitors to differentiate from one another. Characteristically, fragmented industries are easy to enter because of low entry barriers, as delineated by Porter's Five Forces model (see exhibit 2-4). Examples of highly competitive or fragmented industries are dry cleaning, bicycle couriers, and small corner stores.

Approaches to competing in fragmented industries are often limited by the very nature of the industry. However, potentially effective competitive tactics include:

- Focus very carefully on low costs and process innovations that minimize costs. When a firm is expanding, it should apply a "formula" approach to duplicating plants and offices. This minimizes both the capital and operating costs of the expansion.

- Look for unrecognized market niches where customers are not having their needs met. A firm may be able to take a focused differentiated or focused low cost approach to such a small market. Sometimes competition is less intensive in smaller, less dense markets. It may be possible for a company to focus on these markets in an efficient and effective manner. This is one of the strategic approaches that Wal-Mart took when it established itself as one of the top competitors in the very competitive merchandise/retailing industry.

- Constantly look for new trends in technology, government policies, international relations, etc., that enable your firm to take advantage of a newly created market, or to build new competitive advantages and barriers to entry.

- Are there alternative approaches to the standard business model that would provide the company with a competitive advantage? Examine Porter's Five Forces Model and look for ways to change the way business is done. Often firms in fragmented markets become lethargic and miss opportunities for competitive improvement. Investigate things such as economies of scale, forward or backward integration, economies of scope, etc., to change the nature of the business model and, thus, the competitive forces. This approach often requires considerable creativity combined with a certain environmental change that enables an aggressive firm to take advantage of opportunities.

GENERIC STRATEGIES BASED ON THE LIFE CYCLE

Emerging Stage Industries

Emerging industries are recently formed industries resulting from technological changes, changes in customer needs, or legal and political changes. Characteristically, firms in emerging industries face uncertainty in key competitive dimensions, such as technology. If the environment conspires to change the nature of that competitive advantage, and it is no longer effective, the firm loses its ability to support its competitive position. For example, a firm may have a strong technological advantage that is nullified when a new technology becomes available. An example of an emerging industry is biotechnology. Competitive tactics in high-tech and e-commerce industries is covered more thoroughly in Chapter 8.

Competitive tactics for coping in an emerging industry include:

- Ensure that the firm has strong capabilities so that it can contend with the uncertainty in the environment.It is critical that top managers are knowledgeable and aware of the competitive advantages and associated environmental forces. This ensures rapid action if changes appear to be taking place. The firm may also want to supplement its in-house strengths with external forecasting capabilities.
- Concentrate initially on the competitive advantages that are vital to learning and creating better products and services for the customer. Avoid costs and investments that are not associated with the critical advantages and success factors in the industry, if at all possible. For example, many technology companies avoid the costs of manufacturing. Rather, they concentrate all of their limited resources on product/service improvement. Manufacturing can be subcontracted to low cost manufacturers in low cost countries. This assumes that manufacturing process development is not a critical part of the emerging industry.
- Cooperate with other companies in the industry to build a product or service standard and create customer awareness. Many emerging industries have successfully done this including the firms behind the VHS tape format, and the original IBM PC.
- Often the market is initially quite fragmented. Attempt to select and focus on a customer base or segment that will be a reference point for customers that are considering adopting the product or service. Often, the customers that are key reference groups are large companies—companies that are very demanding and have a reputation for buying the best product or service that you are offering. Your

initial strategy should be to design your product and service for this market. It will enables easier market entry and adoption. These high quality customers also enable you to attract interim resources, such as financing and knowledgeable-capable workers.

- Strive for an early entry into an industry if there appears to be potential entry barriers, such as brand awareness that will develop over time. Otherwise, wait until the costs of uncertainty have been eliminated.

High Growth Stage Industries

A high growth industry is one that has gone through the emerging stage and now faces fewer technical uncertainties, but many market and competitive uncertainties. Examples of high growth industries are the mobile computing and DVD industries.

In high growth industries, market growth is very high and this tends to moderate competitive pressures because competitors are just trying to meet market demand. However, despite the moderated competitive climate, it is a period where winners and losers shape their eventual ability to compete in the industry. Therefore, it is critical for companies to develop specific competitive advantages that enable them to be winners when demand slows and competition becomes very intense. During the emerging stage, core competencies are often technologically related, but in the high growth stage, marketing competitive advantages becomes important.

Some competitive tactics that enable firms to best position themselves to be winners during the high growth stage are:

- Focus on production volumes and economies of scale. Focusing on high volumes of production and broad distribution channels enables a firm to grab market share quickly, and if market share is important (as it is in many industries), then your company has the initial advantage. Furthermore, customers are often just looking for the product at any price because demand is outstripping supply. Such a high volume and high market share strategy is particularly important in industries that have high fixed costs, such as high-tech industries. In these industries, high volume enables the companies to cover fixed cost activities, such as research and development, much more effectively than companies that do not have high revenues.

- Attempt to make your product or service the standard in the market. A company can increase their effective market coverage by licensing their technology to other competitors. Such cooperation can be very effective and may extend into marketing and R&D alliances.

- Build manufacturing capabilities, either internally or externally, with alliances to high volume, low cost outsourced manufacturers. It is important that firms have the ability to fill market demand as it grows quickly because, if the products are not available on the shelves, then it will be very difficult to build market share.

- Develop marketing competitive advantages or capabilities. This includes broad channels of distribution, brand recognition, etc. Again, this strategic focus may help the company develop market share and a product that is the standard in the industry.

- A company must constantly consider new technologies and trends that may move the industry in a new direction. Such technologies could dramatically influence acceptance of its product, particularly if the company that develops the new technology has marketing strength.

Chapter 8 examines strategies and tactics specific to the high-tech and e-commerce industries.

Maturing Stage Industries

A maturing industry is an industry that faces little or no future growth prospects, a condition that often produces intense price competition. As companies move into this stage, power in the value chain evolves forward towards the distributor, retailer, and customer, leaving the firm with less competitive influence. In addition, international competition increases and the ability to effectively differentiate oneself may decline. Therefore, firms must build competitive advantages that maximize cost advantages and/or seek focused markets that are looking for specialized services or products. New customer or product trends may also enable a company to differentiate itself for a time. Examples of industries in the mature stage are the grocery food, restaurant, and clothing industries. Firms in these industries constantly attempt to reinvent themselves in an effort to maintain a competitive advantage over rival firms. For instance, firms in the clothing industry attempt to reinvent their business model by moving production to low cost overseas locations, integrating forward into retail operations, and continually adjusting to new product, production, and service trends.

Some alternative competitive tactics used in a mature market environment include:

- The strategy of a firm must focus on low costs and improved customer service. This is a difficult transition because many of these activities, such as manufacturing and customer service, are not activities that the firm has concentrated upon in the past. The activities that it has concentrated upon in the past, such as R&D, are not required or are much less critical to the survival of the firm now. If a firm cannot make this transition in activities, possibly it should look to merge with a firm that has these capabilities.

- The firm may have to consider aggressively competing internationally to gain the economies of scale and scope that are necessary in a mature business.

- The organization must evolve into a disciplined cost efficient and effective operation where managers focus on controlling costs, quality, and service—things that are important to the customers. Often, this change is not easy because the organization, during the emerging and growth stages, has accumulated unnecessary departments, people, and managers.

- Firms could also consider establishing forward focused alliances or integrating forward. This strategic approach may preempt the evolution of power forward in the value chain. However, the manager is cautioned to analyze carefully the pluses and minuses of forward integration before doing so.

- The firm may have to concentrate more on process innovation compared to product innovation. During the growth stage, product design and getting the product out at any cost is the critical concern. However in the mature stage, cost competition will force companies to concentrate on process innovations that make their overall operations more efficient and effective.

- A final option is to recreate the growth cycle by adapting resources and capabilities to new market needs. This strategic alternative is discussed more thoroughly later in this chapter.

Declining Stage Industries

A declining industry faces a shrinking market volume. Competition in such an industry becomes extremely intense, particularly if high barriers to exit exist. A barrier to exit is defined as an impediment to the firm if it wants to get out of an industry. An example of a high exit barrier problem is when a firm invests a lot of capital on production capacity, and this capacity is not useable in another industry. Then, when the firm contemplates abandoning the business and writing off the investment, the owners will be reticent about taking such a strategy because of the large investment loses. An example of a Canadian industry in decline is the fisheries industry, which is facing low fish stocks and a moratorium on fishing in many regions.

In general, four alternative strategies are available to a firm in this situation. They are to take a leadership position, seek a niche position, divest, or harvest. A firm that takes a leadership position must decide if it can capture such a competitive position given its competitive advantages relative to its rivals. The leadership position must clearly put the firm in a low cost or better value leadership position relative to its competitors. Furthermore, the managers must be fairly certain that it can attain such a position; otherwise, it is a very high-risk strategy given that considerable investment is often necessary. Reinvestment strategies are particularly effective if the decline is not permanent (i.e., demand eventually stabilizes). One tactic firms often take when confronted with a declining market that has no clear leader is merging or acquiring other firms in the industry. This may create a clear leader if economies of scale and scope are important in the industry.

An example of a firm using the industry leadership approach in a declining industry is the case of Fisheries Products International (FPI), where Vick Young, the CEO, completely redefined the company's competitive position in the industry by refocusing the company from a fish catcher to a value-added fish processing company. The company now concentrates on importing fish, and then it processes the fish to make specialty products, and re-exports the fish to customers that demand such value-added products.

Seeking a niche position is a good strategy for a firm that does not have a leadership position in the overall market, but can develop a leadership position in a niche market. An important consideration for the firm adopting this strategy is that the characteristics of the niche (e.g., small size, or unusual customer demands) and competitive advantages developed by the firm must make it very difficult for the overall industry leader to attack this niche. Sometimes this strategy is combined with a harvest strategy.

A harvest strategy is one in which the firm has decided to eventually discontinue the business. However, in the short-term, the firm keeps its prices high, minimizes reinvestment costs, and allows its market share to slowly decline, while maximizing its profits. If forecasts for the industry are for long-term decline, then a harvest strategy is the only viable option for a portion of the companies in the industry.

A divestment strategy is the most obvious strategic alternative in a declining industry. Yet, it is often one of the most difficult strategies for managers and owners to adopt because the managers may be without a job and the owners may have to accept a low price. The task of a manager taking this strategy is to make the firm look valuable to other firms in the industry.

SMALL BUSINESS OR ENTREPRENEURIAL GENERIC STRATEGIES

Entrepreneurs must develop unique competitive advantages because they do not have the breadth of competitive advantages that a larger business has in the same industry. Rather, the successful small business must focus its capabilities in developing very specialized competitive advantages. Some of the more generic strategies and competitive advantages used by small firms are:

- Focus on small niche markets—ones that are small enough to not attract the attention of the larger companies in the business. Such an approach may mean focusing on a specific customer or type of unique product. Some small businesses also focus on a particular part of the value chain (as seen by a larger company), and they provide a unique product or service for companies willing to use them as part of their value chain.

- Small companies often provide better service to the customers. Focusing on specific customers and services enables the entrepreneur to provide more value to the customers.

- Small entrepreneurial companies often are faster at making decisions and providing products and services, particularly if it is a made to order product or service. Speed can be important as a competitive advantage because of its dynamic nature. Decision-making and R&D speed, for example, could provide a small company an ongoing competitive advantage over some of its larger rivals.

- Small entrepreneurial firms have tremendous flexibility in formulating and implementing strategy. This may provide them with a competitive advantage if change or flexibility is required. Some small companies are extremely efficient and effective in businesses that require a lot of top management control, an example of which is specialized consulting firms.

STRATEGIC EVOLUTION IN THE LIFE CYCLE PROCESS

Businesses plagued with products in the latter stages of their life cycle may be able to revitalize the products by adding new technological advances or redesigning the products for specialized markets. Such an action may create a growth stage by appealing to customers and needs that have not been fulfilled yet. This process can delay the decline of a product, and, in some cases, may lead to a completely new life cycle.

Exhibit 4-3 illustrates how the Canadian telecommunications service industry is evolving. The leading companies are developing new products, new technologies, and new customer segments in their quest for continued market growth. As shown in the exhibit, the average telephone service is a mature and possibly in decline product. However, several years ago, the companies developed new growth products (e.g., call waiting, Internet services, and local mobile services) that are now growing rapidly. Many of these same companies are now developing emerging technologies and products that will be the growth of tomorrow (e.g., ATM data services, integrated voice/data networks and lines, and global mobile satellite phone services).

exhibit 4-3   Product Evolution in the Canadian Telecommunications
Industry

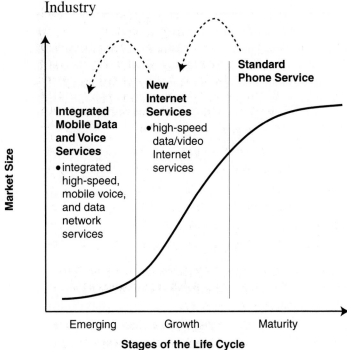

Exhibit 4-3 illustrates how telecommunication companies are attempting to evolve into new life cycle stages by redefining their product, customer, and service focus. They are altering their competitive positions by refocusing their competitive advantages on these new products and markets. This, of course, requires parallel changes in competitive advantages (i.e., resources, knowledge, and capabilities) within the firm.

The difficulties of reinventing one's life cycle are not minor. First, a firm that refocuses on a new product may devote so many resources to its refocusing effort that the old products and competitive position are neglected. This may leave the firm worse off if the new market segment does not develop as predicted. Second, sometimes new products require resources and capabilities (i.e., competitive advantages) that the entering firm does not have compared to other potential competitors. This makes the firm less competitive in the new market segment. An example of this is Kodak's difficult evolution into digital photography when many other electronic companies possibly have more appropriate competitive advantages and positions. Therefore, firms must be careful when refocusing their efforts on emerging products. Strategies should be adopted that develop products that maximize the firm's intrinsic competitive advantages, and the firm should take care to not neglect their underlying mature products.

SUMMARY

Exhibit 4-3 summarizes the questions and issues managers would consider based on the topics examined in this chapter.

Summary of The Competitive Tactics Analysis

Defining the Generic Competitive Strategy and Position

A basic tactical evaluation of strategy should examine a firm's position. Generic positions evolve around the dimensions of differentiation, low-cost, and focus. A manager must understand how different competitive positions require unique and support competitive advantages. It is then important to make sure that the firm's competitive position is well served by the available competitive advantages in the firm.

Tactics for Standard Competitive Threats

There are four standard threats to a firm's overall competitiveness in an industry. They are substitution, imitation, holdup, and slack. Managers must assess which competitive threats are potentially threatening their firm. Then they must devise tactics for holding off or eliminating the threats.

Examining Common Tactics for Specific Industry Environments

There are a number of industry environments in which firms tend to use common tactics. The environments examined in this chapter are small business, highly competitive, emerging, developing, and mature industry environments. It is important that managers understand the tactics that work in these environments because they can use them and they can expect rivals to also use them.

Innovative Tactics

Managers must attempt to develop innovative new tactics that make sense for their specific situation. It is only through such bold innovative development that managers can leap ahead of rivals competitively.

Additional Notes and Recommended Readings

Adler, P. S., McDonald, D. W., and MacDonald, F., "Strategic Management of Technical Functions." *Sloan Management Review*, Winter 1992, pp. 19-38.

Deming, W. E., *Out of the Crisis* (Cambridge, Mass.: MIT 1986). P. 31.

Foster, John, "Scenario Planning for Small Businesses." *Long Range Planning*, February 1993, pp123-129.

Hamel, G., "Strategy as Revolution," *Harvard Business Review* 74 no. 4, 1996.

Paul Nutt, and Robert Backoff. "Transforming Public Organizations with Strategic Management and Strategic Leadership." *Journal of Management*. Summer 1993, pp. 299-348.

Phillip Waalewijn, and Peter Segaar. "Strategic Management: The Key to Profitability in Small Companies." *Long Range Planning*, April 1993, pp.24-30.

Schnarrs, S., *Managing Imitation Strategies: How Later Entrants Seize Markets from Pioneers* Free Press, 1994.

See Michael E. Porter, *Competitive Advantage: Creating and Sustaining Superior Performance* (New York: Free Press, 1985), chap. 9.

See Michael E. Porter, *Competitive Strategy: Techniques for Analyzing Industries and Competitors* (New York: Free Press, 1980), chap 11.

Stuckey, J, and White, D., "When and When Not to Vertically Integrate." *Sloan Management Review* pp. 71-83. 1993.

Venkatesan, R., "Strategic Outsourcing: To Make or Not to Make." *Harvard Business Review*, pp. 98-107, 1992.

chapter 5 Organizational Design and Structure

We live by alliances, partnerships, networks, and friends. You don't do anything on your own. Things move fast around here. We're in a virtual world with people and research all over the world available to us through the internet. It isn't what you know any more, it's how you use what you know and what everybody else does.

JIM GRAY, COFOUNDER AND CHAIRMAN OF CANADIAN HUNTER EXPLORATION

I used to design products, now I design organizations and businesses.

JOHN ROTH, EX CHAIRMAN OF NORTEL

Resources and people with skills and knowledge must be organized appropriately to produce strong, sustainable competitive advantages and capabilities. As was stated in Chapter 3, it is often the complex linkages between activities that produce the real sustainable competitive advantages in a firm. This makes the task of organizational design a critical top management function.

Ultimately, the purpose of organizational structure and coordination management is to convert the resources available to the firm into competitive advantages, competitive capabilities, core competencies, and sustainable competitive advantages and capabilities. These advantages must be methodically organized and coordinated, otherwise, the resources are not effective in the firm and they do not synergistically produce the value required. This notion of organizing and coordinating is illustrated in exhibit 5-1, and it probably represents an aspect of management that occupies the greatest amount of top management's time. Both Jack Welch, past chairman of GE, and Louis Gerstner, chairman of IBM have stressed that their firms' abilities to organize resources is better than competitors, and they continuously attempt to upgrade this ability. It is also understood by good managers that this ability to organize and coordinate is critical in adapting and reacting quickly to emergent strategic issues that come at the firm. This chapter will examine organizational coordinating issues, and Chapter 6 will examine organizational structuring issues.

MANAGING ORGANIZATIONAL DESIGN

Organizational design can be broken into two aspects: organizational structure and organizational coordination. Organizational structure is the process of separating people and tasks that do similar things into separate units for the purpose of managing them efficiently.

exhibit 5-1   Relationships Among the Major Organization Design
               Variables

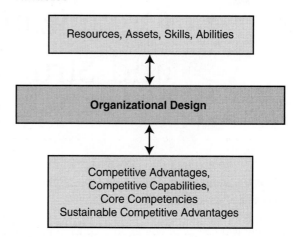

Firms require organizational structure to separate tasks, activities, and competitive advantages into groupings that enable efficient operation and management. Separating organizations into different like-minded units enables the people and activities in that unit to work in an integrated way to complete the task, and it enables management to quickly identify where a problem exists because similar activities are grouped together.

Defining an organizational structure can occur on a functional basis or on some other basis, but the purpose is to group people and activities that work on similar tasks together. However, the other aspect of organizational design is coordinating integration between the different units that have been divided up structurally. This dichotomy of having to break up activities to ensure they are efficient, and then bringing them together to ensure effectiveness using coordinating activities is an important top management function.

Exhibit 5-2 illustrates how managing organizational structure divides a company into groups. The degree to which a company must be divided up depends upon the size and complexity of the organization, as is shown in exhibit 5-2. On the other hand, once an organization is divided, managers must integrate the various groups using coordination mechanisms. Organizational coordination integrates and synchronizes so that the various groups are working to fulfill the firm's overall strategy and objectives. As shown in exhibit 5-2 organizational coordination re-integrates using various coordination mechanisms.

Exhibit 5-3 illustrates some of the important elements of managing organizational structure and managing organizational coordination. This chapter discusses organizational structure, and Chapter 6 explains managing organizational coordination.

ORGANIZATIONAL STRUCTURE

There are essentially four strategy-related forms to organization: (1) functional specialization, (2) geographic organization, (3) decentralized business/product divisions, and (4) matrix structures featuring dual lines of authority and strategic priority. Each form relates structure to strategy in a different way and, consequently, has its own set of strategy-related pros and cons. Each of these forms is discussed in the following sections.

exhibit 5-2   Relationships Among the Major Organization Design
Variables: Dividing the Work Versus Integrating the People
and Work Activities

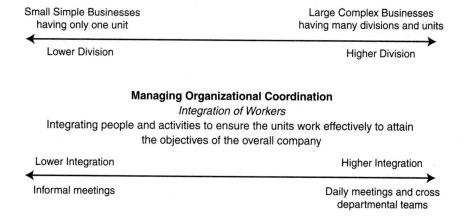

Managing Organizational Structure
Division of Workers
Dividing people and activities into efficient and manageable units

Small Simple Businesses having only one unit	Large Complex Businesses having many divisions and units
Lower Division	Higher Division

Managing Organizational Coordination
Integration of Workers
Integrating people and activities to ensure the units work effectively to attain
the objectives of the overall company

Lower Integration	Higher Integration
Informal meetings	Daily meetings and cross departmental teams

exhibit 5-3   Relationships Among the Major Organization Design
Variables and Their Components

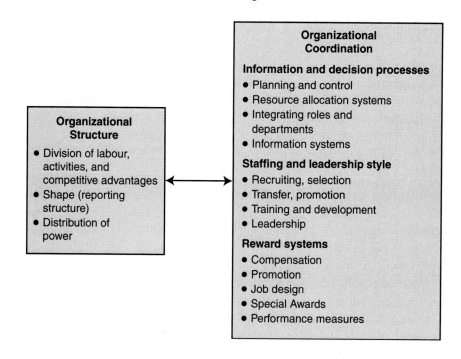

**Organizational
Structure**

- Division of labour,
  activities, and
  competitive advantages
- Shape (reporting
  structure)
- Distribution of
  power

**Organizational
Coordination**

Information and decision processes
- Planning and control
- Resource allocation systems
- Integrating roles and
  departments
- Information systems

Staffing and leadership style
- Recruiting, selection
- Transfer, promotion
- Training and development
- Leadership

Reward systems
- Compensation
- Promotion
- Job design
- Special Awards
- Performance measures

THE FUNCTIONAL ORGANIZATION STRUCTURE

A functional organization structure tends to be effective in single-business units where key activities revolve around well-defined skills and areas of specialization. In such cases, in-depth specialization and focused concentration on performing functional area tasks and activities can enhance both operating efficiency and the development of a distinctive competence. Generally speaking, organizing by functional specialties promotes full utilization of the most up-to-date technical skills, and it helps a business capitalize on the efficiency gains to be had from using specialized personnel, facilities, and equipment. These are strategically important considerations for single-business organizations, dominant product enterprises, and vertically integrated firms, moreover, they account for why the firms usually have some kind of centralized, functionally specialized structure.

Deciding what form the functional specialization will take in a firm must account for variations in customer-product-technology. For instance, a technical instruments manufacturer may be organized around research and development, engineering, production, technical services, quality control, marketing, personnel, and finance and accounting. A municipal government may, on the other hand, be departmentalized according to purpose: fire, public safety, health services, water and sewer, streets, parks and recreation, and education. A university may divide up its organizational units into academic affairs, student services, alumni relations, athletics, buildings and grounds, institutional services, and budget control. Two types of functional organizational approaches are diagrammed in exhibit 5-4.

The Achilles heel of a functional structure is getting and maintaining tight strategic coordination across the separated functional units. Functional specialists, partly because of how they are trained and the technical "mystique" of jobs, tend to develop their own mindset and ways of doing things. The more functional specialists differ in their perspectives and their approaches to task accomplishment, the more difficult it becomes to achieve both strategic and operating coordination among them. They neither "talk the same language" nor have an adequate understanding and appreciation for one another's strategic role and problems. Each functional group is more interested in its own "empire" and promoting its own strategic interest and importance (despite the lip service given to cooperation and "what's best for the company"). Tunnel vision and empire building in functional departments impose a time-consuming administrative burden on a general manager in terms of resolving cross functional differences, enforcing joint cooperation, and opening lines of communication. In addition, a purely functional organization can be myopic when it comes to promoting entrepreneurial creativity, adapting quickly to major customer-market-technological changes, and pursuing opportunities that go beyond the conventional boundaries of the industry.

GEOGRAPHIC FORMS OF ORGANIZATION

Organizing according to geographic areas or territories is a rather common structural form for large-scale enterprises whose strategies need to be tailored to fit the particular needs and features of different geographical areas. As indicated in exhibit 5-5, a geographic organization has its advantages and disadvantages, but the chief reason for its adoption is that it normally improves performance when a market-oriented geographically divergent focus is important strategically.

exhibit 5-4   Functional Organizational Structures

A. The building blocks of a "typical" functional organization structure

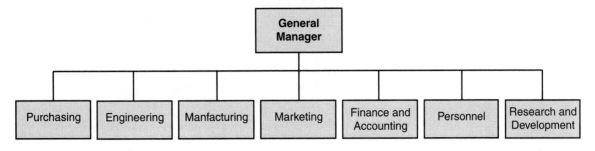

B. The building blocks of a process-oriented functional structure

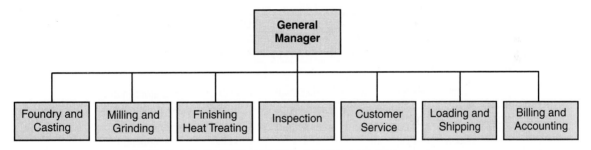

Advantages

- Enhances operating efficiency where tasks are routine and repetitive
- Preserves centralized control of strategic results
- Allows benefits of specialization and learning/experience curve effects to be fully exploited
- Simplifies training of management specialists
- Promotes high emphasis on craftsmanship and professional standards
- Well suited to developing distinctive competencies in one or more functional areas
- Structure is tied to key activities within the business

Disadvantages

- Poses problems of functional coordination
- Can lead to inter functional rivalry, conflict, and empire building
- May promote over-specialization and narrow management viewpoints
- Limited development of general managers
- Forces profit responsibility to the top
- Functional specialists often attach more importance to what is best for the functional area than to what is best for the whole business
- May lead to uneconomically small units or under-utilization of specialized facilities and manpower
- Functional myopia often works against creative entrepreneurship, adapting to change, and attempts to restructure the activity-cost chain that threatens the status of one or more functional departments

In the private sector, a territorial structure is typically utilized by chain store retailers, power companies, cement firms, railroads, airlines, the larger paper-box and carton manufacturers, and large bakeries and dairy products enterprises. In the public sector, such organizations as the Canadian Red Cross and religious groups have adopted territorial structures in order to be directly accessible to geographically dispersed clientele.

exhibit 5-5   A Geographic Organization Structure

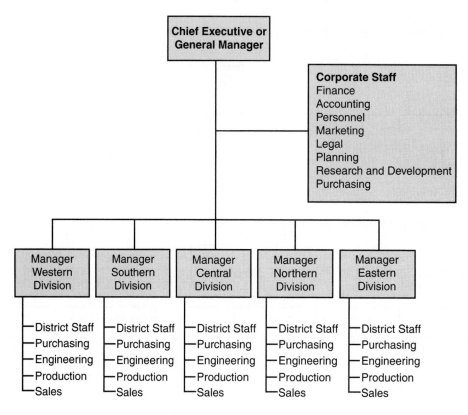

Advantages

- Allows tailoring of strategy to needs of each geographic market
- Delegates profit/loss responsibility to lowest strategic level
- Improves functional coordination within the target geographic market
- Takes advantage of economies of local operations
- Area units make an excellent training ground to higher level general managers

Disadvantages

- Greater difficulty in maintaining consistent and uniform company wide practices
- Requires a larger management staff, especially general managers
- Leads to duplication of staff services
- Poses a problem of headquarters control over local operations

An example of a company that has a geographic structure within Canada is Re/Max Real Estate Company. This company has somewhat of an unusual structure below its geographical structure because of the franchise nature of its local offices, which are all independently owned and operated. As shown in exhibit 5-6 Re/Max has three geographical divisions: Western Canada, Ontario and Atlantic Canada, and Quebec. Re/Max developed in a geographical organizational structure because real estate is by its nature a relatively local business: contacts are local, real estate economic trends are local, and marketing and sales approach tend to take on a regional approach based upon language, aggressiveness, and sophisticatedness of the sales approach.

exhibit 5-6   Re/Max's Organizational Structure

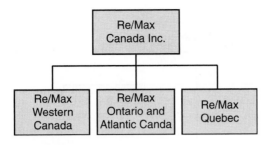

DECENTRALIZED BUSINESS UNITS

Grouping activities along business and product lines has been a trend among diversified enterprises for the past half century, beginning with the pioneering efforts of Du Pont and General Motors in the 1920s. Separate business/product divisions emerged because diversification made a functionally specialized manager's job incredibly complex. Imagine the problems a manufacturing executive and his or her staff would have if put in charge of, say, 50 different plants using 20 different technologies to produce 30 different products in 8 different businesses/industries. In a multi-business enterprise, the needs of strategy virtually dictate that the organizational sequence is corporate to line of business to functional area within a business rather than corporate to functional area (aggregated for all businesses). The latter produces a nightmare in making sense out of business strategy and achieving functional area coordination for a given business.

From a business strategy implementation standpoint, it is far more logical to group all the different activities that belong to the same business under one organization roof, thereby creating line-of-business units (which then can be subdivided into whatever subunits suit the key activities/critical tasks making up the business). The outcome is a structure that fits strategy and also makes the jobs of managers more doable. The creation of separate business units, or strategic business units (SBUs), as they are sometimes called, is then accomplished by decentralizing authority to the SBU business-level manager. The approach, very simply, puts entrepreneurially oriented general managers in charge of the business unit, giving them enough authority to formulate and implement the business strategy that they deem appropriate, motivating them with incentives, and then holding them accountable for the results. However, when a strong strategic fit exists across related business units, it can be tough to get autonomy conscious business-unit general managers to cooperate in coordinating and sharing related activities; each general manager tends to want to argue long and hard about "turf" and about being held accountable for activities not totally under his or her control.

A typical line-of-business organization structure is shown in exhibit 5-7, along with the strategic pros and cons of this organizational form.

This decentralized structure, having three separate business groups, has been adopted by Maple Leaf to ensure that each one of the groups focuses exclusively on developing the competitive advantages that will make that particular type of business a success. This separation of skills and capabilities into a distinct business units ensures that there is a clarity about the business and how it can generate value for its specific customer.

***exhibit 5*-7**   A Decentralized Business Division Type of Organization Structure

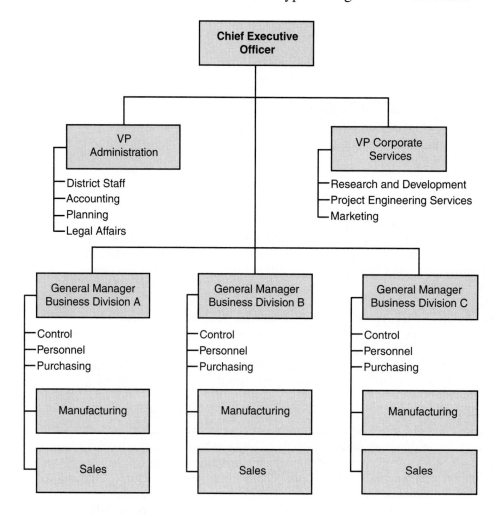

Advantages

- Offers a logical and workable means of decentralizing responsibility and delegating authority in diversified organizations
- Puts responsibility for business strategy in closer proximity to each business's unique environment
- Allows critical tasks and specialization to be organized to fit business strategy
- Frees CEO to handle corporate strategy issues
- Creates clear profit/loss accountability

Disadvantages

- Leads to proliferation of staff functions, policy inconsistencies between divisions, and problems of coordination of divisional operations
- Poses a problem of how much authority to centralize and how much to decentralize
- May lead to excessive divisional rivalry for corporate resources and attention
- Raises issue of how to allocate corporate-level overhead
- Business/division autonomy works against achieving coordination of related activities in different business units thus blocking to some extent the capture of strategic fit benefits

exhibit 5-8   Maple Leaf Foods Inc.'s Organizational Structure

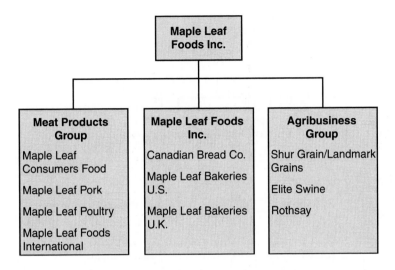

MATRIX FORMS OF ORGANIZATION

A matrix form of organization is a structure with two (or more) channels of command or responsibility. The key feature of the matrix is that product (or business) and functional lines of authority are overlaid (to form a matrix or grid). Managerial authority over the activities in each unit/cell of the matrix is shared between the product manager and the functional manager—as shown in exhibit 5-9. In a matrix structure, subordinates have dual responsibilities: to their business/product line/project head and to their base function. The outcome is a compromise between functional specialization (engineering, R&D, manufacturing, marketing, accounting) and product line or market segment or line-of-business specialization (where all of the specialized talents needed for the product line/market segment/line of business are assigned to the same divisional unit).

A matrix-type organization is a genuinely different structural form and represents a "new way of life." One reason is that the unit-of-command principle is broken: two reporting channels, two bosses, and shared authority create a new kind of organization climate. In essence, the matrix is a conflict resolution system through which strategic and operating priorities are negotiated, power is shared, and resources are allocated internally on a "strongest case for what is best overall for the unit" type basis.

The impetus for matrix organizations stems from the growing use of strategies that add new sources of diversity (products, customer groups, technology, and lines of business) to a firm's range of activities. Out of this diversity comes product managers, functional managers, geographic-area managers, new-venture managers, and business-level managers—all of whom have important strategic responsibilities. When at least two of several variables (product, customer, technology, geography, functional area, and market segment) have roughly equal strategic priorities, then a matrix theoretically can be an effective structural form. A matrix arrangement promotes internal checks and balances among competing viewpoints and perspectives, with separate managers for different dimensions of strategic initiative. A matrix approach

exhibit 5-9   A Matrix Organization Structure

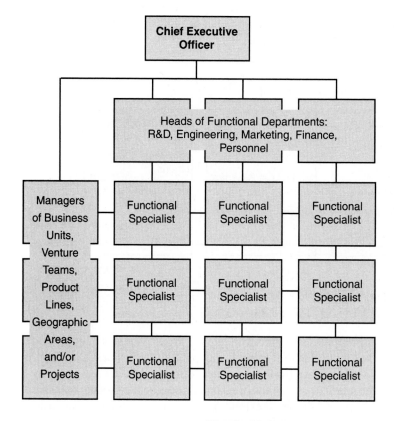

Advantages

- Permits more attention to each dimension of strategic priority
- Creates checks and balances among competing viewpoints
- Facilitates simultaneous pursuit of different types of strategic initiative
- Promotes making trade-off decisions on the basis of "what's best for the organization as a whole"
- Encourages coorperation, consensus building, conflict resolution, and coordination of related activities

Disadvantages

- Very complex to manage
- Hard to maintain "balance" between the two lines of authority
- So much shared authority can result in a transactions logjam and disproportionate amounts of time spent on communications
- It is hard to move quickly and decisively without getting clearance from many other people
- Promotes an organizational bureaucracy and hamstrings creative entrepreneurship

thus allows each of several strategic considerations to be managed directly and to be formally represented in the organization structure. In this sense, it helps middle managers make trade-off decisions from an organization wide perspective. Most applications of matrix organization are limited to certain important functions rather than spanning the whole of a large-scale diversified enterprise.

A number of companies shun matrix organization because of its chief weaknesses. It is a complex structure to manage; people often end up confused over whom to report to for what. Moreover, because the matrix signals that everything is important and, further, that everybody needs to communicate with everybody else, a "transactions logjam" can emerge. Actions turn into paralysis, since, with shared authority, it is hard to move decisively without first considering many points of view and getting clearance from many other people. Sizable administrative costs and communications inefficiency can arise, as well as delays in responding quickly. Even so, there are situations where the benefits of consensus building outweigh these weaknesses.

NETWORK ORGANIZATIONAL FORM

 Another form of organization that is becoming more popular in highly professional service firms is the networked organizational form (shown in exhibit 5-10). This organizational structure promotes equality and the sharing of information across and throughout the organization on an equal basis. Usually, there are two criteria that make this type of organization effective. The first is that each group is essentially self supportive in day-to-day activities, and the second is that all groups are highly educated professional employees or partners that want to operate on a quasi-entrepreneurial basis. However, these individuals have formed this organizational network because it provides them access to specialized knowledge, information, or relationships that may exist in another group. Often, informal communication methods are used widely, although some companies attempt to formalize some of these interactions in an effort to improve coordination. Examples of firms that tend to operate in this manner are law firms and consulting firms.

exhibit 5-10   A Network Organizational Form

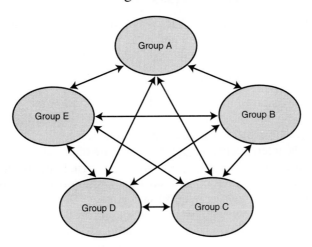

Advantages
- Tends to promote entrepreneurial qualities in an organization
- Is efficient if the groups tend to work independently on a day-to-day basis and each group is responsible for developing, producing, and delivering a product
- Professionals like to work in this type of environment

Disadvantages
- Coordination is not always done when it should be because the groups are used to operating independently
- Can duplicate some overhead costs
- Formal coordination mechanisms that promote interaction are very hard to install and get to work

An example of a networked organization is McKinsey & Associates, which has offices in most major business nations around the world. There is a formal chairman and board of directors for the company. However, for day-to-day operations, major national offices are almost entirely independent operational. Nonetheless, information and expertise spread throughout the different offices is shared throughout a variety of mechanisms, including a database system that defines expertise in different offices, email, and even borrowing personnel from other offices on a short-term basis. Furthermore, remuneration, hiring, and promotion systems in the organization are formulated to encourage consultants to actively share information and expertise. Clearly, the greatest struggle facing these types of operations is enabling and motivating individuals to actively support the interaction between nodes or offices in the network.

COMBINATION AND SUPPLEMENTAL METHODS OF ORGANIZATION

A single type of structural design is not always sufficient to meet the requirements of strategy. When this occurs, one option is to mix and blend the basic organization forms, matching structure to strategy, requirement by requirement, and unit by unit. Another is to supplement a basic organizational design with special-situation devices, such as project manager/project staff approaches, task force approaches, or venture teams.

INTERNATIONAL ORGANIZATIONAL FORMS

There are a variety of ways a manager can design for international activities in his or her firm. The most common approaches are:

International Division

The international division is an international business division that is simply added onto the domestic structure, as shown in exhibit 5-11. This type of structure is typical of a firm having a relatively simple product or functional structure that requires a manager to look after the international operations, which are often sales and marketing related. The structure is appropriate for a firm that is not highly geographically diversified. An international division is usually the first international structural form adopted by a firm as it develops an international strategy. The formation of the international division is an acknowledgment that the international market has become important enough to warrant a top decision maker that focuses entirely on its strategy and performance. Managers also acknowledge that they must establish an organizational form that links them more closely with their international customers.

Multidomestic Structure

A multidomestic structure is a more evolved international geographical structure, and is shown in exhibit 5-12. This international structural form segments the markets based on the similarity of culture, language, product desires, distribution channels, etc. Divisions are established in markets that have similar characteristics. It should also be noted that often activities such as product research and development, marketing, purchasing and finance are relegated to the local/head office divisional level. The

exhibit 5-11   The International Divisional Structure

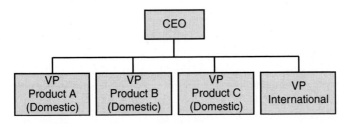

objective of the multidomestic structure is to move the key functional processes and activities to a location close to the customer.

Managers use the multidomestic structure when they are using a multidomestic strategy, as described in Chapter 10. This structure enables the firm to carry out the decentralized market specific strategy in the most effective manner possible. The role of head office in the multidomestic structure is to provide management personnel, skills, and direction to the international divisions, as well as to coordinate the sharing of technology and information among the divisions.

Global Product Structure

The global product structure is illustrated in exhibit 5-13. In a global product-division structure, the firm focuses each of its product lines on a broad scope of international markets. This structure enables each business product division to locate its value chain activities in international locations that maximize the business's overall competitive advantages. For example, in one division, production may be done in Asia, R&D in North America, and marketing in various regions around the world, all of which maximizes the efficiency and effectiveness of the different functions globally for the company. The objective of this structure is to locate parts of the business where they will be most competitive globally.

The global product-division structure is applied to firms that are taking a global strategy internationally (see Chapter 9 for a more thorough description of global strategy).

exhibit 5-12   The Multidomestic Divisional Structure

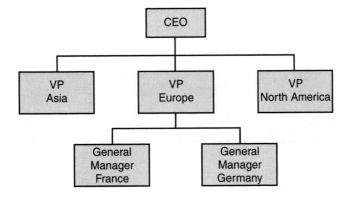

exhibit 5-13   The Global Product-Division Structure

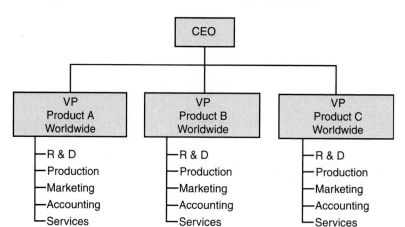

Mini-case:
Illustration of Structure-Strategy Linkages

The following mini-case can be used to assess alternative organizational structures. Suggested discussion questions follow this case.

T. G. Bright and Co., Limited—1986*

In 1977, T. G. Bright and Co., Limited (Brights) of Niagara Falls, Ontario, sold a wide range of wine products in Ontario in eight categories – sparkling, rosé, white table, port, sherry, appetizer, red table, and other (which included such diverse products as Muscatel, Mazel Tov, and sacramental wine). Through wholly owned subsidiaries, Brights also offered additional selections in many of these eight categories in other provinces.

It was a small firm ($14 million in sales) with over half its sales volume in Ontario (see exhibit 5-15), most of its manufacturing in Ontario, and a product line which had not digressed from wine. Its 1977 organization is reflected in exhibit 5-16.

By 1980, Brights' organization was modified to include a second regional operations manager (see exhibit 5-16). A third production facility in Quebec had been acquired in 1979. With this acquisition, the proportion of sales in Quebec—27 percent in 1979—was expected to increase so that Brights would have the largest non government operation in Quebec.

exhibit 5-14   Percentage Share of Canadian Wine Market

	Ontario	Quebec	Rest of Country
Brights' Sales	55%	27%	18%
Total Canadian market	34	32	34

---

* This case was prepared by Professor Paul W. Beamish as a basis for classroom discussion. Copyright © 1986 by Paul W. Beamish

exhibit 5-15 1977 Organization

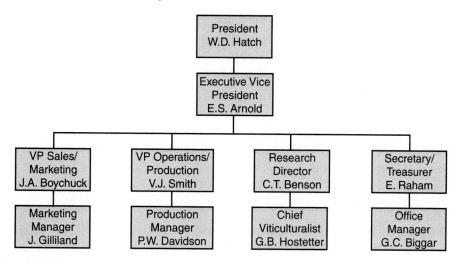

Source: Derived from list of officers and executives in 1977 annual report.

exhibit 5-16 1980 Organization

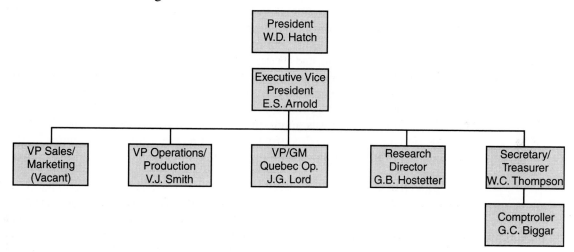

Two other organization changes were made:

1. Hatch became chairman and Arnold became president, with the position of executive vice president dropped.

2. The position of vice president, sales/marketing, had been filled for a few months but of late had been vacant and was being managed by the president.

In late 1980, Bright's formed a joint venture with the Inkameep Indian Band of Oliver, British Columbia, to establish a winery in BC's Okanagan Valley. In 1984 and 1985, small winery operations were established in Manitoba and Nova Scotia, respectively. Sales in 1984 were nearly $38 million, net of excise and sales tax.

In 1985 a limited import operation in wines and spirits under the name of Wines of the Globe was established. (In 1984 the Province of Quebec modified its regulations to permit the bottling of imported wines by local wineries.)

Brights' non-restaurant sales were through provincial government outlets, small grocery stores (in Quebec), and company-owned retail outlets. The company operated over 20 retail outlets in Ontario, with perhaps half being located in Toronto.

In order to keep pace with changing consumer tastes, Brights' product mix had been steadily shifting away from fortified wines to those with lower alcohol levels. In addition, a greater proportion of sales was in white rather than red wines. With the purchase of a Quebec cider company in 1978, Bright acquired the ability and license to produce cider. Brights had also introduced a wine cooler, which combined specially fermented wine and pure spring water.

Grapes were supplied from three sources – company-owned vineyards, purchases from other grape growers, and concentrate and bulk purchases from other countries. Grapes purchased from local growers in Southern Ontario (and, to a lesser extent, the Okanagan region in BC) were the primary source of supply.

By 1985, Brights had once again modified its organization structure (see exhibit 5-17).

The chairman, W. D. Hatch, died in 1985. The chairman's position was not reflected in the 1985 annual report list of fixers and executives. In lieu of a vice president, sales/marketing, a staff director of marketing was appointed to work with the regional vice presidents. The previous vice president/general manager of Quebec Operations had left the company. His replacement held the title of vice president/ general manager Eastern Division.

In 1986, W. C. Thompson resigned and G. C. Bigger became secretary. The designation for the three vice president/general managers changed from being in charge of Operations, Quebec Operations, and BC Operations to being in charge of the Central Division, Eastern Division, and Western Division, respectively.

Carling O'Keefe Limited, Toronto, Ontario, announced on June 26, 1986, that its wholly owned subsidiary, Jordan & Ste-Michelle Cellars Ltd., had been sold (including substantially all of its assets) to T. G. Bright and Co., Limited.

The purchase price was approximately $30 million. It was estimated that the transaction resulted in a loss to Carling O'Keefe Limited of approximately $7,750,000 after tax, or 36 cents per common share. The business had been unprofitable in 1986.

Jordan & Ste-Michelle Cellars Ltd. had wineries in St. Catharines, Ontario, and Surrey, British Columbia, and, until September 1985, had operated a winery in Calgary, Alberta. Except for 33 company-operated retail stores in Ontario, all sales were made

exhibit 5-17   1985 Organization

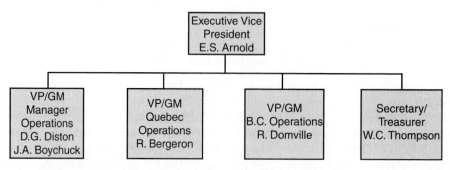

Source: List of officers and executives from 1985 annual report.

through outlets operated by provincial liquor boards. The company had recently entered into a joint venture to manufacture and distribute cider products for the U.S. market.

At the time of the sale, the gross income for Jordan & Ste-Michelle Cellars Ltd. was almost identical to that of Brights. The acquisition meant that Brights was now the largest winery in Canada by a large margin.

Discussion Questions

1. In 1986, Brights had a regional structure. What alternative forms could it have adopted?
    a. Why, then, did it adopt a regional structure?
    b. How big does a company have to be to justify a regional structure?
2. Why did Brights have a functional structure in 1977, given the arguments for a regional?
3. Why was the position of executive vice president eliminated in 1980? Why was the position of vice president, marketing, kept vacant in 1980/81? Why was the position of vice president, marketing, ultimately eliminated and replaced with a staff director of marketing?
4. What might occur now that the acquisition has occurred?

Summary of Organizational Design and Structural Issues

Strategy and Organizational Fit

The organizational structure and coordination design elements enable the resources, assets, and skills to be integrated into efficiently operating sets of competitive advantages and capabilities.

Designing an appropriate organizational approach is an important managerial task.

The basic design of an organization must be appropriate to the firm's overall strategy as well as the firm's characteristics. In particular, strategic issues that necessitate organizational design are:

- Strategic diversification
- Business complexity
- The specific competitive position of the firm

Strategy and Organizational Structure Fit

The organizational structure must fit the overall strategic objectives of the firm and its competitive environment. For example, if the firm is in an international competitive environment, it must adjust its strategy so that it is effective in this complex environment. Some strategic concerns that tend to influence the organizational structure are:

- Customers' requirements—low-cost versus specialized services and features
- The complexity and size of the firm
- The number of different businesses within the firm
- Whether the firm operates in an international market environment or not, and do the different international environments require different or similar competitive advantages
- The KSFs in the firm and industry. If it is production, then production will be highlighted in the structure, etc.

Types of Organizational Structures

The following generic organizational types were considered in the chapter:

- Functional
- Geographic
- Decentralized
- Matrix
- Network
- International, Multinational, and Global

Conclusion

Organizational structures are theoretically laid out in this chapter. However, in reality, firms design their structures to meet their specific strategic objectives and demands. This means that most firms become permutations of several different generic types. Furthermore, managers constantly evolve organizational structures incrementally to ensure that the firm stresses the strategic factors that are important at the particular time.

Additional Notes and Recommended Readings

A more thorough treatment of matrix organization forms can be found in Jay R. Galbraith, "Matrix Organizational Designs," *Business Horizons*, February 1971, pp. 29.

An excellent critique of matrix organizations is presented in Stanley M. Davis and Paul R. Lawrence, "Problems of Matrix Organizations," *Harvard Business Review*, May-June 1978, pp. 131-42.

Bahrami, Homa. "The Emerging Flexible Organization." *California Management Review*, Summer 1992, pp. 33-52.

Bartlett, C.A., and Goshal, S., "Matrix Management: Not a Structure, a Frame of Mind." *Harvard Business Review*, pp. 138-145, 1990.

Beamish, Paul, Peter Killing, Donald Lecraw, and Allen Morrison, *International Management*, Second Edition, Richard D. Irwin Inc., Burr Ridge, Illinois, 1994.

Krackhardt, David and Jeffrey Hanson. "Informal Networks: The Company Behind the Chart." *Harvard Business Review*, July-August 1993, pp. 104-113.

Peters, Thomas J. and Robert H. Waterman, Jr., *In Search of Excellence* (New York: Harper & Row, 1982), pp. 306-7.

Spitzer, Quinn and Benjamin Tregoe. "Thinking and Managing Beyond the Boundaries." *Business Horizons*, January - February 1993, pp. 36-40.

chapter 6 Organizational Coordination

On remunerating managers using stock options "As a result, there's more pressure on people to perform. They have their own money at work, and now they're virtually running their own show. It's amazing the impact that has on a management team. I mean, suddenly you have guys working at night, turning off office lights at night, suddenly you have guys driving home from work thinking about ways they can make more money for the company."

JERRY SCHWARTZ, CHAIRMAN OF ONEX

Our organization is very intense, it's very unbureaucratic.

LAURENT BEAUDOIN, CHAIRMAN BOMBARDIER INC.

Chapter 5 explained that organizational structure and coordination are necessary for molding the disparate resources, skills, and knowledge in a firm into competitive advantages and capabilities that produce a successful overall strategy. In this chapter, organizational coordination is examined.

Organizational coordination is vital to the strategy process because it links, controls, and motivates the people and capabilities that drive a firm to its success. Many top managers in big companies, such as GE, have focused considerable effort on increasing the coordination effort. It should be noted that coordination involves many different potential practices and processes including those delineated in exhibit 6-1.

ORGANIZATIONAL COORDINATION

There are a number of different mechanisms for coordination. The classical formal approaches are: direct control or supervision; managing inputs; managing activities, action, and processes; managing and remunerating based upon output metrics; and managing organizational culture (i.e., beliefs and norms). There are also informal coordination mechanisms, which is sometimes called mutual adjustment. All of these types of coordination approaches have one common objective: to get all the individuals, teams, and divisions in an organization coordinated and working towards a united goal. The formal coordination mechanisms are described more fully in the following sections.

1. ***Direct control or supervision*** is the conventional hierarchical approach to management control imposed on subordinates. This approach to control is effective if the employees being controlled are unskilled and/or temporary in nature: or

exhibit 6-1

Information and Decision Processes

- Planning and control
- Resource allocation systems
- Integrating roles and departments
- Information systems

Staffing and Leadership Style

- Recruiting, selection
- Transfer, promotion
- Training and development
- Leadership

Reward Systems

- Compensation
- Promotion
- Job design
- Special award

when the operation is very standardized. It can also be very effective in some cultures where such control is the expected approach to management. Another situation where it can be useful is when there is considerable risk involved in the operation and things must be controlled rigorously. An example of this latter situation is the army or high-risk operations, such as oil rigs. The downside to this type of coordination is that it does not motivate the workers to become better or work harder. This type of coordination is used heavily in assembly line operations, such as at Ford and GM.

2. ***Managing inputs*** is where managers actively manage the inputs into an operation. Inputs may consist of the hiring of employees, supply inputs, funding, training, conferences, etc. Input coordination and management mechanisms have become the in vogue approach for leading edge managers because it stresses the need to carefully manage resources as they enter your organization and prior to the point of installing them as competitive advantages and capabilities. An example of this is the rigorous hiring management that good companies are now completing. These companies realize that the hiring process is relatively inexpensive compared to the training and firing process. In addition, this approach to coordination underscores the importance of inputting new knowledge, skills, and experiences so that the organization and individuals improve continuously. Firms that use this type of approach are firms with highly professional and skilled staff, including consulting firms.

3. ***Managing activities, action, and processes*** is done by many firms and involves developing policies, procedures, and assembly line type operations. This mechanism is particularly useful if the activities and processes in a firm are operationally monitored, scheduled, and planned. Examples of these types of approaches to coordination include just-in-time systems, various types of assembly lines, and Kanban systems, which is a process map of individual activities that

tends to coordinate separate activities. The only concern with this type of coordination approach is that it can restrict the creative and upgrading process, particularly from workers involved in the activities.

4. ***Managing remuneration***, or compensation, based upon output metrics is widely used in the private sector. This type of approach attempts to motivate employees and groups of employees to meet certain output targets. Often, the output targets are financial or operational, but they can also be subjective output targets, such as customer satisfaction. The advantage of this type of management coordination mechanism is that it is very easy to align the output target with the overall goal towards which managers are attempting to coordinate and direct people toward. The important criterion for using this type of coordination approach is that the output metric must be measurable and controllable by those being measured against it. Almost all firms use this approach to some degree, although sales departments use this approach very effectively to motivate employees to either develop new customers, sell to old customers, improve customer satisfaction, or just increase sales levels.

5. ***Managing organizational beliefs and norms*** (i.e., group and organizational culture) is one of the more difficult approaches to coordinating groups and individuals. It is difficult because creating a positive organizational culture is more of an art than a science. However, some managers are very effective at doing it. Important ingredients to establishing an appropriate organizational culture include leadership style, working environment, hiring employees with the correct attitude (particularly if their attitude is known in the industry), and having the right structure and ancillary management coordination techniques present. Some firms actively attempt to manage this by giving prospective employees attitude quizzes prior to their hiring. In some functions, this has proven to be a very effective tool for hiring. Examples of firms where culture is important are small creative firms, such a high-tech entrepreneurial firms and advertising firms.

Informal Coordination

Using informal management coordination, called mutual adjustment, is much more complex and difficult because it is not directly controlled by management. Rather, what occurs is that management facilitates the effective coordination of information through various mechanisms in the hope that informal coordination will occur. What one is looking for are employees and groups of employees that effortlessly communicate, give council, take advice, discuss and debate issues, as well as pass on information and knowledge in a seamless and efficient manner. The term "mutual adjustment" is used for this type of coordination because it describes how workers mutually adjust to each other in an informal but active manner. Small entrepreneurial firms tend to do this better than larger firms because they are small and have no barriers to interaction and coordination because of the lack of structure and formal roles. However, in larger firms, managers must actively develop the attributes that enables for such an informal coordination process to take place.

The benefits of mutual adjustment are numerous, but two of the most important are the readiness to respond quickly and adaptability. Alacrity results because individuals can communicate and coordinate immediately rather than having to wait for formal mechanisms to kick in. This enables the coordination to be both prompt and enthusiastic. However, adaptability is the more important benefit because it enables mangers, employees, and groups to coordinate on complex, abstract, and often uncertain projects and issues. In these situations, formal communication and coordination techniques have a difficult time because of the standardization and need for conformity to norms in the organization. This makes the informal approach particularly important in firms and organizations that deal with uncertain, complex, and abstract issues—examples include high-tech firms and research institutes. However, leading edge firms, such as GE and IBM, are attempting to instill more informal coordination because of the benefits of such an approach. The only concern with this approach is that it can require considerable time and cost to develop this in a large corporation that is accustomed to a more classical formal coordination process.

Managers use a wide variety of mechanisms to instill mutual adjustment in their firms. Some of the mechanisms and tactics used to instill this type of approach to coordination are:

- Often, this type of coordination approach is mandated for certain parts of the organization—at least, as a principal approach to coordination. The departments that would be most suitable would be those that deal with complex, abstract, and uncertain issues and concerns.

- Some of the primary attributes that managers want to develop that instill mutual adjustment are:
  - Employees must develop relationships with other people in the organization. Managers should be particularly interested in developing relationships and interaction among departments that rely upon one another. This can be done by locating the departments or groups close together. In addition, employees, particularly new employees, can be rotated through several key departments. This enables them to develop contacts and knowledge about the individuals in the various departments. Other methods of facilitating relationships include socializing, putting individuals from different parts of the organization in project teams, etc.
  - It is also important that employees understand the problems and activities that other departments face. When employees understand the issues being faced in other departments, they then know intuitively when they should pass on information or when they should consult the department with a particular issue. Developing this understanding requires that the employees become familiar with the operations and knowledge that is contained in the various departments throughout the firm. Facilitating this can be done by using some of the techniques considered for developing relationships described above. However, it can also be done through different types of information sharing sessions that take place on an ongoing basis.
  - Having employees that are naturally inclined to interaction with others is important to developing informal coordination abilities in the organization. Managers can facilitate this by hiring individuals that have values and attitudes that facilitate interpersonal interaction.
  - Developing an organizational culture that encourages interaction is very important. The features of a good organizational culture are:
    - As little politics in the organization as possible
    - All individuals are respected and valued
    - An organic attitude where different approaches and voicing alternative opinions is quite acceptable

- A culture where employees are encouraged to discuss issues affecting them and their team with their superiors in an open and solution driven context

There are a wide variety of mechanisms that can facilitate such an organizational culture including leadership, interactive sessions, where employees and managers interact openly on issues and concerns in an organization, etc. An example of a very effective tool is GE's workout sessions where employee groups consider solutions to a wide variety of problems in their unit during a multi-day facilitated round table session. Then on the last day, the manager is brought in and he or she has several minutes to say yes or no to the solutions developed by his group. During this solutions address session, the manager's bosses are also watching and this means that the manager has to answer the question in a thoroughly rational and un-political manner. These sessions not only facilitate the open discussion of cross-corporate problems, but they also tend to eliminate politics, something that is thought to be dysfunctional to the informal coordination process.

When managers develop approaches to coordination in their firm, they rely on many different types of mechanisms. In fact, the average company uses dozens of different coordination approaches, and often different types of coordination are used in different parts of the organization. Using numerous coordination mechanisms is beneficial because they often reinforce and stress slightly different issues that require coordination. Furthermore, some mechanisms are good for coordinating individuals while others are better for coordinating groups. This is not to say that a company is better off adopting as many mechanisms as possible. Clearly, simplicity of coordination enables employees to understand what managers are trying to stress in the organization. It also should be noted that coordination devices often must be put in place at interfaces between an organization and other organizations that fit in the firm's business model. For example, Wal-Mart must coordinate very closely with its suppliers using a number of different approaches.

The most difficult decisions that managers face regarding these coordination approaches are ensuring that the mechanisms are working in unison rather than at cross purposes, ensuring that the best mechanism is being used in the appropriate environment in the business model and organization, and finally, what coordination mechanisms are going to best provide for continuous improvement and a healthy evolution of the firm's strategy.

SPECIFIC COORDINATION ISSUES AND APPROACHES

Managing the various coordination processes in a company is vitally important because it ensures that different departments, teams, and individuals are working cohesively on trying to fulfill the company's overall mission and objectives. Some important and widely used management coordination tactics are described in the next sections.

Information and Decision Processes

"Processes are overlaid across the structure to allocate resources and coordinate activities not handled by the department structure." These information and decision processes include planning and control systems (for such things as budgets, schedules, and forecasts), integrating mechanisms (to enable coordination and cooperation to take place among tasks and functional areas), and information systems (to collect, analyze, and disseminate information and knowledge both formally and informally throughout the organization). In any organization, it is critically important that the information and knowledge pertinent to a specific decision be provided to the decision maker. This means that decision processes must either be decentralized or information processes must convey critical information to the individuals making the decisions.

Reward Systems

Perhaps the most easily understood element of organization design is reward systems. Decisions on compensation packages (however they are composed), on promotions (accompanied with any combination of such things as bigger offices, more status, a free parking space, increased holidays, a private secretary, etc.), on ways of awarding outstanding performance, and on the design of jobs (and who gets the more interesting or high-profile assignments), all can be designed in such a way as to reinforce desired behaviour.

Managers design reward systems so that individuals and teams focus on the firm's strategic objectives. The eventual design must consider and support job efficiency and effectiveness, core competitive advantages and positions, and individual as well as group values, preferences, and expectations. Often, these diverse needs are difficult to fulfill in a large complex company that face ever changing environmental and strategic forces. However, reward systems are important motivators and useful tools for evaluation of employees in an organization.

Staffing and Leadership Style

People are critical to an organization's success and long-term performance. Getting (recruiting, selecting), grooming (training and developing), and retaining (transferring, promoting) personnel are crucial activities in every organization. All of these activities ensure that a company hires, and retains the most motivated, skilled, and effective people in its organization, because, over the long-term, an organization is only as good as the people in it.

Training and developing skills is becoming particularly important to firms because of the advent of new technology and processes. Pertinent skills for personnel in a firm range from general business skills, to industry specific knowledge, firm specific knowledge, and job or task specific knowledge and skills. As one moves higher in the organization, a broader spectrum of theses skills is required; yet, it is the more task specific skills that often have to be taught at the lower levels in an organization.

Top managers also have leadership styles that help motivate and direct employees to fulfill the firm's objectives. The classical leadership dimensions in the business literature are identified in exhibit 6-2. These dimensions are autocratic, democratic, structural, considerate, transactional, and transformational. It should be noted that the second and third dimensions are not necessarily mutually exclusive. In other words, a leader can have qualities of both structural and considerate, or transactional and transformational simultaneously. The first dimension of autocratic and democratic is mutually exclusive in that a leader cannot be both simultaneously.

exhibit 6-2   Dimensions of Leadership Style

Autocratic versus Democratic Leadership Dimension (Note: these two dimensions are mutually exclusive, although most leaders would vary somewhere between the two extremes)	An **autocratic leadership** dimension is where the leader tends to make unilateral decisions, dictate work methods, provide only short-term goals, and give feedback only when things go wrong. This type of leadership style is sometimes necessary when a firm faces a crisis and immediate action is required.	A **democratic leadership** dimension is a leader that tends to involve group members in decision-making and the determination of work methods, provide longer-term objectives, and give complete information feedback and coaching. A democratic leadership style is almost essential when the critical knowledge in the organization is dispersed throughout the employees in the organization. This is the case in law and consulting firms, for example.
Structural and Considerate Leadership Dimension (Note: a leader can have both of these dimensions, as they are not mutually exclusive)	A **structural leadership** dimension involves focusing on basic managerial functions, such as planning, coordinating, and controlling. The focus is on achieving activity results. Typical behaviour includes emphasizing deadlines and the quantity and quality of work to be accomplished. Such an approach is particularly useful if employees know what they have to do, little interaction is required between tasks and the manager, the job can be objectively measured and evaluated (when the task is mundane and repetitive), or when the organizational culture and employees are very logical and structured in their social thinking and activity patterns.	A **considerate leadership** dimension involves focusing on building mutual trust with subordinates, respecting their ideas, and showing concern for their ideas. The leader is friendly towards subordinates, engages in two-way conversations, and expresses concern about their welfare. Such an approach can be appropriate when the task is very difficult to measure and evaluate, the employee is learning about the task and social structure in the organization, the task involves intimate contact with others including the manager, or when the organizational culture and employee are emotional in their social, thinking and activity patterns.
Transactional and Transformational Motivational Leadership Dimension (Note: a leader can have both of these dimensions as they are not mutually exclusive)	The **transactional leadership** dimension involves motivating employees to perform to expected levels of performance by clarifying responsibilities, and the means to achieve their goals, and by exchanging rewards for performance. This type of leadership style may be best suited to motivating employees that are involved with repetitive, mundane tasks and whose output is easily measured.	The **transformational leadership** dimension involves motivating employees to transcend expected levels of performance by articulating a compelling vision of the future, which is consistent with their values, and inspiring them to focus on broader missions that go beyond their immediate self-interest. Transformational leaders provide subordinates or "followers" with individual consideration by engaging them in activities that are tailored to their individual needs and will contribute to their personal development. They stimulate followers intellectually by offering them new ideas and encouraging them to think in new ways about old problems. This type of leadership dimension may be particularly important for firms going through change or taking a leadership role in the development of its industry.

Other dimensions that are important to consider in a leader is his or her knowledge and experience in the industry and company, risk preferences, creativity, and intrinsic motivation to get the job done. Since leadership styles are not easily changed, it is important for a firm to select an appropriate leadership style for its particular strategic situation and organizational characteristics.

Probably the greatest failing when organizations are designed is the lack of consistency between (a) the organization design variables and (b) the strategy variables. Often companies develop problems when their strategy changes, but the organizational design variables are not commensurately adjusted to maintain the desired consistency and fit.

Specific examples of normative configurations of strategy and organizational variables that constitute a fit are shown in exhibit 6-3. The three strategic approaches considered are three different product strategies: single or dominant business, related diversified, and unrelated diversified.

HOW ORGANIZATIONS EVOLVE AS STRATEGY EVOLVES

The Stages Model

In a number of respects, the strategist's approach to organization building is governed by the size and growth stage of the enterprise, as well as by the key success factors inherent in the organization's business. For instance, the type of organization that suits a small specialty steel firm relying upon a regionally focused strategy is not likely to be suitable for a large, vertically integrated steel producer doing business in geographically diverse areas. The organization form that works best in a multi-product, multi-technology, multi-business corporation pursuing unrelated diversification is, understandably, likely to be different yet again. Recognition of these differences prompt researchers to formulate a model linking changes in organizational characteristics to stages in an organization's strategic development.

The underpinning of the stages concept is that enterprises can be arrayed along a continuum, running from very simple to very complex organizational forms, and that there is a tendency for an organization to move along this continuum towards more complex forms as it grows in size, market coverage, and product-line scope and as the strategic aspects of its customer-technology/business portfolio become more intricate. Four distinct stages of strategy-related organization structure have been singled out.

Stage I   A Stage I organization is essentially a small, single-business enterprise managed by one person. The owner-entrepreneur has close daily contact with employees at each phase of operations. Most employees report directly to the owner, who makes all the pertinent decisions regarding objectives, strategy, daily operations, and so on. As a consequence, the organization's strengths, vulnerabilities, and resources are closely allied with the entrepreneur's personality, management ability and style, and personal financial capabilities. Not only is a Stage I enterprise an extension of the interests, abilities, and limitations of its owner-entrepreneur, but its activities are typically concentrated in just one line of business. For the most part, Stage I enterprises are organized very simply and the owner-entrepreneur makes most top-level functional decisions.

exhibit 6-3   Strategy-Organization Fit

Strategy	Dominant Business Vertically Integrated	Unrelated Diversified Growth through Acquisition	Related Diversified Growth through Internal Development, Some Acquisition
Strategic focus and task focus	• Degree of integration • Market share • Product line breadth	• Degree of diversity • Types of business • Resource allocation across discrete businesses • Entry and exit businesses	• Realization of synergy from related products, processes, technologies, and markets • Resource allocation • Diversification opportunities
Structure and decision-making style	• Centralized functional • Top control of strategic decisions • Delegation of operations through plans and procedures	• Highly decentralized product divisions/profit centers • Small corporate office • No centralized line functions • Almost complete delegation of operations and strategy within existing businesses • Control through results, selection of management, and capital allocation	• Multidivisional/profit centers • Grouping of highly related business with some centralized functions within groups • Delegated responsibility for operations • Shared responsibility for strategy
Information and decision process	• Coordination and integration through structure, rules, planning, and budgeting • Use of integrating roles for project activity across functions	• No integration across businesses • Coordination and information flows between corporate and division levels around management information systems and budgets	• Coordinate and integrate across businesses and between levels with planning, integrating roles, integrating departments
Rewards	• Performance against functional objectives • Mix of objective and subjective performance measures	• Formula-based bonus on ROI or profitability of divisions • Equity rewards • Strict objective, impersonal evaluation	• Bonus based on divisional and corporate profit performance • Mix of objective and subjective performance measures
People and careers	• Primarily functional specialists • Some inter functional movement to develop some general managers	• Aggressive, independent general managers of divisions • Career development opportunities are primarily intradivisional	• Broad requirements for general managers and integrators • Career developments cross functional, inter divisional, and corporate-divisional

Stage II   Stage II organizations differ from Stage I enterprises in one essential respect: The increased scale and scope of operations create a pervasive strategic need for
management specialization and force a transition from a one-person management to
team management. However, a Stage II enterprise, although run by a team of managers
with functionally specialized responsibilities, remains fundamentally a single-business
operation. This is not to imply that the categories of management specialization are
uniform among large, single business enterprises. In practice, there is wide variation.
Some Stage II organizations prefer to divide strategic responsibilities along classic

functional lines—marketing, production, finance, personnel, control, engineering, public relations, procurement, planning, and so on. In vertically integrated Stage II companies, the main organization units are sequenced according to the flow from one vertical stage to another. For example, the organizational building blocks of an oil company usually consist of exploration, drilling, pipelines, refining, wholesale distribution, and retail sales. In a process-oriented Stage II company, the functional units are sequenced in the order of the steps of the production process. Stage II companies have also developed more formal reporting and information systems upon which to manage and make decisions.

Stage III   Stage III embraces those organizations whose operations, though concentrated in a single field or product line, are large enough and scattered over a wide enough geographical area to justify having geographically decentralized operating units. These units all report to corporate headquarters and conform to corporate policies, but they are given the flexibility to tailor their unit's strategic plan to meet the specific needs of each respective geographic area. Ordinarily, each of the semiautonomous operating units of a Stage III organization is structured along functional lines.

The key difference between Stage II and Stage III, however, is that, while the functional units of a Stage II organization stand or fall together (in that they are built around one business and one end market), the operating units of a Stage III firm can stand alone (or nearly so) in the sense that the operations in each geographic unit are less dependent on the other units to carry out businesses. Firms that could be characterized as Stage III include many large breweries, cement companies, and steel mills having production capacity and sales organizations in several geographically separate market areas.

Stage IV   Stage IV is typified by large decentralized, multi-product, multi-market enterprises. Corporate strategies emphasize diversification. As with Stage III companies, the semiautonomous operating units report to a corporate headquarters and conform to certain firm-wide policies, but the divisional units pursue their own respective line-of-business strategies. Typically, each separate business unit is headed by a general manager who has profit-and-loss responsibility and whose authority extends across all of the unit's functional areas except, perhaps, accounting and capital investment (both of which are traditionally subject to corporate approval). Both business strategy decisions and operating decisions are thus concentrated at the business-unit level rather than at the corporate level. The organization structure at the business-unit level may be along the lines of Stage I, II, or III types of organizations. A characteristic Stage IV company is Canadian Pacific.

Movement through the Stages   The stages model provides useful insights into why organization form tends to change in accordance with product/customer-technology relationships and new directions in corporate strategy. As firms progress from small, entrepreneurial enterprises following a basic concentration strategy to more complex strategic phases of volume expansion, vertical integration, geographic expansion, and line-of-business diversification, their organizational structures evolve from a simply unitary form to functionally centralized to multi-divisional decentralized organizational forms. Firms that remain single-line businesses almost always have some form of a centralized functional structure. Enterprises predominantly in one industry but slightly diversified typically have a hybrid structure; the dominant business is managed via a functional organization, and the diversified activities are handled through a decentralized divisional form. The more diversified an organization becomes, irrespective of whether the diversification is along related or unrelated lines, the more it moves toward some form of decentralized business-unit form.

However, it is by no means imperative that organizations begin at Stage I and move in a lock step sequence toward Stage IV. Some firms have moved from a Stage II organization to a Stage IV form without ever passing through Stage III, while other organizations exhibit characteristics of two or more stages simultaneously. And finally, some companies have found it desirable to revert to more focused and centralized forms of organizations after having been a decentralized organization.

About 90 percent of the Fortune 500 firms (nearly all of which are diversified to one degree or another) have a divisionalized organization structure with the primary basis for decentralization being line-of-business considerations. Exhibit 6-4 summarizes some of the common organizational changes required in the transition from Stage I to Stage IV.

One final lesson that the stages model teaches is worth reiterating. A reassessment of organization structure and authority is always useful whenever strategy is changed. A new strategy is likely to entail new or subtly different skills and key activities. If these changes go unrecognized, especially the subtle ones, the resulting mismatch between strategy and organization can pose implementation problems and curtail performance.

exhibit 6-4 Common Organizational Changes Required in Transitions

	Entrepreneurial Single Business Stage I to Professional Single Business Stage II	Professional Single Business Stage II to Professional Multibusiness Stages III & IV
Structure	• Move from ill-defined functional specialization to well-articulated functions • Almost total centralization converted to substantial functional responsibility, authority • Integration by entrepreneur gives way to various integrating devices	• Move from functional to product/market (business-unit) specialization • Development of corporate functions to manage business-unit portfolio • Delegation of operating and some strategic discretion to units • Integration across units by corporate functions
Business decision processes	• Move planning and resource allocation from an extension of entrepreneurial preferences to more objective processes • Increasing use of functional (sales, costs to budget) performance criteria	• Move planning and resource allocation focus from functional departments to business-units • Strategic goals (market share, profits) used to assess and control businesses
Personnel decision processes	• Move to more systematic procedures and objective criteria for staffing, training, and assessing individual performance • Rewards less subject to personal relationships, paternalism	• Further development of systematic procedures with broadening to emphasize the development of general managers • Rewards variable in relation to business-unit performance
Leadership style	• Move from a personally oriented, hands-on domination of operations to a less-obtrusive style emphasizing leadership and integration of functional units relative to strategic needs	• Senior management further distanced from operations • Symbolic and context setting aspects of style become more critical • Leadership in relation to corporate business-unit strategic needs

ORGANIZATIONAL REENGINEERING

Organizational reengineering is a management technique that has been efficient and effective at focusing the organization on satisfying the customers' demands. Organizations that are particularly appropriate for reengineering include organizations that are large and bureaucratic, have not changed in many years, or where modern technological and business system changes have not been adopted. The objective of organizational reengineering is to make the organization more efficient and effective at focusing on the customers' needs and desires. Some of the characteristics of the reengineered organization include:

- Customer satisfaction drives all processes in the organization
- The company is organized around processes not functions
- The organization has a flatter structure
- Interdisciplinary teams manage many things across functional boundaries
- Teams and personnel are rewarded based on process performance
- Responsibility and appropriate training is provided to all members

Many companies are now considering the organizational reengineering process in place of downsizing or just layoffs. The process for completing reengineering involves the following steps:

1. Get all of the top managers enthusiastically committed to making the move from a non-integrated orientation to an integrated process orientation. This is often one of the most difficult steps.

2. Analyze and identify key processes that support core competitive advantages and that support customer product and service desires. Each of the processes should be linked to a customer product or service outcome.

3. Organize the business around the processes, not functions. This means that multi-functional teams will normally complete the processes. All processes should be directly linked to the customer in some way.

4. Eliminate unnecessary activities or steps in these processes, and eliminate unnecessary processes in the organization that do not support these objectives. They are often designated as key processes.

5. Appoint a manager or supervisor as the "owner' of each key process, and empower employees by giving them the necessary information and allow them to have responsibility for changing the process and achieving the process's goals.

6. Revamp the reward system so that it supports the team who gets the process done most efficiently and effectively. Rewards should also be given for retraining, flexibility, and creativity in designing and accomplishing the process. Performance objectives must be set on a regular basis and they must be linked to customer satisfaction.

SUMMARY

Managers must break an organization and its workers into groups (e.g., teams, functions, departments, etc.) to ensure activities are carried out efficiently, but then they are forced to integrate these groups through various means to ensure that the activities are coordinated properly. This chapter examined organizational control and coordination issues. The next chapter examines how a manager breaks the organization into groups.

Summary of Organizational Coordination Issues

Organizational coordination is important because it helps motivate, control, and direct the efforts of disparate people and resources in different units within a company.

Designing Integration and Coordination Techniques

Integrating and coordinating activities, resources, assets, and skills in an organization is vitally important. Managers use a variety of formal an informal techniques. Some of the more important techniques are:

Formal
- Information systems and decision-making routines
- Reward systems
- Promotional, hiring and firing processes
- Formalized meetings, reporting, and communicating demands
- Leadership style
- Training

Informal
- Informal communication and leadership
- Encouraging people to interact informally
- Motivating people in a direction compatible with the overall purpose of the organization

Other approaches include:
- Leadership style
- Information processing system

Stages Model of Organizational Development

A firm evolves from a small, simple, single business organization through to a complex multinational and business firm. Each of these stages of operation require specific organizational design requirements. In general, the organizational design becomes more complex as the business evolves.

Additional Notes and Recommended Readings

A. D. Chandler, *Strategy and Structure* (Cambridge, Mass.: MIT Press, 1962), p. 14.

Denton, K.D., "Creating a System for Continuous Improvement," *Business Horizons*, pp. 16-21, 1993.

Farkas, G and Wetlaufer, S. "The Ways Chief Executive Officers Lead" *Harvard Business Review*, 74 no. 3, 1996.

For an excellent documentation of how a number of well-known corporations revised their organization structures to meet the needs of strategy changes and specific product/market developments, see E. R. Corey and S. H. Star, *Organization Strategy* (Boston: Division of Research, Harvard University Graduate School of Business Administration, 1971).

Fry, Joseph N. and J. Peter Killing, *Strategic Analysis and Action* (Scarborough, Ont.: Prentice-Hall Canada, 1986), p. 202.

Garvin, David. "Building a Learning Organization." *Harvard Business Review*, July - August 1993, pp. 78-91

Goshal, Sumantra and Christopher Bartlett. "Changing the Role of Top Management: Beyond Structure to Process." A two part series, *Harvard Business Review*, Part I November- December 1994, and Part II January - February 1995.

Hammer, Michael and James Champy, *Reengineering the Corporation.* Harper Collins, New York, 1993.

Herzberg, F. "One More Time: How Do You Motivate Employees" *Harvard Business Review*, pp. 109-120, 1987.

Jay R. Galbraith and Robert K. Kazanjian, *Strategy Implementation*, end ed. (St. Paul, Minn.: West Publishing, 1986), p. 114.

Pfeffer, J. and Veiga, J.F., "Putting People First for Organizational Success." *Academy of Management Executive.* Pp. 37-48, 1999.

Salter, Malcolm S., "Stages of Corporate Development," *Journal of Business Policy*, Spring 1970, pp. 23-27; Donald H. Thai, "Stages of Corporate Development," Business Quarterly, Winter 1969, pp. 32-45; Bruce R. Scott, "The Industrial State: Old Myths and New Realities," *Harvard Business Review*, March April 1973, pp. 133-48; and Chandler, Strategy and Structure, chap. 1.

Salter, "Stages of Corporate Development," pp. 34-35.

Simons, R. "Control in an Age of Empowerment" *Harvard Business Review*, pp 80-88, 1995.

chapter 7 Strategy and Stakeholders' Preferences and Ethics

The things one can do with money can be dangerous, but if it's looked at as a means to an end, to doing something for the good of the family or mankind, then it becomes useful.

PETER ENG, CHAIRMAN OF ALLIED HOLDINGS, INC.

I am basically very conservative – people just perceive that I am a big risk taker.

PAUL DESMARAIS, CHAIRMAN OF POWER CORP.

Strategic planning may seem to be a highly rational and reasoned process within the organization. However, the formulation of strategy is often influenced by the values of certain strategic stakeholders in the organization, and different stakeholder groups must be convinced of the value of executing the strategy based on their desires before the strategy can be successfully implemented. Top managers must understand the values, perceptions, and ultimately, the behaviour of various stakeholder groups to realize a successful strategy outcome.

Stakeholders and their values are also the core elements that produce an organization's culture. Culture is a vital ingredient to the success of a strategy. For example, imposing an aggressive entrepreneurial strategy onto a company having a bureaucratic culture will probably not be effective. Managers must understand the nature of their organizational culture, and how one might change such a culture by changing the nature and content of the strategic stakeholders in the firm.

In this chapter, the role of stakeholder preferences and ethics in strategy formulation and implementation are considered. The chapter will also describe the concept of corporate culture, corporate ethics, and stakeholder pressures since they influence, and are influenced by, managerial preferences.

MANAGING PREFERENCES

Everybody has individual preferences that influence his or her decisions and ultimately behaviour. Preferences are derived from an individual's basic values. These values are modified through a person's experience, personal goals, beliefs, attitudes, and competencies. In this context, a manager's task is to unify the preferences and ultimately the employees' behaviours, in a way that supports the competitive advantages and the strategic direction of the firm. To do this, a manager must confront two issues. First, managers must develop a shared set of preferences and behaviours for their organization, and second, they must ensure that the shared organizational preferences are appropriate for the strategic direction of the company.

MANAGING ORGANIZATIONAL WIDE PREFERENCES AND BEHAVIOUR

Personal preferences must be assimilated into group preferences if management is to have a consistent set of preferences to guide strategic decision-making. Managers attempt to guide their organization's preferences, and inform their stakeholders of their preferences, by developing a vision and mission statement. A vision statement is a statement that describes the top management's vision of what the firm should represent and strategically be sometime in the future (e.g., five or ten years hence). A mission statement sets the guidelines and describes in very general terms how the firm is going to accomplish its vision. Within these statements one often finds a description of the firm's corporate ethics, preferences, and a portrayal of the desired business culture for the firm. One of the goals of these statements is to provide all of the stakeholders with a general description of the company's preferences and ethical principles, and demonstrate how they apply to the overall strategy of the company.

Getting agreement on common and shared preferences by all individuals in an organization is not an easy task. This assimilation process is accomplished through a complex process in which power and leadership often play instrumental roles. Power and leadership enable certain individuals in a business to dominate the formation of group preferences and culture. For this reason, any assessment of firm and group preferences must consider who the powerful people in the organization are, how they see the situation, and what they think should be done. There are both formal and informal leaders in an organization, and both can shape the culture and preferences of a group within the organization. Managing this process requires considerable top management skill and leadership. This process and the participatory groups are described more thoroughly below in sections on the stakeholders, and corporate ethics sections within this chapter.

Stakeholders' Preferences

Managers are increasingly expected to consider a growing number of stakeholders when formulating strategy. A stakeholder is an individual or a group with a personal interest in the business. Each stakeholder depends on the business in order to realize goals, while the business depends on them for something they provide to the business. General classes of stakeholders who directly influence managers' decisions include shareholders, management, employees, financiers, suppliers, customers, community, and government. Illustrative preferences of these stakeholders and how they encourage managers to meet them are presented in exhibit 7-1. Managers often reflect the preferences of stakeholders they see as important to their performance. Thus, the marketing manager will tend to reflect customers' interests, and the financial manager will tend to reflect financiers' interests. Stakeholders often share common interests, because of their involvement in the business.

exhibit 7-1   The Interests of Stakeholders

Stakeholder	Preferences and Expectations	Ways Stakeholders Exert Influence on the Business
Shareholders	• Appreciation in the value of stock dividends • Social responsibility	• Buying and selling stock • Election of directors • Proxy fights • Public expression of satisfaction or discontent through the press or at annual meetings
Managers	• Participation in decisions • Authority/power • Compensation (salary, bonuses, benefits) • Opportunity for advancement • Job security	• Taking/leaving jobs in the firm • Commitment to work • Quality of work
Employees	• Compensation (wages, benefits, profit sharing) • Participation in workplace decisions • Safe working conditions • Opportunity for advancement • Job security	• Strikes • Absenteeism • Workplace grievances • Quality of work • Union activity
Financiers	• Orderly repayment of principal and interest • Further opportunities for sound investment of monies • Timely disclosure of events	• Willingness to lend additional funds • Covenants in the loan agreements • Enforcement of covenants • Credit rating interest rates charged
Suppliers	• Continued, consistent orders • Prompt payment	• Prices charged • Credit terms • Delivery performance • Willingness to meet special demands • Supply priority during periods of shortage • Technical assistance • Recommendations to other suppliers
Customers	• Satisfactory products or services • Satisfactory price/quality relationship • Fair adjustment practices (warranties, responses, etc.)	• Amount purchased • Word of mouth advertising • Complaints, returns, claims • Product liability suits • New product ideas
Community	• Continuity of employment • Continuity of payment of taxes • Environmentally sound activities • Actions socially sound employee • Participation in community activities	• Boycotts, protests, demonstrations • Awards by community groups • Pressure on government
Government	• Continuity of employment • Continuity of payment of taxes • Environmentally sound activities • Advance national objectives (ROD, exports, job creation) • Satisfy regulations	• Subsidies, tax concessions • Regulations • Licenses, permits • Awards by government • Enforcement of regulations
Other Interest Groups	• Interested in social, moral, environmental, cultural, and community issues	• Boycotts, protests, demonstrations • Educating the consumers and public

Which stakeholders' preferences management seeks to satisfy involves difficult choices. Sometimes compromises must be made among the various competing stakeholders' preferences. It is management's responsibility to conciliate and ultimately decide between competing stakeholder groups' preferences. This clearly requires strong managerial abilities. However, sometimes management decides to favour one stakeholder preferentially over another. Such a decision may be based upon rational considerations or the stakeholder power. Factors influencing the potential power of stakeholders are outlined in exhibit 7-2. When executives in large firms were asked, "who is really important to the business?" customers were seen as most important,

exhibit 7-2   Potential Power Held by Stakeholders When Seeking to Influence Strategic Decisions

Stakeholder	Degree of Potential Power	
	Is High If	Is Low If
Shareholders	• Controlling block of shares with an active interest in the company • Many shareholders that have a common interest in what the company does • Shareholders hold stock so they can exert influence over management decisions	• Shares are widely held by uninterested shareholders • Shares are widely held by shareholders with heterogeneous interests • A dominant CEO strongly influences elections to the board
Managers	• A dominating CEO leads management • The management team has been in place for a long time • Compensation is heavily influenced by performance-based bonuses	• The board of directors dominates decision-making
Employees	• Belong to a strong union • The company has a tradition of good employee relations	• Unskilled labour force • High unemployment
Financiers	• The company is highly leveraged • The company has defaulted on the covenants in the loan agreements	• The company generates the investment money it needs internally
Suppliers	• Limited sources of supply • Switching costs are high	• Many alternative suppliers
Customers	• Few possible customers • A few customers buy a significant proportion of the output • Customers possess a credible threat for backward integration	• Many possible customers • The company's product is unique
Community Government	• A single-industry town • Regulations provide government with control over company activities • Government approval is required for mergers and acquisitions • The government can provide grants, licenses, and special tax benefits	• The company has facilities in many locations • Firm is an international firm with the ability to move operations outside of the country • If the country does not have any attractive resources or markets
Other Interest Groups	• If they can influence the actions of some of the other stakeholders such as customers and government	• If they cannot influence other stakeholders

followed by themselves, subordinates, employees, and bosses. Those who were least important, in order of declining importance, were stockholders, elected public officials, government bureaucrats, and other interest groups.

The following questions are relevant when determining the influence of stakeholder interests:

- Which stakeholder interests are most important?
- Will any stakeholders be injured by the proposed decisions?
- Should and can strategy be changed to accommodate stakeholder expectations?
- Is it possible to negotiate a compromise?
- Should and can certain stakeholders be replaced?

These questions also raise ethical considerations about "what is right" and "what is wrong," which is addressed later in the chapter.

MANAGING CORPORATE CULTURE

Corporate culture is defined as the common preferences held by those working in the firm about the way things are done. It gives rise to norms, routines, and informal rules that people follow in the firm. It also provides them with a common understanding of what is considered important and standards of performance. Good managers attempt to influence and shape the firm's culture so that it provides the firm with a competitive advantage in either efficiency or effectiveness.

From the strategic perspective, a corporate culture must be closely linked to a firm's business strategy. A culture that is closely linked to the firm's strategy and environment often produces stellar performance results. For example, firms in the advertising business benefit from having a very creative culture, while a firm in health care may benefit from having a caring, yet efficient culture. In particular, organizational culture has a direct impact on how well a strategy is implemented. Consequently, many managers try and proactively manage their organizational cultures by hiring the appropriate people and putting in place organizational environments, rewards, and systems that promote a specific culture. The only downside to having a strong culture is if the strategy has to change, and changing an organization's culture is not easily or quickly done. Another situation where organizational culture may be detrimental is when two firms merge and there organizational cultures are different.

An example where two different cultures coexist in a company is Bell Canada and CTV, both subsidiaries of BCE Inc. Bell Canada has a much more traditional hierarchical and conservative culture, while CTV has a flatter more organic structure. Administering over such diverse cultures and strategies poses considerable difficulty for BCE. It is speculated that BCE will divest itself of media type businesses to focus solely on communication businesses. Exhibit 7-3 contrasts the characteristics present in these organizational cultures.

Exhibit 7.3 illustrates how an organizational culture is often related to the business and organizational environment and, ultimately, the strategy. For example, we see that Bell Canada's organizational decision-making, systems and style is focused on economizing and efficiency, while CTV's has a more market and customer satisfaction focus.

Another interesting management decision that should have considered the interests of more stakeholders and the organizational culture was the transition of Seagram's from a liquor company to a multimedia company. The business changed from a rather staid conservative liquor operation to a firm that required an entrepreneurial

exhibit 7-3   A Contrast Between Bell Canada and CTV's Culture

Organizational Trait	Bell Canada	CTV
Demographics of Organization	*Very large organization* • Employees tend to be slightly older than average organization • Many do not have university or college degrees	*Medium sized organization* • Employees tend to be younger • Most have university or college degree
Organizational Style	• Hierarchical, staid, and steeped in boss fear • This style is somewhat a result of its previous monopoly position that it had a decade ago	• Flatter organization with a more liberal and freewheeling style
Organizational Systems	• Highly centralized information systems • Most employees paid on a straight salary basis	• Centralized and decentralized information systems • Most employees paid on a straight salary basis
Leadership Style	• Career Bell and government executives who tend to emphasize a very formal top-down management style	• Career media executives who have a more democratic style
Decision-Making Style	• Centralized and bureaucratic • Most lower level decisions have specific rules of process and constraints • More complex decisions take considerable time and may require written authorization	• More decentralized, fast moving, and somewhat entrepreneurial • In the media business executives must delegate some responsibility to ensure news and market trends are quickly and accurately portrayed
Business Strategy	• Focuses on lowering costs and adding new services when market becomes large enough • Generally, not a market leader	• Focuses on developing programming that is creative and being a market leader in the programming content it focuses upon
Business Environment and Performance	• Oligopolistic • Core business is mature and has low growth • Competition is increasing in some segments • Moderately profitable	• Oligopolistic to competitive • Market growth is modest • Competition is increasing in almost all segments of this business, particularly international competition • Moderately profitable

organic organizational culture. Furthermore, shareholder stakeholders saw their ownership change from a conservative income generating company to a highly volatile cash demanding company.

Culture in an organization can range between strong and weak. A strong culture greatly influences the behaviour of organizational members. Evidence for the strength of a culture is found in exhibit 7-4. In general, businesses with strong cultures are likely to have better performance. However, a strong culture is not a sure road to success. A strong culture may become a liability if it does not fit with the requirements of changing business environment and strategy. Nor is a strong culture necessarily self-sustaining. It can break down when rapid growth brings in new people faster than they can be socialized into the culture.

exhibit 7-4   Evidence of the Strength of a Culture

Character of the Culture	Evidence of Character
Strong	• Members share preferences about how to succeed • Members know the activities the business must carry out well to be successful • Standards of achievement are well established • "Heroes" in the organization personify values and provide tangible role models to follow
Weak	• Members have no clear preferences about how to succeed • Members do not agree on beliefs that are important • Different parts of the business have different beliefs or preferences • "Heroes" of the business are destructive or disruptive • Rituals are disorganized, with organizational members either "doing their own thing" or working at cross-purposes

The compatibility between culture and strategy, sometimes called *cultural risk*, can be examined using a logical process. First, the key tasks arising from the strategy are determined. Next, the behaviour required to perform the tasks satisfactorily is determined. This is compared with the behaviour arising out of the current corporate culture. If required behaviour is similar to the actual behaviour, culture poses no risk to the implementation of strategy. If it is different, culture can present so much risk that it is a barrier to the pursuit of a strategy.

The strategist can deal with cultural risk in several ways. One approach is to ignore culture and plunge ahead. Since a good fit is needed between culture and strategy, this approach nearly always invites disaster. Another approach is to manage around culture, either by performing the tasks in ways more in line with the current culture, or, more drastically, by modifying the strategy so that different tasks are required. A third approach is to change the selected components of culture that affect critical organizational activities. For example, a company facing a more competitive environment found that it needed to improve its relationships with customers. It reoriented the culture to fit its new strategy and environment by promoting the slogan "the customer is always right" to employees and customers, and by training employees to respond courteously and promptly to customer requests.

MANAGING BUSINESS ETHICS

Business ethics are related to a society's ethics. Some people know when they are acting unethically, yet they are motivated to do so by various incentives. Yet, what are ethics? Ethical decisions and behaviour are concerned with acts that have impact on the welfare, personal rights, and justice of other people or things. Ethical behaviour is what society considers right and the norm to ensure that social calm and order are maintained.

Some national cultures can have different ethical norms than others. For example, in some countries giving ex-gratia payment (i.e., a bribe) is considered entirely acceptable, while in other countries it is both immoral and illegal. Therefore, it is critical that managers fully understand what the ethical norms are for the country they are considering doing business within.

At this time, business is facing possibly the most difficult ethical challenges it has ever faced in North America. The excesses of some business executives during the 1990s appear to have shaken the public's confidence in business leaders. Some of the more notorious events that have occurred in the first half of 2002 include:

- During 2002, many major companies have had to restate their earnings records for the past several years because of accounting "mistakes" including Xerox, Halliburton, Elan, Bristol-Myers Squib, Harken Energy, Vivendi, Global Crossing, Tyco, Qwest Communications, Enron, WorldCom, and Merck.

- Some of these companies, such as Arthur Anderson, Enron, Tyco, Qwest Communications and WorldCom, are under criminal investigation for making accounting "mistakes" of billions of dollars. Several of these companies have applied for bankruptcy.

- President Bush and Vice President Cheney have been involved in business dealings with questionable accounting practices.

- Remuneration for top managers is very high and arguably unfair. For example, the top management team (i.e., seven employees) at Global Crossing cashed in over $1.3 billion dollars in stock options, which had been paid out in remuneration, prior to the company going bankrupt.

A *U.S. News* Poll conducted in 1999 indicated the amount of trust the public had in top management was appallingly low. In this poll, the public indicated that they thought 89 percent of politicians, 60 percent of business owners, 73 percent of CEOs of Fortune 500 companies, and 55 percent of accountants cheat. Given the above business news during 2002, these poll figures are probably low.

Managing ethical behaviour in a company is not an easy task. One way in which large companies attempt to do this is through a *Statement of Ethical Conduct and Behaviour*. This statement lays out appropriate behaviours and potential penalties for employees in the company. Yet the most important ethical influence in a firm is provided by the managers' day-to-day conduct with employees and customers. If managers participate in marginal activities, then employees will be encouraged to do so. In addition, managers must be fully versed in ethical conduct and discipline measures so that they can provide guidance to employees when necessary. Ultimately, managers must attempt to demonstrate consistent implementation of ethical business conduct and punish those that deviate from such behaviour.

Formulating ethical guidelines can be difficult because of the differences in what is viewed as ethical behaviour in different regions. Nonetheless, a good starting point is to strive to satisfy the ethical norms of all of your stakeholders. For example, if your business is done in several countries, the most stringent ethical principles should be adopted, otherwise, those stakeholders, including customers, owners, and employees, could take issue with your ethical standards, and business performance could suffer. Ultimately, all people must take responsibility for their actions and must consider the long-term consequences of their behaviours to their career, family, and personal prospects.

Ethical standards cannot be taught in classrooms or derived from readings textbooks. Moral values and ethics are the result of interacting with your parents, friends, and the leaders of your community and organization. It is through this evolution of building values that ethics are instilled in people. As future business leaders, it is incumbent upon us to communicate strong ethical values and demonstrate them in our behaviour. Leaders that demonstrate such ethical character will enhance their reputation as well as their company's. The pay off for strong ethics is not necessarily immediate, but, in the future, when customers develop loyalty to your brand, and shareholders demonstrate trust and faith in your ethical decisions.

Questions that should be asked when assessing a company's ethical guidelines are:

- Would the manager like to have that behaviour done to him/her?
- Is there evidence that any of the firm's stakeholders have adopted or oppose this ethical belief?
- Has an ethical principle been ignored because of short-term profitability? And has the manager considered the long-term consequences and arguments for such behaviour?
- Are the committees and organizational processes democratic that establish and control the ethical guidelines?

MANAGING THE FIT BETWEEN PREFERENCES AND STRATEGY

Preferences, at both the group and individual level, are directly related to the components of strategy. Some organizations, particularly not-for-profit organizations, have preferences for kindness and cooperation. Yet, other organizations, particularly those in tough competitive situations, have preferences for efficiency, effectiveness, getting the job done, and aggressive competitiveness.

These preference differences are related to an organization's competitive environment and strategy, and they must be mirrored in the management's preferences. Yet, some manager's have their own preferences that push the company in a specific strategic direction. For example, entrepreneurs often have gambler instincts and they want their company to grow at all costs, often using highly risky strategies. However, a bureaucrat manager is risk averse and is more willing to curtail short-term growth by taking strategies that maintain long-term stability. In this context, the entrepreneur perceives the environment to be full of opportunities, while the bureaucrat sees mostly threats and danger. This difference in perceptions, and thus, preferences must be understood by anybody who works with or employs the manager. If you understand the preferences of your manager, you can and should customize arguments and strategic formulations that consider his or her perspective. For example, if you have been asked to assess a risky growth strategy by an entrepreneur, you would be well advised to not just discredit the strategy to him or her unless the evidence is overpowering. Rather, you should make him or her aware of the potential concerns, suggest strategic tactics that might ameliorate the concerns, and advise him or her to delay the growth until certain strategic concerns and objectives are met. This latter approach does not confront in a blunt way his or her preferences, but forces the manager to consider modifying the strategy so that the risk is ameliorated.

Managers have preferences for the types and levels of goals, and where and how the company competes (i.e., competitive positions). Managerial preferences are important to strategy in other ways as well. Preferences for uncertainty influence the trade-off between risks and rewards, and determine the margin of safety sought to ensure competitive success, financial continuity, and organizational survival. Preferences about self-sufficiency influence the degree of independence sought from key stakeholders. And finally, preferences about how to lead and manage will influence the culture of the firm as these preferences shape decisions about how to keep employees committed, motivated, and loyal, and decisions about how to best use employees' talents.

Other preferences that influence manager's decisions may be related to power, friendship, or personal gain. Advisors, employees and employers to top managers must understand the manager's preferences so that they can take into account these preferences when providing advice to him or her. Either the advisor should understand the manager's preferences and perspective of the firm's environment, resources, organizational capabilities, and strategic "fit," or the advisor should attempt to convince the top manager that his or her perspective, and, therefore, preferences are errant. Changing a top manager's preferences and perspective is not easy. Often it is easier to change top managers than to convince the manager that a different preference would be appropriate.

MANAGING THE RELATIONSHIPS AMONG STRATEGY, PREFERENCES, AND CULTURE

Managerial preferences and culture influence strategy. For example, a preference for growth to satisfy a need for achievement or recognition can encourage managers to follow a strategy of diversification. However, the firm may lack the resources, or there may not be environmental opportunities to follow such a strategy. Therefore, there must be a fit among a firm's environment and strategy and its preferences and culture (exhibit 7-5).

When there is a major gap between the preferences and cultures held, versus those required, either the strategy must change or the preferences and culture must change. As stated previously, it is not easy to change stakeholders' preferences or the organization's culture. Making such changes should be considered carefully as they require considerable effort and may upset the strategic/organizational fit of the company even more. However, if stakeholders' preferences and the organizational culture changes are deemed necessary, then managers should begin making the changes as soon as possible. Some issues that must be addressed in this process are:

Leadership: Often a change in leadership is necessary because it not only signals to the organization and stakeholders that a change is going to take place, but the business can select a leader that embraces the desired preferences and cultural attributes.

Signaling a change in preferences and culture: Quite often it is necessary for the management to overtly signal to stakeholders and employees that a change is going to occur specific to preferences and culture. Changing leadership, changing personal in the organization, changing the organizational structure and systems or just informing the relevant parties can do this. However, sometimes shocks are necessary for organizational cultures to initiate change.

***exhibit* 7-5**   Strategic Gap Analysis: Culture and Preferences

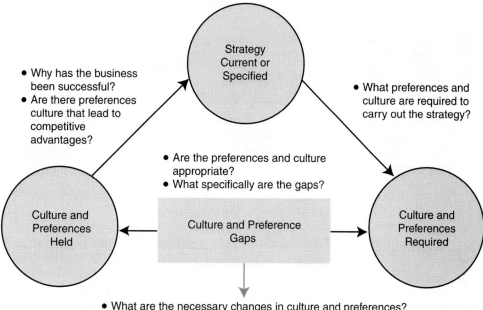

Changing the organizational culture: Subtle cultural change can occur over time by changing an organization's structures and systems, strong and coercive leadership techniques, and by bringing in workers having the desired cultural values. More radical change may require wholesale changes in employees and organizational attributes. However, in both cases, it is imperative that management understands how it wants to change the culture, and that it monitors the behaviour in the organization to ensure that the correct changes are occurring. All too often, a company attempts to make these changes without controlling the process.

Changing external stakeholders can be done by clearly indicating a change in products, services, or business objectives. Again, the magnitude of the change will dictate how fast and how many stakeholders will abandon the company. Managers must, also, control this process. For example, if some investors abandon a company due to changed objectives, management must manage the transition to new investors. In fact, some companies continuously try to coerce good (e.g., loyal, quality-based, and long-term vision) external stakeholders to get involved with their company.

Summary of Stakeholder and Organizational Culture

Stakeholders

Stakeholders must be characterized in terms of their attitudes, desires and power because they can have a profound influence on the direction and ability to execute a strategy. Key stakeholders include owners, managers, workers, unions, customers, and suppliers.

Organizational Cultures

An organizational culture is produced from the values of the key and powerful stakeholders within a firm. Managing an organizational culture is important because it enables the firm to execute a strategy more effectively as the workers are in favour of the strategy because of their perceptions and desires.

Ethical Conduct in Management

Ethical conduct is vitally important to a manager because it influences his or her future reputation. Furthermore, managers must be leaders of ethical conduct, both inside and outside their organizations, because companies that demonstrate an ethical standard will have greater loyalty, brand reputation in the market place. Unethical behaviour may produce quick gains but often lead to long-term disappointment and failure.

Changing Organizational Stakeholders and Culture

Changing organizational culture involves changing key stakeholders or at least some of the representatives of this stakeholder group that are the leaders of the attitudes and behaviour in the group. It is critically important to ensure that your stakeholders are aligned with the firm's overall strategy.

Additional Notes and Recommended Readings

According to T. Deal and A. Kennedy, a strong culture has almost always been the driving force behind continuing success in American business. In *Corporate Cultures* (Reading, Mass.: Addison-Wesley, 1982), p. 5.

Additional coverage of this topic can be found in 1. C. MacMillan and P. E. Jones, *Strategy Formulation: Power and Politics*, 2nd ed. (St. Paul, Minn.: West Publishing, 1986).

Additional sources of information on ethical questions are R. E. Freeman and D. R. Gilbert, Jr., *Corporate Strategy and the Search for Ethics* (Englewood Cliffs, N.J.: Prentice Hall, 1988); S. W. Gellerman, "Why 'Good' Managers Make Bad Ethical Choices," *Harvard Business Review*, July-August 1986, pp. 85-90; and L. L. Nash, "Ethics without a Sermon," *Harvard Business Review*, November-December 1981, pp. 79-90.

Additional sources of information on managerial preferences are G. Donaldson and J. W. Lorsch, *Decision Making at the Top* (Now York: Basic Books, 1983), chaps. 5 and 6; J. N. Fry and J. P. Killing, *Strategic Analysis and Action*, 3rd ed. (Scarborough, Ont.: Prentice-Hall Canada, 1995), chap. 8; and C. R. Schwenk, "Management Illusions and Biases: Their Impact on Strategic Decisions," *Long-Range Planning* 18, no. 5 (1985), pp. 74-80.

Badaracco, J.L. *Defining Moments: When Managers Must Choose between Right and Wrong*, Harvard Business Review Press, 1997.

Badaracco, J.L., "Business Ethics: Four Spheres of Executive Responsibility." *California Management Review*, Spring 1992, pp. 64-79.

Discussion of the personal system in relation to needs and behaviour is found in most texts dealing with organizational behaviour. One good example is A. R. Cohen, S L. Fink, H. Gadon, and R. Willets, *Effective Behavior in Organizations*, 4th ed. (Homewood, Ill.: Richard D. Irwin, 1988), chaps. 7 and 8.

Kotter, J.P. and Heskett, J.L., *Corporate Culture and Performance*, Free Press, 1992.

Malcolm Morgan. "How Corporate Culture Drives Strategy." *Long Range Planning*, April 1993, pp. 110-118.

Poster, B. Z., and W. H. Schmidt, "Values and the American Manager: An Update," *California Management Review*, Spring 1984, p. 206.

Savage, G.T., T. Nix, C.J. Whitehead, and J.D. Blair. "Strategies for Assessing and Managing Organizational Stakeholders." *Academy of Management Executive*, May 1991, pp.61-75.

Schneider, B., Gunnarson, S.K., and Niles-Jolly. "Creating the Climate and Culture of Success", *Organizational Dynamics*, pp. 17-29, 1994.

Stark, Andrew, "What's the Matter with Business Ethics?" *Harvard Business Review*, May-June 1993, pp. 38-48.

The differences are described in greater detail in: Andrew Kupfer & Kathleen C. Smyth, "AT&T's $12 Billion Cellular Dream," *Fortune*, December 12, 1994. pp. 100-112.

The role of culture in successful business organizations has been popularized in Great Britain by W. Goldsmith and D. Clutterback, *The Winning Streak* (Harmondsworth, Middlesex, England, Penguin Books, 1985) and in the United States by T. Peters and R. H. Waterman, *In Search of Excellence* (New York: Harper & Row, 1982). Additional sources of information on corporate culture are J. Barney, "Organizational Culture: Can It Be a Source of Sustained Competitive Advantage?" *Academy of Management Review*, July 1986, pp. 656-665; S. Davis, *Managing Corporate Culture* (Cambridge, Mass.: Ballinger, 1984); and T. Deal and A. Kennedy, *Corporate Cultures* (Reading, Mass.: Addison-Wesley, 1982).

chapter 8 High Technology and E-Commerce Strategies

My strategy is to be in every high-growth area of telecommunications.

JOHN ROTH, EX CHAIRMAN OF NORTEL

My father taught us that you either grow or die; you can't stand still, and it's better to lead than to follow.

JIM SHAW, CEO OF SHAW COMMUNICATIONS

High technology encompasses a wide assortment of industries, including communication, data transmission, computer hardware and software, micro-electronics, aerospace, biotechnology and pharmaceutical, new exotic materials, data transmission, etc. The commonality is the uncertainty and opportunity that technology provides in these industries on a daily basis.

High technology presents managers with a variety of different strategic concerns as well as opportunities. Many of them are related to the extreme uncertainty and speed of change that occur in the environment, while others are related to the intrinsic nature of high technology in the market place. The uncertainty in the high-tech business environment results from a wide variety of interacting factors. Some of the more significant ones are:

- **Basic technological change** occurs at a tremendous rate and this translates into even faster product and service development cycles for the marketplace. Moore's law of technological change, developed by a founder of Hewlett Packard and Intel, states that technological complexity doubles every year. This was a very insightful conjecture back in the mid 1960s because during the 1990s computer microchip technology doubled every year and a half.

- **Markets and customer desires** are evolving as new technologies bombard the market. These changes produce changes in customers' desires. New markets can be created; old markets can disappear; markets can merge, such as the voice, data, and video transmission markets (e.g., cable, Internet, and phone); and segments of markets are almost always continually evolving. These changes make it very difficult for high-tech companies because they not only have difficulty predicting technological changes, but they also have difficulty predicting markets and customers' desires and the resulting market evolutions.

- **Industry competitiveness** is continually changing because of the influx and failure of companies on an almost daily basis. The e-commerce and Internet service provider industries demonstrate how competitiveness can change as markets grow and then slow, new technologies and market tastes change competitive dynamics making for a highly dynamic and fluid industry where both companies are both entering and exiting the business simultaneously. For example, Rogers Cable in 2002 was entering the ISP business while @Home was declaring bankruptcy.

- *Legal and government regulation* may also be influencing some of these businesses. Patent regulation on new science and product developments are one source of change. However, in some of these industries, such as communication, biotechnology, pharmaceutical, and the media industries, government regulation influences market characteristics, and ultimately, the competitiveness of the industry. These changes can turn a company's competitive environment into a cut-throat caldron of activity. An example is the telephone industry where deregulation has changed Bell Canada's competitive position from one of monopoly to a highly competitive and uncertain market environment.

Each of these elements of change produces uncertainty that must be actively managed by top managers.

In this chapter, we will examine two important high-tech strategic issues. The first is the different types of technological innovations that have impact upon firms. This topic will be looked at from the perspective of both the small entrepreneurial firm and the large established firm. Then, the high-tech start-up will be examined. And, finally, strategies in e-commerce will be examined briefly.

TECHNOLOGICAL CHANGE AND STRATEGIC MANAGEMENT

Technological change has been studied under many names and from many perspectives. However, one of the more important studies, by Clayton Christensen, at Harvard, examined failures in the computer hard disk drive industry—an industry that has seen considerable technical change during its evolution. During the period from 1976 to 1995, 129 firms entered this industry, and, astonishingly, 109 firms failed during this same period. Only one firm, IBM's disk drive division, lasted the duration of the period.

Christensen found two types of technological change represented very different strategic situations and they were sustaining versus disruptive technological change. Christensen subsequently applied his findings to other industries and found similar conclusions.

A *sustaining technological change* is when the change pushes the products and services along the same value dimensions that are presently stressed in the market. For example, in the computer monitor industry, the price, size, clarity and lack of flicker were important dimensions upon which customers purchased monitors. Monitor manufacturers continually attempted to lower prices, improve clarity, etc. so that they would be competitive in the market. This is sustaining technological change because it sustains the dimensions that the products are presently judged upon, and it also tends to sustain the major companies that have built competitive advantages in the industry. In effect, this technological change represents the continual improvement of a product or service over time, which is what the vast majority of technological changes entail. Sustaining technological change also tends to emphasize the same value adding activities in the value chain or business model. The change only modifies or improves one or two of the activities, such as production.

A *disruptive technical change* is when a new product or service is developed that does not support the same value dimensions that are stressed in the market. It is when one or more completely new value dimensions are stressed. Usually, when a new disruptive technology is introduced into the market, it is perceived to satisfy the prior dimensions of value poorly, and therefore, most customers find it disappointing. An example is when flat monitor screens were first produced. Most clients found flat screen monitors were terribly expensive, had poor resolutions, and were small in viewing size compared to normal monitors. Thus, most customers did not buy the product. The only benefits of the first generation of flat monitors were their small size, which enabled them to go into portables, and on crowded desks. These new value dimensions initially attracted some customers. However, as the technology evolved it became better and cheaper and began to attract a much larger segment of the market.

Disruptive technological changes are particularly dangerous for established competitors because at first these new technologies are viewed as inferior, as stated above, but over the longer term, they evolve into products that can provide many customers with greater value than the original technology. And if this evolution occurs relatively quickly, the disruptive technologies can overwhelm the established industries in the business. There are many examples of small entrepreneurial companies developing disruptive technologies and eventually overwhelming established companies. In other instances, these disruptive technologies only partially replace established competitors. Examples include computers replacing typewriters, desktop computers replacing many mainframe and mini computers, telephones replacing teletype, email replacing regular mail, etc. We will now look at the dynamics of these technical changes.

Disruptive technical changes are often overlooked by large, mainstream companies for a variety of reasons, some of which include:

- ***Inferior product or service:*** The disruptively derived product or service, initially, is much inferior to the product or service that the principal competitors are producing for the mainstream market. Often the price is higher, the quality is lower, and features are limited. Thus, if a product assessment or a customer survey is done, the results clearly state that the mainstream product is superior and mainstream companies are reticent to support the product.

- ***Tiny market syndrome:*** Initially, the disruptive product has a very small market because it is inferior in so many ways and only appeals to a few customers. Thus, when a large company is financially analyzing whether they should invest in the technology, they deem it to be too small a market compared to their mainstream market, which often is thousands of times larger. Furthermore, R&D, new production facilities, and new sales and marketing efforts are costs that are best supported by large markets. Managers, therefore, choose the sustaining technological development rather than the disruptive technological change based on sound financial analysis.

- ***New value added activities:*** Because the disruptive technology is such a discontinuous type of product or service, it often requires entirely or almost entirely different value chain activities to support it (e.g., production, R&D, marketing, after sales servicing, etc). This means that a large established company in the mainstream market will have to completely change its value chain or business model to adapt to the new technology. Many established firms resist this large investment in resources, knowledge and activities until it is too late.

- ***Market and technology uncertainty:*** The uncertainty of disruptive technologies can be problematic because 99 times out of 100, the technology will fail, but the difficulty occurs when a company comes up with a winning disruptive technology. Even when managers are aware of a disruptive technology, the uncertainty makes normal market forecasting and investment analysis impossible initially in disruptive technologies. When a disruptive technology is invented, the market is non-existent and, therefore, there is no available information on the growth, market volume, market acceptance, pricing, competition, customers' desires, etc. This makes it impossible for managers to apply the normal management decision-making tools of forecasting and investment analysis that are required by large firms. ROI analysis requires information, and if you have none, how is one going to justify an investment of millions of dollars?

- ***Investment in sustaining technology:*** Firms that have the opportunity to invest in technological change often select sustaining technological over disruptive technological change. This is because sustaining technological change investment initially provides much better returns on investments than those in disruptive technological changes because of the market share and being able to use established value chain activities in the company. This means that the firm's resources get devoted to sustaining technological change product development and commercialization rather than disruptive based products.

- ***Organizational norms and processes:*** In small firms that tend to develop disruptive technologies, the small market and revenue mean that the company must operate on a shoestring budget in a highly flexible yet aggressive manner. Workers must work incredibly long hours for little initial pay, hoping that they will get future payouts in stock options. These firms also have organizational cultures that are organic, informal, and highly productive in nature because everyone has a sense of "belonging and ownership." In these organizations, decisions are made quickly and workers are willing to do what ever job is necessary to get the product out the door.

On the other hand, established firms have much more formalized structures and processes. Workers are motivated based upon promotions and increasing their remuneration. Furthermore, they often have highly standardized job classifications that are efficient in large operations, but inefficient in smaller ones. In summary, established firms do not have the required organizational characteristics to develop a disruptive technology efficiently and aggressively compared to a small, highly flexible, lean mean entrepreneurial company.

For all of these reasons, established firms tend not to develop disruptive technologies. Rather, it is technologically-based entrepreneurs who tend to do it because they revel in the uncertainty and the making of intuitive decisions. They accept the poor performance because entrepreneurs tend to be eternal optimists and envisage the potential in the technology. Finally, these firms are quite willing to build a unique value chain or business model because they do not have an investment in resources, assets, capabilities, and personnel that are specific to any another business model.

Examples of entrepreneurial firms that have developed disruptive technological products are Apple computer in the desktop computer industry rather than IBM, low cost digital cameras were developed by Epson and Logitech rather than Kodak and

Canon, and a variety of biotech companies developed the latest biotech drug therapies rather than the large pharmaceutical companies.

These two types of technological changes create opportunities for different types of business tactics, some of which are described in the following sections.

Sustaining Technological Change Tactics

This is where established firms have the competitive advantage. Their competitive position has focused on this market and they have developed all of the prerequisite competitive advantages to compete effectively in this market. Therefore, they can adapt and accommodate these competitive changes fairly readily into their business model.

Entrepreneurs and small firms must be very cautious about developing sustaining technological change products because they will be entering the competitive market of the established firms. Established firms not only have the R&D, production, and infrastructure capabilities, but they also have intangible abilities, such as strong customer relations, brand awareness, and a strong external distribution channel. This makes it extremely difficult for a firm that is attempting to enter this market for the first time. Corel made the initial mistake of trying to compete directly with Microsoft when it first bought WordPerfect and it spent a tremendous amount of money before it reoriented itself to a focused niche strategy.

If the small firm or entrepreneur finds itself entering a market based on sustaining technological change there are several strategic approaches that may help it survive, which are:

- They should attempt to operate in a niche market that is tangential to the main market. This may enable it to develop products that are particularly suitable to a specific user and the established firms are focused more on the main market segment. Norton Utilities has used this strategy to survive against Microsoft by developing utility software. Microsoft dabbled in this market but decided it was not large enough to interest it. Out-focusing the large companies in a niche is probably the most viable strategic approach available to small companies.

- Small companies must be prepared to re-position themselves when they are in a market that has become large enough to attract the attention of major firms, particularly if these small firms have not the competitive advantages with which to compete with the larger firms. Developing a variety of associated opportunities may enable small firms to flexibly re-position themselves as this occurs. It must be admitted that this is a difficult strategy to implement. However, a number of Canadian companies in the high-tech sector have managed to do this, one being Cognos, which had a software product that Microsoft challenged. Cognos then moved into the market intelligence software business.

- Another approach is to associate yourself with companies that have competitive advantages, whether it be suppliers, customers, or complementary products. For example, a number of companies have built up a mutually beneficial relationship with Microsoft, including Norton and Corel. These companies use Microsoft's name and abilities to improve their products features and image. The concern with this strategy is that this relationship may provide the larger company with knowledge about how to enter your business. In essence, you are playing with the potential executioner. Yet the risk is often necessary and must be actively managed during the growth of the small company's market.

Disruptive Technological Change Tactics

Disruptive technological change also creates a market and competitive environment that suggests certain strategic tactics would be best implemented by certain types of companies. These are:

- Entrepreneurial companies have the best prospects for becoming a leading firm in an industry if they focus their development efforts on disruptive technological change. This type of technological change has inherent risks of failure, but the benefits, if successful, are immense.

- Established firms should actively develop tactics to deal with disruptive technological change. First, managers must clearly understand the danger that disruptive technological change poses. Then a variety of tactics are available to managers, which include:
  - Develop market, competition, and technical scanning mechanisms that feedback changes to the appropriate managers. In addition, there should be processes that track disruptive technologies once they are identified, which monitors their development.
  - Attempt to develop associations and alliances with companies developing disruptive technologies in your particular industry. This may provide you with inside knowledge on capabilities that are necessary as well as the potential success of the technology. Formalizing these relationships using a joint venture or merger may become important if their technology gains momentum in the market.
  - Develop organizational mechanisms to nurture disruptive technologies in your firm. Essentially, the organizational mechanisms that effectively develop disruptive technology are distinctly separate from the established firm's main organization. To accomplish this, there are different strategies from minority ownership to full ownership. Newbridge was successful at developing disruptive technology by allowing workers who had these ideas to start companies outside of their organization. Newbridge acted as a venture capital holding firm and owned a significant, but usually minority, ownership share of the new company. This enabled the firm to develop its own aggressive mean and lean organizational style while also relying on Newbridge to help it with any important capabilities, such as helping it develop distribution networks, or establish customer relationships. The only downside to this approach was that several times a competitor acquired one of the firms, potentially stripping Newbridge of a valuable capability. Nortel took a less aggressive approach by allowing the innovators to setup their own organizational unit separate from Nortel's, but owned by Nortel. Nortel would provide the workers with "internal shares," which would ultimately be based on the "firm's" success. If the technological development proved not to be critical to Nortel's businesses, they often spun it off, an example being Entrust Technologies. This approach enabled Nortel to control the development of distributed technology, but it also may have stifled some entrepreneurial drive in these new units.

In conclusion, developing tactics appropriate for different technological changes is very important. In particular, managers of established firms must recognize that disruptive technologies pose a risk to their firm and must be monitored very carefully, while entrepreneurial firms must understand the risk of following sustaining technological development.

It should be noted that this notion of a change in a business model can also be extended to non-technical industries where new ideas are developed that focus on a new class of customers. Examples are Costco in the large format, low priced warehouse retail outlet rather than other established retailers.

MANAGING HIGH-TECH START-UPS

Managing high-tech start-ups, particularly when a disruptive technological change is occurring, presents more than the normal entrepreneurial concerns because, not only is there market uncertainty, but also there is the ambiguity of the future technological and competitive dynamics. One tool that is very useful in entrepreneurial development is the product growth cycle, and it is also applicable to the development of high-tech products, shown in exhibit 8-1. There are three important stages during the high-tech growth cycle and each of them has distinct characteristics and unique customers, as is described in table 8-1.

Geoffrey Moore describes the stages in this cycle in greater detail in his books *Inside the Tornado* and *Crossing the Chasm*. Moore has also identified two points in the cycle that present particular difficulties, and they are the Chasm and Tornado, illustrated in exhibit 8-1.

exhibit 8-1   High Technology Product Growth Cycle

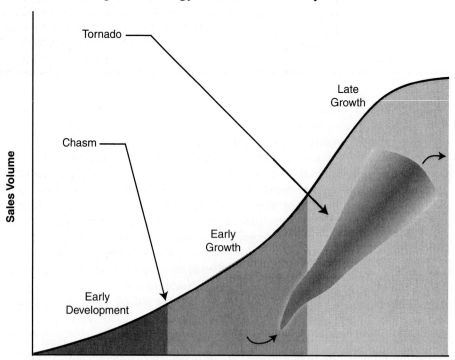

table 8-1   The Stages of High-Tech Development

Stage	Characteristic	Customers
Early Development	• Product is in the development stages and features are being added as R&D focuses its efforts on the product • Market acceptance is gradual as the product attempts to define its utility and value early inthis stage, and in the latter stages it has found its utility but it is being improved	• *Experimental User* – customers are technology enthusiasts or visionaries who strive to be at the leading edge of technology • During the first part of this stage, technology "geeks" want to be on the leading edge • Near the latter part of this stage, there are the few individuals who have realized the utility of the product and are willing to take some risk when developing competitive advantages • Users are willing to assemble the product with other devices to create a useful product for themselves
Early Growth	• The product now has defined value to customers • Market acceptance and growth is beginning to develop as different segments of the market begin to understand the benefits of the product • Some companies are purchasing the product based on the product's attributes	• *Pragmatist* – are customers who are the primary technological purchasers in a firm • They are not high-risk purchasers and want clear evidence of the quality and utility of a product before they adopting a product • These users want the product to be provided in a complete form, including any services or additional equipment that may be required
Late Growth	• The product has developed broad market acceptance and now it is a given that everybody purchases the product • Most companies are purchasing the products and the purchasing decision is based upon the brand reputation of the product	• *Conservative User* – are customers who are late adopters and generally speaking have a pessimistic attitude towards technology, but have accepted the utility of this product because of the established brand reputation and value. These buyers only buy a product after it has become the standard in the industry and an essential purchase.

Adapted from Moore's Crossing the Chasm

The Chasm occurs between the early development stage and the early growth stage. It is point at which many high-tech companies begin to incur difficulties in their growth. The Chasm occurs because the experimental users who buy the product in the initial stage are willing to take risks and are willing to buy an incomplete product and assemble a complete solution. Experimental users make decisions intuitively and are motivated by future opportunities and possibilities. However, the pragmatists, who purchase in the early growth stage, are low-risk purchasers who want the benefits assembled for them and provided to them as a total solution. Their purchasing decision must be supported with financial analyses, and they consult with their colleagues when making a decision. These customers are low-risk purchasers and only want to buy products that provide them positive benefits.

Based on the above characterizations, the experimental users view the pragmatists as obsolete traditionalists, while the pragmatists see the experimental users as perilous risk takers. Consequently, the experimental users are not going to be good sales representatives for the product in the eyes of the pragmatists. The pragmatists are also looking for a complete solution to his or her problem while the experimental users are willing to concoct a solution from diverse sources. And, the pragmatists require information about the usefulness and applicability of the product and assurances that the product is going provide them with benefits immediately. These dramatically different customer groups make the progression from one customer group to the other extremely difficult because they are so dramatically different and require completely different approaches to the marketing task.

In the early development stage, the firm must focus on product and technical development. But then, in the early growth stage, the firm has to develop a market perspective very quickly. In particular, managers must understand what pragmatic customers desire, and they must offer a complete product solution containing all the necessary services for this new customer. This is a huge evolution for most firms and management. Because of this, the Chasm becomes a point where many growing firms have trouble moving beyond their technical origins and orienting themselves to their new customer set. Consequently, many firms do not make it across the chasm and continue to focus on experimental users.

It is important for managers to realize that firms that move across the Chasm fastest have the best chance of dominating their market space in the future. It is also a fact that the majority of small high-tech companies do not successfully move beyond this point. To simplify the process of developing capabilities specific to these new pragmatic customers, firms must simplify and focus on one segment of the market. One of the biggest mistakes managers can make is to market to many segments in the hope that one will become successful. This is a poor strategy because it stretches the firm's capabilities too thinly; the number of different product offerings becomes unwieldy; and a complete solution is offered to no one. Competition that takes a focused approach will be more successful than a company that remains unfocused.

To get past the Chasm, it is important that managers take several tactical steps. They include:

- Managers must focus their product on one clearly selected and defined customer group that is predominately composed of pragmatists. The customers in the selected group would ideally require a similar product and information to close the sale. This minimizes the complex demands a growing firm faces as it begins to take a market orientation. Some managers have difficulty focusing on one segment, but it is imperative that the company makes this leap of faith because an unfocused approach almost certainly results in failure. An example of a company taking such a focused approach is Research In Motion (RIM), a Waterloo based company selling personal information management devices that focused on the financial industry in an attempt to move beyond the Chasm. Some of the attributes that make a segment valuable to focus upon are:
  - The segment is made up of a large number of influential, yet demanding pragmatic customers that will, ultimately, influence the brand reputation of the product. This accomplishes two things. First, market pressures force the firm to offer a first-class complete product, and second, these customers provide a powerful endorsement when the firm begins to market to other segments.
  - Complete product solutions and information on the value of the product to the customers can be readily developed for the segment. This enables the sales to proceed as quickly as possible.
  - The targeted segment should have minimal direct competition. You do not want to be fighting tooth and nail over an initial market segment while other companies capture alternative segments and move onto the next stage of growth and development.

● The firm must develop an integrated full solution product that provides the customer with a turnkey solution to their needs. Pragmatic customers are not sophisticated technologists and, therefore, they are not willing to assemble a solution as the prior experimental users were. Developing a complete solution also requires that the firm understands the customer's needs specific to the usage of the product, the information that will be required to sell the product, the add-on services necessary, and the additional features and peripheral products that will be needed to provide the complete solution to the customer.

● A firm can outsource or align itself with other firms that provide parts of the product solution. However, it is critical that the firm develop a thorough understanding of the market and how to market to customers. Furthermore, the firm must develop brand recognition under its name because, as the market matures and other segments are entered, a brand image becomes important.

After crossing the Chasm, managers must now aggressively begin building market share by conquering other market segments in a succession of conquests. The company that wins the majority of a market habitually obtains insurmountable sustainable competitive advantages, such as brand image, patents, economies of scale and scope in the crucial R&D and marketing activities, and having a proprietary technical standard that all customers want to buy (See the note below on sustainable competitive advantages in the high-tech industry).

During this growth phase, focus continues to be important but now it means focusing on targeting one segment after another until the majority of the broader market is captured. To win new market segments, the firm must draw upon its developing brand image and reputation, which has so diligently been developed in prior segments. The selection of subsequent segments should be consistent with the objectives defined in the initial crossing of the Chasm stage. That is, they should include influential customers, direct competition should be avoided if possible, and it is helpful if the complete solution developed for the first market segment satisfies customers in subsequent segments with minimal modifications.

The importance of winning this battle to become market leader cannot be over stated. During the early growth stage, one or a few companies typically become the market leaders enabling them to dominate the market during the high growth and volume periods of growth, which is a time of extraordinary profits for winning companies. In high-tech jargon, these market leaders are referred to as "gorillas," while other competitors are called "chimps." The gorillas have built overpowering sustainable competitive advantages, while the chimps are often delegated to focusing on niches within the main market. Several of the critical competitive advantages developed by gorillas in high-tech industries are described in the note below (exhibit 8-2).

exhibit 8-2 Note on Sustainable Competitive Advantages in High-Tech

The reason the Tornado is such an important phenomenon is that certain high-tech sectors enable the gorillas to develop insurmountable competitive advantages. Some of these competitive advantages are:

● Network externalities are present when customers use products to interact either directly or indirectly. This interaction demands that the products are standardized so they can work with one another. For example, telephones, computer hardware and software, and PIMs are all most useful if they enable the user to share information and interact with one and another. Therefore, customers demand that a product conforms to the most widely used technical standards in the industry. Sometimes these standards are agreed upon standards within competitors in an industry (i.e., open standards), such as telephone standards, but more often they are owned by companies (i.e., closed standards), such as Microsoft Windows or cell phones. Companies that have developed a standard, such as Microsoft, have competitive advantages that make it very difficult for others to encroach on their market space. Microsoft is continuously trying to move the market away from open standards to its proprietary standards for exactly this reason. In fact, Microsoft has been accused and convicted of using its other proprietary standards, or network externalities, such as the Windows operating system, to force others to adapt to its newly introduced standard. This indicates how important network externalities are to sustainable competitive advantage.

- In an industry of high fixed sunk costs, companies that have the leading market share obtain an important competitive advantage because these firms can reinvest a tremendous amount of money into R&D and marketing compared to the competition. For example, Microsoft has captured more than 90 percent of the Office suite market, and the competition has less than 10 percent. Therefore, if the variable cost for the program CDs and the packaging is $50, the selling price is $150, and the total market volume is 100,000 units, Microsoft will have more than $9 million (after variable cost is subtracted) to spend on R&D and marketing, while the competition will have less than $1 million. Thus, the firm with the largest market share has an intrinsic advantage in developing and promoting new products.

- Patent and copyright protection provides an advantage to companies in certain industries. For example, Intel and Microsoft both have enjoyed competitive advantages due to legal protection, which has discouraged competitors from copying or imitating their products. Intel more recently ran into problems with AMD, which won the right to imitate Intel's products. Industries, such as biotechnology and pharmaceutical, enjoy strong patent protection. The importance of patent protection is illustrated by the fact that industries with good patent protection tend to have higher than average profitability.

- Finally, brand image and reputation, most of which result from the above competitive advantages, is a very powerful competitive advantage. This is particularly true when the technologies are new and purchasers are uncertain of the technologies' quality and abilities. Therefore, they purchase the most reputable one, which is most often the one with the most market share. An example of this is how many companies buy computers from some of the more reputable vendors when less costly and probably just as capable computers are available through smaller vendors.

Clearly, the strength of a company's capabilities and the advantages it builds while crossing the Chasm provide it with the basis upon which a market leader is born. Yet, there are tactics that must continue to be stressed during this growth stage, which include:

- Attempt to develop a standardized product that satisfies the needs of the majority of users in this market. This not only includes features, but also services and price. The approach that is best taken is to focus on the key market segments as one evolves from one segment to the next so that your company ends up servicing the important and major customer segments in the market. This marginalizes other companies' positions who are forced to focus on sub-optimal segments. The importance of this market focus and the selection of it cannot be stressed strongly enough. This is because the winner may not necessarily have the best technical product, but they almost certainly have the best market skills, including widely available product at a reasonable price.

● Attack competition relentlessly to become the market leader in all segments. This means attacking them at all points in the value chain, as well as attacking their customers through aggressive marketing tactics. Many of the tactics involve locking up the important distribution and supplier channels, preying upon any mistake made by competitors. For example, if a firm has quality problem, use every means to magnify this problem in the eyes of the customer.

This is a major transition point where a firm either becomes a market leader or a struggling marginalized competitor and aggressiveness is important. A vivid example of such aggressiveness is Microsoft, which has incurred numerous legal challenges because of its aggressive attitude in the market place.

During the early growth stage, one company usually begins to dominate, a product standard takes hold in the market and a "Tornado" is set in motion (shown in exhibit 8-1). A Tornado is when the market suddenly takes off around a specific standard. It is named a Tornado because of the violent nature with which growth takes place and competition is forced to the niches surrounding the broader market sidelines. At this point the market leader suddenly has trouble supplying enough products because demand for its product has gone wild. Yet, competitors may have overcapacity because their product is not selling so well.

Once market demand takes off, the market leader must focus all of its efforts on supplying product and distributing the product as widely as is possible. This is because all customers are convinced of the product's value, and they only want that specific product. The market leader can only fall down if it is not able to supply the volume of product and distribute it effectively during this last stage of growth. A market leader may have to develop external production and distribution capabilities by outsourcing or alliance agreements to enable them to ramp up the necessary capabilities quickly and cost effectively. Furthermore, during this Tornado period the market leader has the opportunity to lower the costs and increase the effectiveness and coordination in its production and distribution network. This even further compromises the "chimps'" competitive positions.

Research has shown that only two or three companies can survive in the broad market during a Tornado and only one of those companies is extremely profitable. The others have normal to marginal profits depending upon the specific market dynamics. Therefore, managers of all the remaining firms must quickly recognize their inferior competitive positions and make a decision as to which market niche they should refocus upon. Firms that make this decision quickly have the advantage of selecting the best and most profitable niches to focus upon. Often the best niches are related products to the product that has become the standard in the Tornado. For example, Microsoft is a gorilla in several markets, including desktop operating systems and office suit software in which it has over 90 percent market share in both. Yet, quite a number of companies have developed related products that occupy niches surrounding these Tornado products, including operating system utilities, such as Norton Utilities, reference management programs, virus software, graphics programs, etc. Indeed, some of these companies, such as Norton, Adobe, etc. have become very profitable and viable firms albeit of a much smaller scale to that of the gorilla.

E-COMMERCE AND THE INTERNET

During the last half of the 1990s, the Internet spawned tremendous e-commerce growth. Subsequently however, many of these businesses ran into difficulties. This poses the question, what is an appropriate strategy for the Internet?

The Internet provides individuals and firms with a tremendous capability of communicating using many different forms of information including data, video, pictures, voice, etc. Furthermore, it can provide this information in real time, or it can store it in a variety of formats for use later. It also enables users to develop large networks of interactivity and conduct searches in many different ways for relevant information on the network. Yet, one of the most interesting possibilities is related to the dynamic facility and interaction with computer programs and other users. This makes it a tremendously innovative and useful business tool.

On the other hand, when one uses the competitive advantage assessment matrix provided in Chapter 5 to assess the quality of this resource, one finds that the actual Internet is not a rare, inimitable, or complex capability. Therefore, as a resource, the Internet is valuable, but it on its own is not a sustainable competitive advantage. Most of the firms that initially developed an e-commerce business failed to understand that they were not developing a sustainable competitive advantage, which is why so many firms failed after a few years of development. In actual fact, e-commerce increases competition by enabling customers and markets to trade information more freely than ever before.

Types of E-Commerce Activities

Internet related businesses can be broken into many different types of operations. One industry sector is the infrastructure providers, which include software and hardware businesses, data communications providers, internet service providers, etc. These companies are very diverse and include firms such as Sympatico, Rogers, Telus, SAP, IBM, Cisco, etc. As a group of businesses, these companies are technology companies but they are not considered e-commerce businesses.

E-commerce activities can be separated into two broad types of operations, and they are ordinary Web sites and commercial Web portals.

Ordinary Web sites are online information sites containing data, video, voice, and multimedia, having numerous pages. Web sites of this sort are for one way communication from the site's manager to the Internet browsing individual. Often, these are individuals or institutions providing information in essentially a one dimensional manner.

Commercial Web portals, on the other hand, are large Web sites that bring together many different users in a multidimensional exchange of information. Portals have not only different customers, but also suppliers of information, and the site facilitates the transaction of information between all of these parties. There are different categories of Web portals, the most prevalent are described in exhibit 8-3.

E-commerce Strategies

E-commerce strategies occur along several dimensions. The first dimension describes the parties involved in the informational transaction, and the second dimension describes the ownership of relationship.

exhibit 8-3   Commercial E-commerce Portals

Type of Portal	Description
General Purpose Portals	• These are Web sites that provide a wide array of information, contain many links to other Web sites and portals, and often contain interactive capabilities, such as a search engine. Examples to this type are Yahoo and AOL.
Vertical Portals	• These are Web sites that are specialized for a specific industry or service, and, as the name suggests, provide a depth of content vertically into an industry or content focus. Examples of this type are Google, Zdnet, CEOexpress, and Cnet.
Corporate Portals	• These are Web sites that are for specific companies. To make these true portals, the Web sites must have multidimensional transactional capabilities, such as online purchasing, downloading of information, or other interactions, such as inventory control, purchasing, etc. Examples of this type of Web site are Dell Computer, and IBM.
Web Hub Portals	• These are Web sites that facilitate information exchange and business transactions by firms in the same or a related industry. Examples include the steel industry, which has a private online Web site that enables the steel distribution centres to find specific types and quantities of steel easily. These hubs can be either private or public.

Any number of parties can be involved in establishing a Web portal. There are three distinct types of commercial portal strategies: business to business (B2B), business to customer (B2C), and business to business to customer (B2B2C) Web portals. The abbreviations describe the parties involved in the portal. Exhibit 8-4 illustrates where these transactions are located within the broader value chain of an industry.

B2B e-commerce is used to connect a company with suppliers or distributors and it enables them to operate more efficiently and effectively. An example of this type of arrangement is the National Bank's outsourcing of all of its computer operations to IBM. This outsourcing is possible due to the interconnectivity of the Internet, enabling the National Bank to move all of its processing needs electronically to IBM, a supplier of computer processing capabilities. By doing this, it enables the National

exhibit 8-4   E-commerce Strategic Interactions

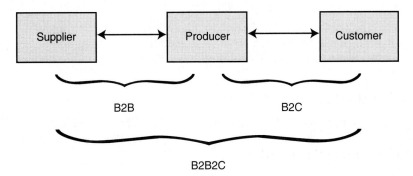

Bank to focus on the strategic concerns of developing financial services and products, and building customer relations. Globally, B2B e-commerce is actually the biggest business segment accounting for US $131 billion in 2000, and it is forecast to expand to $1.5 trillion in 2003. In Canada, B2B transactions are expected to reach $272 billion by 2005 and account for almost 20 percent of all inter-business transactions. (All figures are from Forrestor research.)

B2C e-commerce is when a business sells products or services to end customers. Many retailers have begun to develop e-commerce capabilities to at least provide information about their company and services to the market. The most successful retail e-commerce industries involve products and services that can be most easily transacted over the Internet. That means they can be cost effectively delivered to the customer and the product is standardized so that the customer does not need to have hands on experience, but can query the Web site for the necessary information. An example of an industry that has these qualities is the travel reservation business, which happens to be an industry that is recording the highest sales unit transaction level of any industry on the Internet. On the other hand, auto Web sites have had very few sales but many visitors because buyers want to experience the products in the dealerships. B2C e-commerce accounted for US $111 billion in 2000, and it is forecast to grow to $1.3 trillion in 2003. Gambling is forecast to become the single largest market in this sector.

B2B2C is a more intricate e-commerce network that melds both of the above networks into one network. An example of a business that has used this approach successfully is Dell Computers. When a customer orders a computer from Dell, it automatically is forwarded to the supplying manufacturer in Asia which builds the computer. This enables Dell to provide customized computers, while at the same time minimizing its inventory and delivery time. This is clearly the most difficult strategy to replicate because of the complexities of setting up such a vast network.

Ownership Control—Internal Versus External E-commerce Strategies

One or more user firms can carry out an e-commerce strategy internally, or a third party called a service provider can develop the strategy. During the first five years of e-commerce development, third parties developed the majority of hubs. However, more recently, firms have been moving to internal Web sites. An external provider has some advantages, including providing an independent, unbiased operator who focuses upon the needs of the transactional service. This approach can be helpful when competing firms are sharing a Web portal. An example of such an external service is "Minimidimaxi—Canadian Fashion Stage" which is a portal for the Canadian Fashion industry, and it brings together designers, textile manufacturers, wholesalers, retailers, fashion show producers, styling experts, and media experts.

An internal hub also has advantages. These include directly controlling the content and collecting proprietary information on Web usage. Information collection can be particularly valuable because it enables the firm to assess customer needs and desires directly and privately. An example of this type of portal is GE's light bulb business, which initially had outsourced its e-commerce transactions to a third party service provider. However, when GE realized how large the volume of Internet sales were (e.g., sales were over a million dollars by the second year), they decided to internalize the service. GE now has a policy of keeping all of its e-commerce services internal.

There are also quasi-internally controlled e-commerce portals that are alliances between the partnering companies involved. These are becoming popular as industries develop Web sites to manage transactions efficiently between firms in the industry. Such a partnership ownership arrangement ensures that all parties think they are being dealt with efficiently and fairly. Furthermore, they feel they have some operational control over the portal. An example is the North American aerospace companies' Web portal, which facilitates transactions between aerospace manufacturers as well as with their suppliers.

E-commerce Strategic Issues and Tactics

There are a number of strategic tactics that managers must consider when developing an Internet strategy, and all of them should be aimed at creating a sustainable competitive advantage for the business. Unfortunately, many e-commerce companies initially focused on growth and overlooked the concept of creating long-term competitive advantages, which has resulted in the high failure rate in this industry. Based on this tenet, some important strategic tactics are:

- *Established brick and mortar firms often have an advantage:* Small start-up e-commerce companies should be very cautious about directly challenging an established firm by using a similar business model. Established firms often have built up competitive advantages, such as a brand reputation, and a broad distribution and service network. Consequently, they can evolve into an e-commerce strategy, and it further enhances their intrinsic competitive advantages. Given these large companies competitive advantages, start-ups must avoid direct competition. In fact, eight of the top ten Canadian retail e-commerce sites in 2001 were established companies that developed an e-commerce presence well after many start-up competitors had (see exhibit 8-5).

- *Focus at first:* When both start-up and established companies are starting an e-commerce business, it is important that they focus on a customer segment and overwhelm them with value. The brand reputation and market share growth that results is critical to the establishment of a business over the long run. As a segment is conquered, new segments can be focused upon.

exhibit 8-5   The Top Ten Visited Web Sites in Canada 2001
            in millions of visits

Site	Visits
Amazon.com	9.4
Sears.ca	6.9
Canadiantire.ca	4.7
Futureshop.ca	4.5
Columbiahousecda.ca	4.4
Hbc.com	3.9
Chapters.com	3.3
Hallmark.com	2.5
Cdnow.com	2.2
Magazineoutlet.com	2.2

- *Challenging an established company:* When challenging an established company, the two most fruitful strategies are to take a niche approach and develop a disruptive business model. The niche approach enables a small company to out-focus a larger company, while developing a disruptive business model will provide customers with value that established firms cannot easily duplicate. An example of this latter approach is President's Choice Financial discount banking, which provides low cost banking. Other financial institutions have trouble replicating the strategy because they have a much more costly structure, which includes hundreds of branches with all of their associated operating and capital costs.

- *Value-chain analysis is essential:* It is important to understand where the negotiating power lies when developing an e-commerce business. Value-chain analysis using Porter's concepts provides managers with important information to understanding the power distribution in an industry. The b2b and b2c e-commerce business models actually represent the value chain as illustrated in exhibit 8-4 (i.e., the first b is the supplier and the second b or c is the purchaser in the value chain). An example of such analysis is most established companies are moving from outsourced e-commerce to internally controlled so that they do not give up power to an outsourcer. This has occurred because these established businesses have the competitive advantages and can dictate what occurs with their e-commerce business. For small companies, it is important to understand the potential potency of another firm or industry with whom one is serving or building a relationship. Chapter 4 discussed approaches for minimizing holdup and many of these same concepts apply to dealing with powerful partners.

- *Develop complex sustainable competitive capabilities:* competitors easily copy a straightforward e-commerce strategy. Therefore, it is important that managers consider integrating Internet capabilities into existing competitive advantages and capability. Another objective must be to develop new complex and difficult to imitate competitive advantages, such as brand reputation, a network of suppliers and buyers, which are based upon relationships, and other proprietary competitive advantages that are difficult to imitate. Some e-commerce companies, such as AOL, Goggle, and EBay are trying to build brand reputations, based on trust, quality information and an easily navigated standardized Web portal. Other companies, such as Chapters/Indigo and Canadian Tire are trying to build e-commerce competitive advantages that are complementary to the competitive advantages that exist in their brick and mortar strategies. Thus, it is imperative that managers reflect on how they are going to build sustainable competitive advantages, and what type they will use over the longer term to make it difficult for competition to imitate their strategy.

- *An e-commerce strategy should fit an established company's strategy:* It is important that an e-commerce strategy be consistent with the strategy of an established company's brick and mortar strategy. A similar strategy enables the different operations to share and impart competitive advantages to each other in an integrated fashion if designed properly.

    There is one situation in which a different strategy is acceptable, and that is when a firm is trying to appeal to an entirely different, and usually new and growing, customer segment. At the same time, their present business model does not allow them to be competitive in this new segment. An example is CIBC's development of its President's Choice Financial low cost e-commerce business, which is an alliance with Loblaws. E-commerce strategies that take entirely new strategies must be set up outside of the parent organization because their different business model often uses competitive advantages that are not compatible with the other business.

- *One option is to stay small and focused:* Some e-commerce businesses are able to compete very effectively by just staying incredibly focused and small. This enables them to keep their costs low, while, at the same time, focusing on the small segment of customers they serve, and the products and services they offer. An example is Raincoast.com, a small e-commerce bookstore and publisher operated out of British Columbia. This company has been profitable almost from the day it opened its doors by staying small and focused in comparison to Amazon.com, which has gone for the gorilla position in the market, but has not had a profitable year since its inception some seven years ago.

- *Established firms should develop e-commerce strategies:* Established firms must begin to develop e-commerce strategies because the Internet actually increases competition by enabling firms to expand beyond their natural geographic and resource limitations by using the Internet to establish an e-commerce presence. Almost all industries and business models allow for some sort of Internet strategy to be realized, whether it is just internal coordination, or whether it involves a broader external e-commerce strategy. It is important for these companies to begin evolving e-commerce strategies otherwise competition could gain a competitive advantage by melding their advantages with new Internet abilities. It is also important for the managers to use their Internet strategy to complement their overall strategic focus. For example, Sears's Web service emphasizes appliances and value items, which is consistent with its overall strategy.

E-commerce strategies will continue to evolve as the industry grows over the next decade. In 2000, Canadian e-commerce sales represented less than two percent of all retail sales, and fewer than 14 percent of all businesses have transact sales or purchases over the Internet (as shown in exhibit 8-6). Yet, healthy sales growth is forecast, and in some industries, such as the travel and gambling industries, Internet sales are expected to become significant competitive forces in the industry.

exhibit 8-6 Canadian E-commerce Sales in Various Industries for 2000 (as a percentage of total operating revenue)

Accommodation and food services	1.3%
Information and cultural industries	1.0
Professional, scientific and technical services	0.8
Other industry sectors	0.4
Real estate and renta	0.3
Retail trade	0.3
Transport and warehousing	0.3
All private sector	0.2
Manufacturing	0.2
Finance and insurance	0.1
Wholesale trade	0.1

In conclusion, managers must be aware of the opportunities that e-commerce represents, as well as the competitive threat it poses to established firms in many industries. It is critical that firms begin building e-commerce competitive capabilities and advantages as soon as possible, and that they devise a long-term strategy that builds sustainable competitive advantages in concert with other competitive advantages available to the company either internally or externally.

Summary of Strategies in High-Tech

Two Types of Technological Change

- *Sustaining technological change* is when the technical change moves along technical dimensions that are presently stressed in the industry and by customers historically. Sustaining technical change favours the old guard companies in the industry because the change is stressing dimensions that fit well with their historic competitive advantages.
- *Disruptive technological change* is when the technical change stresses new technical dimensions in the industry and new value to customers. Disruptive technical changes tend to favour new start-up firms in an industry.

Stages of High-Tech Development

There are three important stages in the high-tech industries, which are:

- *Early Development Stage* where experimental users are technical enthusiasts that are trying out new products. Firms during this stage should focus on developing the technical aspects of the product.
- *Early Growth* is where pragmatists demand a product that fulfills an economic need for these relatively leading edge value oriented customers. Firms during this stage should focus on satisfying the needs of a key customer user group. It is important to focus on becoming a standard and building market share during this phase.
- *Late Growth* is where conservative customers are buying the product. Firms during this stage now must focus on providing a "whole product." A firm must continue to stress building market share and becoming the standard during this phase.

Two Elements During the Development Phases

- The Chasm occurs in the transition between the early development stage and early growth stage. In brief, it is when companies do not successfully switch from a technically focused strategy to a marketing focused strategy.
- The Tornado exists during the growth stages of development and it represents the market forces that surround a product standard. During these growth stages, when a product standard is accepted in the marketplace, it takes off and competitors are best advised to move out of the way.

E-commerce Strategy

Developing good e-commerce strategies involves developing strong competitive advantages that make it difficult for competition to imitate your business model. Using Web based technology does not in itself provide such a competitive advantage.

In e-commerce, there are four different types of portals: general purpose, vertical, corporate, and Web-hub portals. In addition, there are three generic value business models that are used, and they are B2Bb, B2C, and B2B2C.

Additional Notes and Recommended Readings

Christensen, C. M., *The Innovators Dilemma*, Harvard Business School Press, 1997.

Geoffrey Moore, Geoffrey, *Crossing the Chasm*, Harper Business, 1991

Geoffrey Moore, Geoffrey, *Inside the Tornado*, Harper Business, 1995

Ghosh, S. "Making Business Sense of the Internet," *Harvard Business Review*, pp 126-135, 1998.

Gulati, R. and Garino, J. "Get the Right Mix of Bricks and Clicks" *Harvard Business Review* pp. 107-114, 2000.

Rosenoer, J, Armstrong, D. and Gates, J.R., *The Clickable Corporation: Successful Strategies for Capturing the Internet Advantage*, Free Press, 1999.

Tapscott, D, Ticoll, D., and Lowy, A. *Digital Capital: Harnessing the Power of Business Webs*, Harvard Business School Press, 2000.

chapter 9 Corporate and International Strategies

We would rather lose some synergy across the groups than hamper decision making and entrepreneurialism within them.

LAURENT BEAUDOIN, CHAIRMAN BOMBARDIER INC.

I think ...when we started here, that we didn't have a lot of focus and didn't have a lot of reason for being." "Over the last five years or so, we've taken the disparate parts of Weston and concentrated them on the baking business. It's been a matter of simultaneous rationalization and rebuilding.

RICHARD CURRIE, PAST PRESIDENT OF LOBLAWS AND WESTON FOODS INC.

Corporate and international business strategies are similar in that both are diversification strategies. Corporate strategy is diversification into different businesses, while international strategy is diversification into different countries. This chapter examines corporate and international strategies. The first section studies the different types of corporate strategy, and the second section briefly describes a number of different international strategies.

CORPORATE

Corporate strategy focuses on the task of selecting what businesses to be in, what businesses not to be in, what businesses to invest in further, and how to coordinate the different businesses. These corporate decisions and their relationship to business strategy are illustrated in exhibit 9-1.

The objective of corporate strategy is essentially the same as business strategy, which is to develop value through the development and advancement of competitive advantages throughout the whole firm. Moreover, a strong business strategy is the foundation upon which a strong corporate strategy is built, just as robust functional strategies are supportive of a strong business strategy. Therefore, firms cannot simply own businesses, but rather they must manage them in a way that increases their value above what they would otherwise have been as independent businesses. Present day corporate strategy can attribute much of its knowledge to resource-based theory.

Managers can grow their firms in a number of different directions, as is illustrated in exhibit 9-2. The two different dimensions firms can grow involve growth into different markets (or customer segments), and growth into new types of products

exhibit 9-1   Corporate Versus Business Strategy

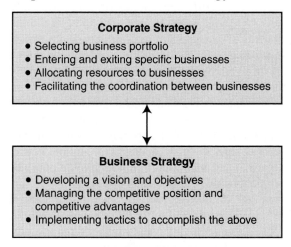

Corporate Strategy
- Selecting business portfolio
- Entering and exiting specific businesses
- Allocating resources to businesses
- Facilitating the coordination between businesses

Business Strategy
- Developing a vision and objectives
- Managing the competitive position and competitive advantages
- Implementing tactics to accomplish the above

exhibit 9-2   Product/Market Growth Strategic Choices

Business Product/Service Growth	Market/Customer Growth	
	Existing	New
Existing	Market Penetration	Market Development
Modified or improved	Product Development	
Completely new and different but associated or related	Related Horizontal Diversification	
Completely new, different and unassociated or unrelated	Unrelated Horizontal Diversification	Unrelated Horizontal Diversification

(or services if it is a service company). Business strategy encompasses the first three dimensions of growth (i.e., market penetration, market development, and product development), because they are types of growth that are all within the confines of one business.

The other three types of growth involve corporate diversification. The defining difference found in these three, and the prior business growth mechanisms, is that the corporate diversification growth modes take the firm into new businesses because the products and services are completely new and different to the company. These different types of corporate diversification are explained more fully below.

DIVERSIFICATION

Firms that expand into new businesses and markets are considered to have taken a diversification approach strategy. Diversification can occur along three different dimensions. Firms can diversify across different industries; they can diversify vertically within an industry; and they diversify across geographic markets. The latter type of diversification, across geographic markets, is international strategy and is looked at in a subsequent section. The different modes of diversification are described in exhibit 9-3.

Previously, a number of management tools have been developed to help manage a company's diversification growth. Some of the more popular ones were matrices that evaluated businesses on a variety of different competitive dimensions. One of the more popular ones was the Boston Consulting Group (BCG) matrix, which evaluated businesses on market growth and relative market share basis, dimensions that captured cash usage and the intrinsic competitive strengths of a business. These tools spawned diversification binges through the 1960s and 1970s most of which were promptly undone in the 1980s. Research has subsequently found that many of these consultant derived tools lacked in both effect and logic. Unfortunately, some consultants still use these tools to "help" their clients grow into new businesses.

Horizontal diversification is when two businesses have value chains that operate concurrently and provide products and services to different customer groups, as is illustrated in exhibit 9-2. As concurrent value chains they can operate separately or they can share integrated value chain activities and competitive advantages, such as competitive capabilities and core competencies. This integration is illustrated by the arrows in exhibit 9-4.

exhibit 9-3   Types of Diversification Growth

Type of Diversification	Description	Example
Horizontal Diversification	• Growth into new businesses and different industry markets	• A retail men's clothing business starts up a hardware store business
Vertical Integration	• Growth into a different business in which one business supplies the other business with inputs used to produce products or services	• A firm that owns a cement business and a concrete block business decides to acquire a construction company
Geographic Diversification	• Growth into different geographic regions	• A North American fast food business decides to expand into Asia

exhibit 9-4   Horizontal Diversification

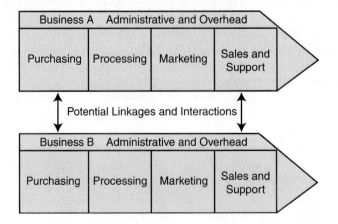

Diversification can produce value at both the corporate and the business strategic level. At the business strategic level, diversification can produce value when the businesses share value chain activities. The sharing of these activities can produce competitive advantages that run through all of the businesses, such as economies of scale and scope in many of the primary activities, including purchasing, production, and sales. In addition, intangible competitive advantages, such as brand reputation, copyrights, and patents can produce value if they are applicable to the all of the businesses. These types of competitive advantages are called core competencies. The key in developing value through horizontal diversification is maximizing the value of these shared and synergistic value chain activities or core competencies.

Corporate level value creation is more elusive. In some companies, operational risk may be moderated. For example, Bombardier has diversified into train and plane manufacturing. The risk in these businesses often occurs because of the large financing cycles between sale deals, which run in the billions of dollars. Having both of these businesses enables them individually to weather difficult periods because the other business has sales. Another potential corporate value is excess to cheap financing and being able to attract very strong management talent. An example of a company that uses inexpensive financing is Berkshire Hathaway, which uses float money from its insurance companies (i.e., the insurance premiums collected from customers) to fund expansion in other companies. In addition, corporate managers may be very good at valuing and purchasing undervalued companies, and then restructuring them to create value.

The costs associated with a horizontal diversification are related to the added costs of a corporate overhead structure that must be added to the businesses, and the costs of managing the integration of any shared activities. In addition, there could be a cost associated with diversifying to the point of not understanding the businesses that a firm owns or having many complex value chain activities, and ultimately, this could contribute to deteriorating performance over time.

The degree of diversification is related to two basic metrics, and both attempt to capture the degree of complexity that has been introduced into a corporation's value chain. The first is the amount of revenue that is derived from the new non-core business(s), and this is a rough indicator of the scale to which the firm has refocused on divergent businesses. Research has shown that firms deriving less than 70 percent of the revenues from a dominant or core business tend to show signs of diversification. The second metric is the degree to which businesses in a company share competitive advantages. Related diversification is when businesses share important competitive advantages, and unrelated diversification is when the businesses do not share, such operational advantages. An example of a related diversification is the three big auto companies' ownership of both car and truck businesses. These businesses have somewhat different value chains, but many of their key competitive advantages are common. An example of unrelated diversification is GM's purchase of Hughes Electronics and EDS both of which were subsequently sold. Hughes, an aerospace electronics firm, and EDS, a firm specializing in computer support and outsourcing services, have very different value chains, and also share almost no similar competitive advantages to those critical in the auto business.

These two metrics provide us with a rough measure of the degree to which a firm is diversified. Exhibit 9-5 describes levels of diversification based upon the above metrics.

exhibit 9-5   Type of Diversification

Type or Level	Description
Low (No Diversification)	• More than 70% of the revenues come from a single business. This is called a single or dominant business diversification and really involves minimal commitment to different value chain activities or businesses.
Moderate (Related Diversification)	• Less than 70% of the revenues come from the dominate business in the corporation, but all businesses share some important competitive advantages, such as R&D, distribution, etc. This corporate strategy is called related business diversification.
High (Unrelated Diversification)	• Less than 70% of the revenues come from the dominate business in the corporation, and none of the competitive advantages at the business level are shared. This corporate strategy is called unrelated diversification.

A strong relationship has been found to exist between the level of diversification and the profitability of firms, as is shown in exhibit 9-6. In this figure, firms having low levels of diversification have average profitability, moderately diversified firms have higher profitability, and firms having high diversification have lower profitability. The difference in profitability is attributed to the ability of the firms to develop competitive advantages across the various businesses. Firms that are independent businesses can attain business specific competitive advantages. However, firms that have diversified into related businesses not only have business-specific competitive advantages, but also gain competitive advantages from sharing advantages. In addition, unrelated diversification suffers because of the complexity of managing different value chains activities that have no relationship to one another.

Canadian Pacific is an example of the performance difference between a high versus low diversified firm. At the turn of the century, Canadian Pacific owned businesses in railroad, oil and gas, shipping, hotels, and coal, making it a highly diversified firm. Corporate managers decided to break it apart, and instantly, financial analysts and

exhibit 9-6   Typical Performance in Diversified Companies

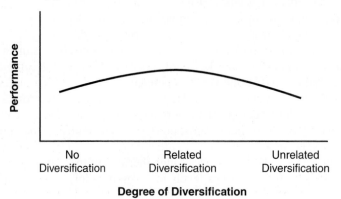

investors increased the stock value of the aggregate companies by approximately 25 percent. This increase in value is a result of the elimination of the corporate overhead, and management in the independent businesses could now focus strictly on developing strong business-specific competitive advantages.

It should be noted that the above generalizations are based upon average performances of the different types of diversification and that individual firms have a wide range of performances. In fact, some highly diversified firms have good performance while many undiversified firms have poor performance, because performance is a result of aspects beyond corporate strategy, such as business strategy and competitive environment. The actual mechanisms that influence the performance of corporate diversification strategy are discussed below.

Based on the above, the question arises, why should a firm contemplate diversification? The reasons for diversifying are described in exhibit 9-7.

Moderate or unrelated diversification can provide benefits related to the individual business operations as well as the overall corporation. In particular, economies of scale and scope through the sharing of value chain activities can make the individual business models much more efficient. An example is Honda's diversification into the related businesses of cars, motorcycles, and small motor equipment, which enables it to share some critical activities, such as mechanical design of its products, and manufacturing process design. Honda has put particular emphasis on the design of efficient and powerful engines, and it has made the design of such engines a core competitive capability, upon which all of its businesses rely heavily. Honda began to build this competitive advantage when its began making motorcycles. Honda then used it to diversify into small cars, and, rather than get into large cars and trucks, it diversified the other direction into small motorized equipment, such as generators, which again relied on its ability to design, develop, and manufacture powerful, reliable, and light engines. In fact, Honda's engine design capability has become so successful that it is one of the leading suppliers of Formula One and Indy car racing engines.

exhibit 9-7 Reasons to Diversify

Moderate or related diversification

- Economies of scale or scope: Develop inter-business competitive advantages related to sharing capabilities, such as brand reputation, distribution relationships and network, advertising economies of scale, technological development capabilities, etc.
- Also can get the advantages delineated below in the high or unrelated diversification

High or unrelated diversification

- Develop financial economies
  - Excess to low cost financial resources both internally and externally
  - Management understands the markets valuation of companies. Furthermore, they know how to restructure companies to create greater value.
  - There may also be administrative economies of scale for the implementation of large scale programs

VERTICAL INTEGRATION

Vertical integration is a form of diversification, but it involves a firm buying businesses that have a linked value chain, as is illustrated in exhibit 9-8. One business supplies product or services for the benefit of the other business(s). An example of such a business is the auto firms' diversification into auto parts manufacturing, which are necessary for the construction of their cars.

Generally, managers select vertical diversification when the businesses provide each other with competitive advantages that are more valuable combined than independent. The most typical situation is when both the supplier and buyer have valuable, rare, and hard to duplicate competitive capabilities and the supplier's capabilities make the buyer's capabilities even more valuable (as well as possibly rarer and more difficult to imitate), and the buyer's capabilities benefit similarly from the supplier. The potential costs and risks associated with the vertical diversification integration as it is often called are related to the dependent relationship created between the two businesses.

Exhibit 9-9 delineates some of the reasons why managers may or may not consider vertical integration a viable strategy from a value creation perspective.

Vertical integration can occur in both the forward and backward directions. Backward integration is when a firm grows into the business of supplying itself necessary products or services. Forward integration is when a firm grows into the business of being a customer or distributor for the products or services it makes. These different types of vertical integration are more fully explained in the sections that follow.

Backward integration, that is, seeking ownership or increased control over suppliers, is appropriate when:

- An organization's present suppliers are especially expensive, or unreliable, or incapable of meeting the firm's needs for parts, components, assemblies, or raw materials.

- The number of suppliers is few and the number of competitors is many.

- An organization competes in an industry that is growing rapidly. This is a factor because integrative-type strategies (forward, backward, and horizontal) reduce an organization's ability to diversify in a declining industry.

- An organization has both the capital and human resources needed to manage the new business of supplying its own raw materials.

exhibit 9-8   Vertical Integration

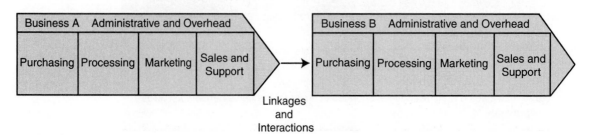

exhibit 9-9   Value Creation in Vertical Integration

Potential for Value Creation

- The greatest potential for value creation is if the two firms being integrated have rare, valuable, and difficult to imitate capabilities or competitive advantages that are critical to both companies. An example are clothing design companies that have vertically integrated into retail stores. For instance, the GAP, Liz Claiborne, and Laura Ashley all have integrated into retail to ensure that their products are advantageously presented to the customers. Furthermore, it enables the designers to get immediate feedback on what is selling and what is not selling in the retail stores so they can adjust their designs and orders to the manufacturers.

Risks of Extra Costs

- If the end product or service produced by the two businesses is cyclical in nature, then a slow down in demand for this industry may cause the other industries to slow production, which may be costly.

- When two firms are integrated, competitors will often not buy or sell to them, thus limiting the flexibility of the integrated firms. Two instances where this can be a burden are:
  1. If the two businesses are not perfectly balanced in regard to production and demand, then one of the businesses will have to either buy or sell to other firms. However, competing firms maybe less than enthusiastic about selling or buying from a business that is owned by a competitor.
  2. There often is less of an ability for either of the businesses to buy or sell to other businesses. This may become an issue if another business develops very strong competitive advantages. If the two businesses were not integrated, then one of them might be able to flourish as the supplier or buyer from the outside company that has the new competitive advantage, but because of the integrated nature of the companies there is less of an opportunity for this to occur.

- The costs of coordinating and managing two integrated businesses can be high simply because everything must be coordinated from design and production through to possible expansion projects.

- The advantages of stable prices are particularly important. This is a factor because an organization can stabilize the cost of its raw materials and the associated price of its products through backward integration.

- Present suppliers have high profit margins, which suggests that the business of supplying products or services in the given industry is a worthwhile venture.

- An organization needs to acquire a needed yet limited resource quickly.

Forward integration, that is, gaining ownership or increased control over distributors or retailers, is appropriate when:

- An organization's present distributors are especially expensive, or unreliable, or incapable of meeting the firm's distribution needs.

- The availability of quality distributors is so limited as to offer a competitive advantage to those firms that integrate forward.

- An organization competes in an industry that is growing and is expected to continue to grow markedly. This is a factor because forward integration reduces an organization's ability to diversify if its basic industry falters.

- An organization has both the capital and human resources needed to manage the new business of distributing its own products.

- The advantages of stable production are particularly high. This is a consideration because an organization can increase the predictability of the demand for its output through forward integration.

- Present distributors or retailers have high profit margins. This situation suggests that a company could profitably distribute its own products and price them more competitively by integrating forward.

Some advantages of vertical integration are to reduce vulnerability by securing supply and/or markets, or to reduce transaction costs by absorbing costs upstream or downstream in the value chain. In general, vertical integration helps a business to protect profit margins and market share by ensuring access to consumers and/or material inputs. Some of the advantages and disadvantages of vertical integration are summarized in exhibit 9-10.

exhibit 9-10   Some Advantages and Disadvantages of Vertical Integration

Advantages	Disadvantages
Internal benefits	**Internal costs**
• Integration economies reduce costs by eliminating steps, reducing duplicate overhead, and cutting costs (technology-dependent) • Improved coordination of activities reduces inventory and other costs • Avoid time-consuming tasks, such as price shopping, communicating design details, or negotiating contracts	• Need for overhead to coordinate vertical integration increases costs • Burden of excess capacity from unevenly balanced minimum-efficient-scale plants (technology-dependent) • Poorly organized vertically integrated firms do not enjoy synergies that compensate for higher costs
Competitive Benefits	**Competitive Dangers**
• Avoid foreclosure to inputs, services, or markets • Improved marketing or technological intelligence • Opportunity to create product differentiation (increased value-added) • Superior control of firm's economic environment (market power) • Create credibility for new products • Synergies could be created by coordinating vertical activities skillfully	• Obsolete processes may be perpetuated • Creates mobility (or exit) barriers • Links firm to sick adjacent businesses • Lose access to information from suppliers or distributors • Synergies created through vertical integration may be overrated • Managers integrated before thinking through the most appropriate way to do so

Source: Strategic Flexibility: A Management Guide for Changing Times, by Kathryn Rudie Harrigan (Lexington, Mass: Lexington Books, D. C. Heath and Company).

RESOURCE ALLOCATION AND COORDINATION

Resource allocation and coordination are two other important tasks that corporate managers must carry out. They are critical to the overall well being of the company. However, these roles must not spawn a corporate staff that becomes costly and may tend to interfere with business decisions in the individual business-units. In fact, some of the most successful corporate offices are small in size. For example, Berkshire Hathaway, a diversified multibillion dollar highly successful company, has a corporate office of 12 people that are housed above a drug store in downtown Omaha, Nebraska. Clearly, this does not represent much of a cost burden to the individual businesses in Berkshire Hathaway. In conclusion, it is critical to minimize the corporate costs that are going to be allocated to the businesses, because most competing businesses are not going to have such additional costs.

RESOURCE ALLOCATION DECISIONS

Resource allocation is an important role for corporate managers because present day investments ultimately drive the future of the company.

For the most part, the decision making for allocating resources to the individual businesses in a corporation follows a well defined process and set of guidelines. All resource allocating processes must have a financial analysis procedure, which evaluates the quality of the project from a financial perspective. The normal financial evaluation approach requires discounted cash flow analysis or some similar financial analysis.

The degree to which corporate managers get involved in managing the allocation of resources beyond the financial evaluation varies. In corporations where the businesses are very integrated and related, the corporate managers may be completely integrated with the business managers. This will enable these managers to both develop and evaluate the investment projects in a manner that considers both the financial and non-financial implications of the project. However, when corporations have more diversified and unrelated businesses it is often more productive if the corporate office just evaluate the business proposals on there financial merits. This is because the knowledge about the business aspects of the project are in the business and it becomes counter productive for the corporate managers to second guess the business managers. Furthermore, the costs of gathering and processing the information necessary to make non-financial decisions can create problems.

For example, Berkshire Hathaway completely allows the businesses to make investment decisions. The corporate office does not even get involved with financial analysis of business decisions unless the business is thinking of acquiring another business. On the other hand, GE, which is also a relatively diversified company, evaluates the financial aspects of the businesses if they are over a specific amount, and will discuss these projects at different types of investment review meetings where the corporate officers get to query the managers who proposed the investments. Bombardier, which is a less diversified company, has corporate officers involved in not only the evaluation of an investment project, but in the development of them. In conclusion, the resource allocation process in companies varies depending upon the diversity of the company. However, all successful companies minimize the redundancy and costs of this decision by either integrating the decision process with the businesses or pushing the decision down to the business level.

COORDINATION PROGRAMS AND DECISIONS

Coordination between businesses in a diversified company occurs to different degrees depending upon how diversified, and, thus, integrated the businesses are in the corporation. In highly diversified firms, often very little coordination occurs between businesses. Berkshire Hathaway is a zealous example of this where managers of the different business-units for the most part have never spoken to one another. GE is a more typical example where the businesses operate independently and coordination at the corporate level occurs through meetings, seminars, and conferences. The goal of these meetings, etc. is to chronicle and share potential competitive advantages that could benefit all of the companies. GE has developed a number of programs that it has implemented throughout all of its businesses including quality control programs, worker training programs, e-commerce programs, etc. These programs are expensive; for example, the quality program, called Six Sigma, cost millions of dollars to role out in all of the businesses. However, its savings over the five years since it was implemented are in the billions of dollars. Most individual businesses would hesitate to expend such an amount of money, but GE can spread the costs over many businesses, and, of course, reaps the rewards from all of these businesses saving money.

Coordination in corporations that have diversified into highly related businesses, or into vertically integrated businesses usually take a much more integrated approach to coordination. This is because it is through the integration and coordination of their value chains that they derive value. For example, Canadian Tire acquired Marks Work Warehouse based on the savings and increase in competitive advantage from integrating and coordinating some of the activities in the two companies. Much of this coordination will probably not be to the head office, but will be directly between the businesses.

Thus, the amount and level (i.e., corporate versus business) of coordination that occurs in a corporation depends upon the diversification, the activities, and the competitive advantages that exist within the businesses themselves. Ultimately, coordination must produce value or it should be eliminated. Furthermore, corporate head office should attempt to push as much coordination down into the businesses where the knowledge exists and costs are lower.

COOPERATIVE STRATEGIES

One of the predominant trends in the past decade has been the increased use of cooperative strategies. Whether in the domestic or international market, more frequent use of joint ventures, licensing, counter trade, and technology/R&D collaboration has been observed. These collaborative arrangements are characterized by a willingness to either share or split managerial control and possibly ownership.

Several opportunities for sharing can come from a cooperative strategy. These include sharing a sales force, advertising activities, manufacturing facilities, and management know-how. A number of potential competitive advantages are associated with each type of opportunity for sharing. Such opportunities include gaining economies of scale in some activities, using another company's specialized assets, knowledge or skill, and lowering the financial risk or increasing the resources put on a project. However, cooperative strategies have an associated cost of managing them, and sometimes the fit can be more illusory than real. For example, salespersons may not be as effective as expected in representing a new product. Despite the difficulties that can arise, a recent trend is the increase in cooperative arrangements between hitherto competing organizations.

Cooperative strategies may be particularly appropriate for Canadian companies because of our small size in the global competitive environment. Cooperative strategies may enable Canadian firms to compete effectively globally.

There are conditions, however, which would suggest the use of one form of cooperation over another. Some of the considerations before deciding on the form of cooperation include assessments of:

- Level of risk (e.g., creating a competitor)
- Synergies/complementary skills to be gained
- Regulations influencing type of involvement
- Managerial and financial resources available to go it alone
- Speed of innovation required

Licensing

The advantages to be gained by licensing depend on the technology, firm size, product maturity, and extent of the firm's experience. A number of internal and external circumstances may lead a firm to employ a licensing strategy:

1. The licensee has existing products or facilities but requires technology, which may be acquired more cheaply or quickly from third parties (licensers) than by internal R&D; the need may be of limited extent or long duration.

2. The licenser wishes to exploit its technology in secondary markets that may be too small to justify larger investments; the required economies of scale may not be attainable.

3. The licensee wishes to maximize its business by adding new technologies.

4. Host-country governments restrict imports and/or foreign direct investment (FDI), or the risk of nationalization or foreign control is too great.

5. Prospects of "technology feedback" are high (that is, the licenser has contractually assured itself of access to new developments generated by the licensee and based on licensed knowledge).

6. Licensing is a way of testing and developing a market that can later be exploited by direct investment.

7. The licensee is unlikely to become a future competitor.

8. The pace of technological change is sufficiently rapid that the licenser can remain technologically superior and ahead of the licensee, who is a potential competitor.

9. Opportunities exist for licensing auxiliary processes without having to license basic product or process technologies.

10. A firm lacks the capital and managerial resources required for exporting or building a regional plant, but wants to earn additional profits with minimum commitment.

Joint Ventures

Joint ventures are appropriate when:

- A privately owned organization is forming a joint venture with a publicly owned organization. There are some advantages of being privately held, such as close ownership; there are some advantages of being publicly held, such as access to equity markets as a source of capital. Therefore, the unique advantages of being privately and publicly held may sometimes be synergistically combined.

- A domestic organization is forming a joint venture with a foreign company; a joint venture can provide a domestic company with the opportunity for obtaining local management in a foreign country and the local managers' knowledge of the foreign economy, politics, and culture. This may also have the residual advantage of reducing risks such as expropriation and harassment by host country officials.

- The distinctive competencies of two or more firms complement each other especially well.

- Some project is potentially very profitable, but requires overwhelming resources and risks.

- Two or more smaller firms have trouble competing with a large firm.

- There exists a need to introduce a new technology quickly.

Outsourcing

A recent strategic alternative, from an investment perspective, is outsourcing. Outsourcing involves contracting out, on a long-term basis, critical competencies or tasks. An example of outsourcing is the contracting out of the computer and information services (CIS) by banks to companies specialized in these businesses. The banks realize that they do not have the expertise or the strategic focus to provide the CIS services to their organization or customers. Therefore, they outsource the task to computer service firms, such as IBM and EDS, which have core competencies in this particular business. In this case, the outsourcing provides lower costs and better services. Critical questions to think about when considering the outsourcing option are:

- Is the competency or task being outsourced a core competency for the outsourcer, and will this activity or core competency provide critical competitive advantages in the future?

- Will outsourcing allow the insourcer to compete with you more directly. (e.g., Intel is now competing with PC computer assemblers such as Compaq)?

- Will outsourcing provide lower costs and higher effectiveness or efficiency, and is this a critical competitive advantage for the firm?

- Do the outsourcer and insourcer trust each other? How can this trust be established or built?

CORPORATE STRATEGIES OF BUSINESS UNITS

As stated earlier, corporate and business strategy in reality cannot be separated. Here we look at how business strategies must be addressed when a corporate strategic decision to either divest or invest in a business has been taken. A corporate decision to harvest an ailing business (i.e., divest or liquidate) versus invest (i.e., retrench or turnaround) is based upon the firm's competitive position and advantages as well as future prospects for the industry. The retrenchment and turnaround strategies are based upon establishing stronger business-based competitive advantages and competitive positions.

When a business is in trouble—whether it is the result of such factors as strong competition, technological turbulence, or escalating interest rates—a different set of strategic choices face the general manager. An attempt can be made to turn the business around, or the business can be immediately divested or liquidated. The business can also be "harvested," which involves optimizing cash flows through such tactics as curtailing all new investments, cutting advertising expenditures, or increasing prices, until the business is sold or liquidated.

The decision of whether to attempt a turnaround depends on the kind of turnaround strategy which is likely to be successful and then whether the firm is willing to bear the risks, devote the resources, and make the management commitment associated with this particular turnaround strategy.

Three corporate strategies for dealing with ailing businesses are discussed in the sections that follow.

Turnaround strategies can be classified as follows:

Efficiency oriented

1. Asset reduction (for example, disposal of assets)
   a. Cost cutting (for example, cutbacks in administrative ROD, marketing expenses)
   b. Market oriented
2. Revenue generation (for example, increase sales by product reintroduction, increased advertising, increased selling effort, lower prices)
   a. Product/market refocusing (for example, shift emphasis into defensible or lucrative niches)

Turnarounds can follow definite stages: (1) change in management, (2) evaluation, (3) emergency, to "stop the bleeding" or "unload," (4) stabilization, emphasizing organization, that is, building, and (5) return-to-normal growth.

Turnarounds are appropriate when an organization:

- Has a clearly distinctive competence, but has failed to meet its objectives and goals consistently over time
- Is one of the weakest competitors in a relatively prosperous growth industry
- Is plagued by inefficiency, low profitability, poor employee morale, and pressure from stockholders to improve performance
- Has failed to capitalize on external opportunities, minimize external threats, take advantage of internal strengths, and overcome internal weaknesses over time; that is, when the organization's strategic managers have become complacent and failed
- Has grown so large so quickly that major internal reorganization is needed

Divestiture, that is, selling a division or part of an organization, is appropriate when:

- An organization has pursued a turnaround strategy and has failed to accomplish needed improvements.
- A division needs more resources to be competitive than the company can provide.
- A division is a misfit with the rest of an organization; this can result from radically different markets, customers, managers, employees, values, or needs.
- A large amount of cash is needed quickly and cannot be reasonably obtained from other sources.

Liquidation, that is, selling all of a company's assets, in parts, for their tangible worth, is appropriate when:

- An organization has pursued both a turnaround strategy and a divestiture strategy and neither has been successful.
- An organization's only alternative is bankruptcy; liquidation represents an orderly and planned means of obtaining the greatest possible cash for an organization's assets. A company can legally declare bankruptcy first and then liquidate various divisions to raise needed capital.
- The stockholders of a firm can minimize their losses by selling the organization's assets.

INTERNATIONAL STRATEGIES AND MODES OF ENTRY

International strategic decisions cover a wide variety of problems and issues. However, some basic international strategies are related to selecting an entry mode for entering a new international market, and defining how the company should coordinate and manage their regional strategies from a corporate perspective.

International Strategies

Strategies for coordinating international business units present managers with two issues: Should the businesses be coordinated globally to produce efficiency, or should they be coordinated locally so that effectiveness in the local markets is maximized?

The globalization approach requires managers to coordinate strategy from a global perspective so that the firm's global competitive advantages from an efficiency perspective are maximized. This approach, called a global strategy, involves providing a standard product or service in all geographic regions. An example of a global strategy is a firm that designs its products in United States because of the technical and design capabilities exist there; it manufacturers products in China because of the low cost of manufacturing; and it sells the products worldwide. Managers select a global strategy to try and maximize the overall global competitive advantage of the firm. Good examples of global industries are the consumer electronic and computer industries where different parts of the company's value chain activities are distributed throughout the world. Activities are placed in locations where they are most efficient and effectively carried out. The real challenge for a manager using this strategy is coordinating the different value chain activities around the world so that the firm's overall global competitive advantage is maximized.

exhibit 9-11   International Strategic Positions and Coordination

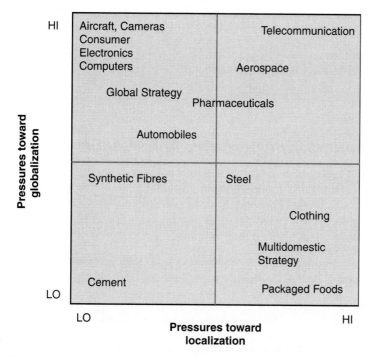

Source: This diagram is used with permission from International Management: Text and Cases, 3rd. Edition, by Beamish, Morrison and Rosenburg, Irwin, Burr Ridge, Ill., 1997.

The localization approach requires managers to coordinate and manage different strategies in different international regions. This approach, called a multidomestic strategy, emphasizes the different regional aspects of business and market demands. A manager would take a multidomestic approach if all of the firm's regional markets had different customer tastes, distribution systems, marketing techniques, and/or product standards. In this situation, each region must be treated differently. To do this, each region is given the responsibility to carry out its own product development, manufacturing and selling so that it most effectively meets the needs of the customers. A good example of this type of business is the packaged food-processing industry. Many of the products in this industry vary regionally based on contents, packaging, and distribution channels. The challenge facing a manager using this strategy is to coordinate the various local strategies so that the brand image is strongly supported, but to diversify decision-making and primary value chain activities into the regions in an effective yet economic manner.

The forces that dictate whether a firm takes a global, or multidomestic or intermediate international strategic position depends upon the pressures of globalization and localization. Pressures for globalization are associated with industries that have extremely intense international competitive pressures and widely adopted international product standards. Pressures for localization are associated with industries having very pronounced regional market differences. Product, service, and knowledge transferability in the industry are also quite important in the global business position, because, if you manufacture goods in Asia but cannot transport them effectively or efficiently to North America, then a global strategy becomes less viable.

Some companies take a dual strategic approach. An example of this is the telecommunications industry where firms must use global technological competitive advantages, yet cater to individual market tastes, product standards, and distribution requirements. This often puts extra pressure on the managers because they have to coordinate a much more complex set of strategic alternatives.

It must also be noted that the global and multidomestic strategies are associated with different types of international organizational structures, which are delineated in this chapter.

International Strategic Entry Mode Alternatives

A major decision managers must face when they are expanding internationally is how to enter a new market. Entry mode selection involves a complex tradeoff decision between having enough market knowledge, having sufficient resources to support the entry mode, and minimizing risks. Some of the concerns specifically related to the various entry modes are delineated in exhibit 9-12.

exhibit 9-12   International Strategic Modes of Entry

Mode	Reasons for Taking Mode	Potential Risks of Using Mode
Licensing Agreement	• Requires few resources particularly capital • Potentially can get an agreement with a firm having the missing resources (e.g., manufacturing, sales force, etc.) • May be the only way for a small company to enter international markets if the product or service does not transport easily • Circumvents import duties and quotes • The licensing firm has minimal risk of income loss because the operational costs are supported by the licenser	• Neither party has complete long-term strategic control over the development of the product • One party may put in more effort than the other party
Exporting	• Requires more resources than licensing but fewer than joint venture and wholly owned subsidiary • May be a good method for a small company to take if the product or service does transport easily	• May incur extra costs associated with transporting, duties, or volume restrictions related to quotes
Joint Venture	• Requires more resources than licensing or exporting, but fewer than a wholly owned subsidiary • The firm shares any income losses with its partners • The potential for learning from the partners is maximized	• The relationship may not last because of differing long-term objectives or values • Operational and capital losses can be higher than in the licensing and exporting options because of greater ownership and operational involvement • The joint venture partner(s), and possibly future competitor(s), may have access to proprietary information and resources in your company
Wholly Owned Subsidiary	• The firm has complete control of the product or service from inception through to sales and distribution • The firm captures all of the profit potential of the product or service	• The firm risks income losses if the product or service does not do well

Summary of Corporate and International Strategies

Both corporate and international strategies represent diversification.

Corporate Strategy

- There are two different types of corporate diversification: vertical integration and horizontal diversification. Horizontal diversification can be broken into related and unrelated diversification.
- Cooperative business corporate strategies consist of licensing, joint ventures, and licensing agreements. Cooperative business strategies have become popular over the past several decades.
- Corporate strategies for business-units pertain to the investment potential for these businesses. These strategies are turnaround, divestiture, and liquidation strategies.

International Strategy

- There are two principal international strategies: global and multidomestic. These strategies are selected based upon pressures towards globalization versus pressures for localization of products and services.

International Entry Modes

- The selection of an international entry mode depends upon the pressures for control, versus having the appropriate international resources. Entry mode is also influenced in many countries by government investment policies.
- Licensing agreement
- Exporting
- Joint venture
- Wholly owned subsidiary

Additional Notes and Recommended Readings

Beamish, Paul, Allen Morrison and Philip Rosenburg, *International Management*, Third Edition, Irwin, Burr Ridge, Ill., 1997.

Campbell, A, Goold, M. and Alexander, M., "Corporate Strategy: The Quest for Parenting Advantage" *Harvard Business Review* pp 12-132, 1995.

Collis, D.J. and Montgomery, C.A., "Creating Corporate Advantage" *Harvard Business Review* pp 70- 83, 1998.

Deming, W.E., *Out of the Crisis* (Cambridge, Mass.: MIT, 1986), P. 31.

For a more complete analysis of turnaround strategies, see Donald C. Geringer, J. M., Paul W. Beamish, and R. da Costa, "Diversification Strategy and Internationalization: Implications for MNE Performance," *Strategic Management Journal* 10, no. 2 (March/April 1989), pp. 109-19.

Hambrick and Steven M. Schecter, "Turnaround Strategies for Mature Industrial Product Business Units," *Academy of Management Journal*, June 1983, PP. 231 48.

Hu, Yao-Su., "Global Corporations are National Firms with International Operations." *California Management Review*, Winter 1992, pp. 66-87.

Michael E. Porter, "From Competitive Advantage to Corporate Strategy," *Harvard Business Review*, May-June 1987. Pp. 43-59

Michael E. Porter, *Competitive Advantage: Creating and Sustaining Superior Performance* (New York: Free Press, 1985), chap. 9.

Porter, M., "From Competitive Advantage to Corporate Strategy" *Harvard Business Review*, pp 43-59, 1987.

Porter, Michael E., *Competitive Strategy: Techniques for Analyzing Industries and Competitors* (New York: Free Press, 1980), chap 11.

Sadtler, David R., "Brief Case: The Role of Today's Board in Corporate Strategy." *Long Range Planning*, August 1993, pp. 112-113.

Thomas J. Peters and Robert H. Waterman, *In Search of Excellence* New York: Harper & Row, 1982.

Wrigley, Leonard, "Divisional Autonomy and Diversification" (doctoral dissertation, Harvard University, 1970).

chapter 10 Managing Strategic Change

Taking your time is not always very efficient, but sometimes absolutely necessary.

PAUL DESMARAIS, CHAIRMAN OF POWER CORP.

I love change.

JEAN MONTY, PAST CHAIRMAN OF BCE INC.

Organizations must constantly deal with change. Managers wishing to make changes in their organization must be both effective implementers and champions of change. The ability to commit to a change and see that it is adopted has become a highly valued skill in an organization.

THE THREE PHASES OF STRATEGIC CHANGE

In broad terms, the process of strategic change can be thought of as having three phases. The first phase is awareness and capability building; the second, commitment and adoption; and the third, reinforcement and recycling (see exhibit 10-1). The most exciting phase for most managers, and certainly the one that receives the greatest emphasis in the popular press is the second one. Managing this phase well is important, but not necessarily sufficient for overall success.

Phase One: Awareness and Capability Building

The first phase in the strategic change process is awareness and capability building. Without widespread awareness of the need for change, most employees will resist change. Such a reaction is understandable given the uncertainty and potential negative outcome that individuals may face.

Even when there exists wide awareness of the need for change, there may not be a shared view of the appropriate direction of change. For example, everyone may be dissatisfied with the firm's performance and recognize the need for change. But should the solution be to retrench, or to take an aggressive, growth-oriented approach? It is important that the employee groups not only be aware that change is necessary, but also understand the type and direction of change required.

exhibit 10-1   Achieving Readiness for and Implanting Strategic Change

Change Target Development and Phases	Potential Obstacles	Common Management Tactics
Phase 1		
Awareness understanding: • Establishing a general appreciation of the need for and direction of change • Building a greater depth of knowledge of the situation, its consequences and potential remedies	• Ambiguous change requirements • Inertial resistance • Information bottlenecks • Limited capacity to understand	• Informal contact, lobbying • Loosening up exercises—target exposure, involvement • Short-term task forces
Capability: • Developing capacity to perform new tasks	• Personnel bottlenecks—inadequate training and experience • Support systems bottlenecks • Behavioural resistance	• Training programs • Support systems development • Personnel changes • Direct coaching
Phase 2		
Commitment: • Developing genuine agreement about and support for the required changes	• Displacement of the problem • Behavioural resistance • Inadequacies, inconsistencies in support and incentive systems • Weak position of power	• Involvement activities • Partial solutions and demonstrations • Negotiations • Coalition building • Coercion • Personnel changes
Adoption: • Achieving change in behaviour, effective performance	• Tangible risk • Lagging resistance, support factors • Poor readiness	• Close monitoring • Intensification and recycling of readiness efforts • Mop-up action
Phase 3		
Reinforcement: • Sustaining effort and diligence in performing new tasks	• Loss of commitment • Resource and organizational inconsistencies	• Rewards for new behaviour • Adjustment of resource and organizational factors
Recycling: • Defining and implementing improvements and new directions	• Problems in linking a series of changes • Complacency	• Training and structuring for flexibility • Continuous challenges for improvement

Source: J. N. Fry and J. P. Killing, Strategic Analysis and Action, end ed. (Scarborough, On.: Prentice-Hall Canada, 1989), figs. 13.5 and 13.6. Reprinted by permission.

Assuming that widespread awareness of the need for, and agreement on the direction of, change does exist—and this is a big assumption—management can then proceed with examining whether it has (or can develop) the necessary capabilities to permit the change to take place. Building capabilities through staff or systems development can be a time-consuming and (in the short-term) not immediately gratifying process. Nonetheless, it is absolutely essential. Just as a hockey coach needs players who know how to skate and who possess hockey sticks, managers must ensure that the organizational capability for change exists.

Phase Two: Commitment and Adoption

With the proper groundwork laid, the manager, as change-agent, can begin placing greater effort on the development of widespread support and enthusiasm for the proposed change. Organizational champions cannot enact changes themselves, particularly in larger firms. They require support throughout the organization from both above and below. Through negotiations and coalition building, they need to get other managers to "sign on," or if this is unsuccessful or too slow, they need to consider various coercive tactics or ultimately personnel changes.

Having developed wider commitment (and mitigated where possible the principal sources of resistance) attention can then turn to actual adoption of the change; people can be hired or moved, money can be spent, assets and resources can be put in place, and people can begin to take on new responsibilities.

What characterizes the commitment and adoption phase is an escalating sense that change is necessary and it is happening. Decisions are being made and acted upon. In contrast, during the awareness and capability phase—even though some resources were being allocated—management still had the option to change their mind, or slow the process.

Phase Three: Reinforcement and Recycling

Even with the change having been adopted, the change process does not end. Follow-up effort and reinforcement are typically required. It may be a less glamorous phase, but it is no less important. Just as a newly purchased automobile will subsequently require scheduled maintenance, service, and parts, so too does a company change require ongoing attention. This ongoing attention is necessary both to reinforce change and to ensure that the organization keeps pace with changes in the environment. Only through a process of ongoing reassessment can the organization improve overall prospects for success.

TYPES OF CHANGE

One of the most significant influences on the way in which the three phases of the change process are managed is the degree of urgency required. When the impact urgency will have on change is considered, we are left with three principal types of change: urgent change, reactive change, and proactive change (see exhibit 10-2).

exhibit 10-2   Pressure for Change

	Type of Change		
	Urgent	**Reactive**	**Proactive**
Necessity for Change	• Pressing or immediate	• Tangible, but not pressing	• Forecast or sometime in the future
Action Required	• Comprehensive	• Diagnostic, plus some clear needs	• Uncertain, but diagnostic at a minimum
Timing for Required Change	• Immediate	• Soon	• Uncertain
Range of Options Available	• Quite constrained due to erosion of competitive position and advantages	• Possibly constrained due to a slight erosion of competitive position and advantages	• Unconstrained except for competitive options available in the industry

Urgent Change

When the necessity for change is urgent, comprehensive action is required, and there is little time for languid decision-making. Action is required now. Urgent change is when the company faces a crisis and the long-term success, and possibly the viability of the organization is at stake. Usually, there are clear signs that change is required. For example, sales and profits have been declining, cash flow is drying up, and other financial and operational performance indicators are poor.

Urgent change often requires a manager that understands the situation clearly and makes the necessary changes quickly, often in a non-participatory manner. Having said this, employees usually are well aware that change is necessary and may even understand more specifically the direction of change required.

Some academics and managers have proposed creating a crisis if there is not one, to instill the need for change in employees. The use of a contrived crisis is inherently risky because the need for change may be questionable, and employee resistance may develop. As well, the general manager who throws his or her organization into a crisis, and is seen to have contrived it, runs a serious risk of losing credibility.

Reactive Change

Unlike urgent change, in a reactive change situation, the necessity for change is not as pressing. Action is clearly required, but sufficient time is available to permit the organization to respond to conditions in a more planned fashion. Abrupt realignment of a firm's strategy or organization is not required.

Generally, the need for reactive change is preceded by some financial and operational performance warnings, but the financial and operational health of the company has not yet been compromised. Some employee groups may be aware that change is necessary, but often they do not understand what type or direction of change will be taken.

Proactive Change

Proactive change enables the company the luxury of developing over time a strategic plan and implementing it because the need for change is forecast. Often financial and operational performance has not been affected, but there may be some strategic performance indicators that are providing some feedback to the managers that change is necessary.

At first this type of change seems easier because management has more degrees of latitude and more time to implement change. However, the difficulty in carrying out this type of change is understanding the extent, timing, and kind of change required given the uncertainty of future events. Furthermore, employees may be more resistant to change because there is no clear evidence that change is necessary.

Given the uncertainty that surrounds it, change is often implemented in an incremental step-by-step approach. This enables managers to edge towards their ultimate goal, but adjust plans and objectives as the uncertainty declines.

Most good managers recognize the value of gaining practice with change through small, logical incremental steps rather than major one-time realignments. As one writer noted:

> An organization that is used to continuous small changes and that has balanced strategic expertise at the top with operating expertise and entrepreneurship at the bottom is probably better prepared for a big leap than is an organization that has gone for several years without any change at all, but now requires a change.
>
> Further, these managers recognize that dealing with change will always create some level of stress in an organization, and too much change all at once, and thus stress, can be fatal. The process of incremental change, or incrementalism, allows the managers to continually adjust to new realities in the competitive environment while also maintaining the organization's ability to implement change.

THE GENERAL MANAGER AND CHANGE

The general manager (GM) is the person most responsible for managing change. His or her task is influenced by:

- Experience and skill in the organization and industry
- Political position in the organization
- Preferences and values
- Style
- Urgency
- Available resources

The implication of such a complex list is that key stakeholders may very well hold different perceptions about what type of change situation exists. As exhibit 10-3 suggests, by plotting an estimate of how each stakeholder may perceive the change situation, it is possible to focus on areas of potential disagreement. The specific type of change, which is obvious to you, may not be obvious to someone else, and vice versa. Further, others may not perceive the need for any change.

exhibit 10-3   Key Stakeholder Perceptions of Type of Change Situation

	Type of Change			
Stakeholder	**No Change**	**Proactive**	**Reactive**	**Urgent**
A				
B				
C				
D				

Tactics for Change

The general manager has a variety of tactics available for implementing change. These depend in part on the manager's skill in coercing people into committing to change, the level and preference for the use of power, and whether this power can or should be exerted directly or indirectly. Exhibit 10-4 lays out four basic tactics for change: giving orders, changing the context, persuasion, and opening channels. Each has advantages and disadvantages and unique characteristics.

Giving Orders

This approach is characterized by the forceful, top-down unambiguous issuance of orders. It has the advantage of being fast, requiring little senior management time. However, low organization commitment and high resistance may result from such an approach. As well, it places heavy reliance on the abilities of the GM to have correctly surmised what change is needed. Not surprisingly, "giving orders" is a tactic frequently observed in an urgent change situation.

Persuasion

Persuasion is a less formal and more time-intensive than "giving orders." It involves negotiation and is more participative in nature. It is a tactic employed by GMs who either do not have a great deal of power or the persuasive skills to get commitment. In order to persuade, additional information may have to be collected to educate the target group on the advantages of the change. If the target groups or individuals see the change as being in their self-interest, greater motivation and commitment will result. Focusing people's attention on the long-term positive goals as well as an external target (such as the customer, competition, etc.) can be helpful. The problems associated with this change tactic are that it may require a lot of GM time, is much slower than giving orders, and may require more of a compromise.

Opening Channels

The subtlest of change tactics has been called "opening channels." It is characterized by a low use of power and by indirect actions. It is slow, informal, consensus oriented,

exhibit 10-4   Tactics for Change

High Use of Power	
Direct Action: Giving Orders	**Indirect Action: Changing Context**
Characteristics • Forceful, top-down, unambiguous, power based	**Characteristics** • Formal or informal, power driven; if the organization or resources are changed as a means of driving a change in direction or behaviour, great attention must be placed on implementation
Pros • Fast • Desired direction clear • Requires little senior management time	**Pros** • Fast (but not as quick as giving orders) • Useful approach when management power cannot be used directly on principal targets
Cons • Low organization commitment • High resistance possible • Places heavy reliance on abilities of the GM	**Cons** • High resistance possible • Risky since action is indirect but power driven • Timing important
Low Use of Power	
Direct Action: Persuasion	**Indirect Action: Opening Channels**
Characteristics • Less formal; time-intensive, participative, negotiated; may require information to "educate" the employees and/or to permit employees to see that change is in their self-interest	**Characteristics** • Subtle, evolutionary, informal; slower; consensus oriented
Pros • Higher organization commitment likely • Greater motivation	**Pros** • High commitment likely • Draws ideas from maximum number of people
Cons • Slower implementation • Requires a lot of GM time for communications • May require compromise • Very slow implementation	**Cons** • Requires a GM with foresight, patience, tolerance for ambiguity • Will require compromise

and takes an evolutionary approach. The objective is to open the channels of communication and interaction in such a way that employees are guided in a particular general direction. The task of the GM is to put in place the conditions (through resource means, such as task forces and training programs) that will enable the organization to more openly consider a particular change.

Realistically, the GM will be unable to exert a great deal of control or precision over the pace at which the change occurs. This is not typically a problem, however, since here the GM has a longer-term focus. Not surprisingly, this tactic for change is often associated with proactive change.

The principal benefits of opening channels are that you often get high commitment, and input will be received from the maximum number of people. It has the disadvantages of being slow and requiring a GM with foresight, patience, tolerance for ambiguity, and a willingness to compromise.

Changing Context

Changing context as a tactic for implementing change is characterized by high use of power and by indirect action. Changing the organization and/or resources are the principal methods employed. Some of the advantages of this tactic are that it is fast (but not as fast as giving orders) and useful when management power cannot be exerted directly on the change target. For example, a GM wishing to make an important acquisition may wish to make the acquisition with the support of senior management. While the GM has wide support, he or she faces some resistance, particularly from one key head office manager who will likely be involved in the acquired company. One organizational solution is to transfer the resisting manager to an unrelated or distant division. Then, the acquisition can proceed with support of management. The GM exerts his or her power by moving the resisting manager, and by this indirect action, achieves the GM's acquisition objective. While moving a manager is a direct action, this tactic is considered indirect because it was not strictly a requirement of achieving the principal change (i.e., making the acquisition). The organization context was changed so as to facilitate achievement of the prime change.

There are inherent risks when using this change tactic. Changing context may not eliminate all the intended resistance, and may create new sources of resistance. Further, changing the context may be more detrimental to the business than allowing the resistance to be present while continuing with the change.

CONCLUSION

This chapter has provided an introduction to managing change. The process of a strategic change has three phases: awareness and capability building, commitment and adoption, and reinforcement and recycling. As exhibit 10-1 noted, there are potential obstacles and common management tactics for each phase.

A significant influence on how the change process is managed is the degree of urgency required. In this context, there are three main types of change: urgent, reactive, and proactive change.

A strategy has not been implemented until the targeted behaviour has changed. In most instances, the task of installing the new strategy and seeing that the behaviour of people in the organization changes is a formidable one for the GM. Yet, with creativity and determination, it is possible.

The tactics available for implementing change depend in part on the GM's skill, status, and degree of preference for the use of power, and on whether or not this power should be applied directly. Exhibit 10-4 noted four basic tactics for achieving change: giving orders, persuasion, opening channels, and changing the context.

Summary of Managing Strategic Change

The phases of change in an organization are:
- Phase 1: Awareness and capability
- Phase 2: Commitment and adoption
- Phase 3: Reinforcement and recycling

Types of Change

The types of change are related to the necessity of urgency of change. The three types are urgent, reactive, and proactive change.

- *Urgent Change* is when the firm is under immediate financial pressure to initiate change.
- *Reactive Change* is when management has become aware, due to financial changes, that change is necessary, and the type of change necessary is fairly obvious to all firms in the industry.
- *Proactive Change* is when management, in its forward-looking planning, realizes that certain changes may be necessary. The uncertainty of change at this stage is fairly high.

Potential Tools and Tactics For Change

The tools and tactics for change available to managers are power, formal orders, persuasion, opening channels, and changing context.

Additional Notes and Recommended Readings

Berling, Robert. "The Emerging Approach to Business Strategy: Building a Relationship Advantage." *Business Horizons*, July-August 1993, pp. 16-27.

Brache, Alan. "Process Improvement and Management: A Tool for Strategy Implementation." *Planning Review*, September-October 1992, pp. 24-26.

Floyd, Steven W. and Bill Wooldridge. "Managing Strategic Consensus: The Foundation of Effective Implementation." *The Executive*, November 1992, pp. 27-39.

Fry, Joesph N. and J. Peter Killing, *Strategic Analysis and Action*, Scarborough, Ontario, Prentice-Hall Canada Inc.1995.

Hamel, Gary and C. K. Prahalad, "Strategic Intent." *Harvard Business Review*, May-June 1989, p. 67.

Hayes, Robert A., "Strategic Planning—Forward in Reverse?" *Harvard Business Review*, November-December 1985, p. 117.

Hurst, David K. "Of Boxes, Bubbles and Effective Management." *Harvard Business Review*, May-June 1984.

James Brian Quinn, *Strategies for Change: Logical Incrementalism* (Home wood, Ill.: Richard D. Irwin, 1980).

Pearson, Christine and Ian Mitroff. "From Crisis Prone to Crisis Prepared: A Framework for Crisis Management." *The Executive*, February 1993, pp. 48-59.

Starr, Marting. "Accelerating Inovation." *Business Horizons*, July August 1992, pp. 44-51.

Wilhelm, Warren. Changing Corporate Culture—or Corporate Behavior? How to Change Your Company." *The Executive*, November 1992, pp. 72-77.

chapter 11 Assessing Strategic Performance

At the end of the day, performance is what really counts.

TONY COMPER, CHAIRMAN OF BANK OF MONTREAL

As we proceed through the year, we expect to see further benefits from our value maximization program.

TRAVIS ENGEN, CEO OF ALCAN

Performance is an important measure for managers to estimate, evaluate, and understand because it indicates whether the firm is achieving its purpose or objective(s). Selecting an appropriate purpose or objective is controversial because different people have different perspectives on what the purpose of a firm should be in society. For example, should it be long-term survival; or satisfaction to its customers and employees; or should it be profitability.

Ultimately, performance in an organization is about long-term value creation. In for-profit firms, value may be related to the value created for owners, or other critical stakeholders, while not-for-profit firms may emphasize value creation for funders and customers.

MEASURING PERFORMANCE FROM A STRATEGIC PERSPECTIVE

Value creation can be measured in a number of ways, including operating margin, percentage of profits to sales, percentage profits to capital employed, percentage profits to assets, the amount of patients treated, customer satisfaction, etc. And if managers set the performance objective as one of these measures, workers will most probably react in very different manners because they can increase each one of these measures using different operating factors.

Based on the above analysis, it is very important that firms select the appropriate measurement for value creation. Strategically, firms tend to have their own individualized approaches that emphasize their strategic objectives and the drivers of competitive advantage in their organization. For example, in some retail businesses strategic core competences are location and the ability to produce sales through having the correct products and service. Therefore, a critical measure of strategic performance is sales per square foot of retail space. A secondary strategic measure might be the amount and speed at which inventory is sold from the store. Inventory is expensive, it must be financed, and the older the inventory gets, the greater the probability it will be out of fashion.

Research provides us with evidence that firms that define a good strategy are best to develop a clear and simple performance indicator that measures the key competitive ability of the strategy to be successful. Sometimes this relates to a core competence or a competitive ability, and sometimes it tends to indicate the assessment of a competitive position dynamic. However, what ever the measure, management should think about the following question in the context of their strategy: *If management could select only one economic performance indicator—profit per X—to systematically strive for and increase over time, what X would have the greatest and most sustainable impact on performance?*

In for-profit businesses two aspects of this performance indicator are important. First, it relates to profit, and second, only one should be selected as the overall key economic performance indicator. The reason the indicator should relate to profit is because profit is the defining performance value in firms, as was stressed above. The reason only one overall key economic performance should be selected is because it simplifies it for everyone in the firm. Everyone is working towards the same target and the explanation for that target is entirely logical and reasonable.

In exhibit 11-1, we examine a number of different firms that have had tremendous success at developing shareholder value. On, average these firms have produced over 300 percent annual value growth for their shareholders over the past 15 years, except for GE ,which has done relatively well, nonetheless. For each firm, we examine the strategic performance indicator that they focused upon to develop such growth, and we examine the strategic driver that made this such a good indicator to select.

The above economic performance indicators are not the only economic indicators used in a firm, rather, they are just the key and most emphasized indicators. In fact, most of these key economic indicators are a result of many other economic indicators coming together from a hierarchy of indicators that result from different units in the organization. Exhibit 11-2 indicates the nature of this hierarchy if Return on Invested Capital (ROIC) was the key economic indicator. If ROIC was not satisfactory, then the manager(s) would move left down the hierarchy of contributors to find out what was negatively having impact on ROIC. This would lead the manager to an indicator that was out of variance and the root problem of the ROIC concern. Managers could then reevaluate their strategy or their measures to rectify the concerns present.

Exhibit 11-3 further delineates how the hierarchy of indicators moves downwards through the organization. As is seen, the key economic indicator, in this case ROIC, is a measure upon which everyone focuses. However, as one moves down through the organizations, different levels and different units are responsible for other performance variables that they can influence, and which ultimately have impact upon the key economic indicator.

An approach that uses this hierarchical measurement approach to evaluate different aspects of the firm from the overall corporate performance down through to individual performance is the Balanced Scorecard. In this approach, management develops key performance indicators, including financial, customer satisfaction, operational and learning growth perspective indicators, at every level and organizational unit in the business—including at the individual level. The process begins at the top of the organization and managers describe clear objectives and goals for the organization over the short- and long-term. Then objectives and goals are developed for the next level in the

exhibit 11-1   Examples of Key Economic Performance Indicators

Company	Performance Indicator	Critical Strategic Issue or Driver
Kroger (grocery business)	• Competitively number one or two in the grocery business for the region served	• Competitive position and location critical in this business—If too much competition, it is not worth investing in the region—sales and profits will always be compromised
GE (conglomerate in many businesses)	• Each business must be competitive—number one or two in its business	• Competitive position in an industry is directly related to profits: as research has indicated, the first two companies in every industry tend to make the majority of the profits—particularly in oligopolistic industries, which is what GE invests in
Nucor (steel industry)	• Profit per finished ton of steel	• Indicates that everything that contributes to the value of every ton of steel is critical in this industry—focuses employees on what they can do to increase this critical value
Gillette (personal consumer product)	• Profit per customer	• Emphasizes value added and differentiated strategy that this company uses—Gillette emphasizes high margin products that are repeatable purchases
Abbott (health prevention devices)	• Profit per employee	• Usually in this industry profit per product is the norm, but profit per employee emphasizes that employees provide good products and excellent customer service
Walgreens (drugstore)	• Profit per customer visit	• Emphasizes that stores be located well (i.e., convenient location), and the store contains a scope of products and services to inexpensively fill customers' needs

exhibit 11-2   Hierarchy of Performance Indicators in a Firm

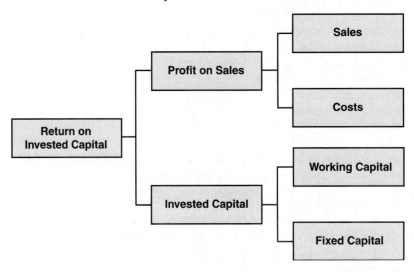

exhibit 11-3   Hierarchy of Performance Indicators

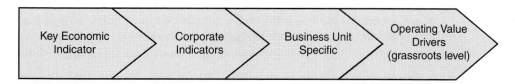

Key Economic Indicator	Corporate Indicators	Business-Unit Specific	Operating Value Drivers (grassroots level)
• Return on invested capital	• Business unit capital invested • Business unit profitability	• Customer mix • Sales force productivity (revenue/expense) • Fixed costs/allocations • Capacity management • Operational yield	• Percent accounts revolving • Dollars per visit • Number of customers • Unit revenues • Billable hours/total payroll hours • Percent capacity utilized • Cost per delivery • Accounts receivable terms and timing • Accounts payable terms and timing

organization. These objectives and goals are vital and support the ability of the overall corporation to reach its goals. Performance indicators are developed at every level that indicate whether the objectives and goals are being met or exceeded. In addition, competitive advantages are identified that must be developed. This process is completed throughout the organization down to the individual level. For example, an individual in the purchasing department has the following objectives and goals:

- Improve the quality of the suppliers' products to a level where 99.99 percent meet the quality guidelines of our process.
- All suppliers pass the ISO9001 quality control standards.
- All deliveries are scheduled in a just-in-time manner, and none of them arrive late enough to halt the production process.
- Suppliers' costs increase by less than 50% of inflation.
- Lower per unit buying costs of the department by 5 percent over the year, while continuing to account for an increased purchase volume of 15 percent.
- A new purchasing assistant must be hired and trained up to level 1A of the Purchasing Managers Associations standards.

An individual in the purchasing department then may have an individual Balanced Scorecard that mandates the individual achieve these things:

- Aid five suppliers (specified) to achieve ISO 9001 accreditation;
- Visit all suppliers under his or her control and complete a engineering activity cost assessment. This will help them manage their costs effectively.

- Find and accredit two new suppliers that are able to supply part x at less than $3.00 per unit, with 99.999 percent quality, and have zero missed deliveries in the last year.
- Develop a training program for the assistant to be hired that will train him or her to level 1A, and that also initiates the individual into the activities.
- Costs per unit purchased must increase less than 40 percent of inflation.
- Automate the purchasing of all products that are purchased daily and are standardized (i.e., require no alteration in specifications throughout the year).
- Study for and pass the Purchasing Supervisory level or the Purchasing Managers Associations standards.

As is seen from the above example, the individual purchasing agent's objectives and goals (or performance indicators) support the achievement of the strategic objectives and goals of his or her department. This approach to managing the execution and performance of strategy throughout the organization is very effective because it clearly delineates everyone's tasks, objectives, and learning goals. And it also integrates everyone's efforts into an overall strategic effort and direction. The complex process of developing a Balanced Scorecard approach in an organization is briefly described in exhibit 11-4.

exhibit 11-4 The Balanced Scorecard Process

The Balanced Scorecard is a technique that translates strategic vision into action. It does this by communicating, incenting, and tracking the achievement of an organization's strategy. The approach uses a four-step process. The main elements of this process are:

1. Clarifying and translating the vision and strategy
   - Clarifying the vision with the top management team
   - Gaining consensus between top managers about the vision and strategic direction
2. Communicating and linking
   - Communicating and educating employees about the vision and strategy
   - Setting goals for functions, teams, and activities in the value chain
   - Linking rewards to performance measures at the team and personal level
3. Planning and target setting
   - Setting targets for business and functional activities to attain
   - Aligning strategic incentives ensuring that the incentives reflect the targets
   - Allocating resources so that activities have the necessary resources
   - Establishing milestones
4. Strategic feedback and learning
   - Articulating the shared vision from various parts of the organization to the top
   - Supplying strategic feedback to all parts of the organization
   - Facilitating strategy review and learning

The Balanced Scorecard has become important because it not only links strategy to performance, but it also assesses performance from a financial, customer, internal-business-process, and learning and growth perspective. By using these pre-cursors to value creation, managers can develop a causal logic that enables them to understand when and why financial performance is being impacted. It also provides management and workers an early indicator (i.e., prior to financial performance) that they can fix immediately. Finally, the approach does a good job of translating the higher -level strategic vision to the lower level functional and operational activities, including developing incentives, priorities, and goals for specific activities.

MEASURING SHAREHOLDER VALUE CREATION

Measuring profitability in a for-profit organization can lead to different outcomes depending how one defines profitability, an issue that was examined briefly in the previous section. Further, just because a firm is profitable, it does not mean it will necessarily survive in the long-term. Shareholders may find the firm is not profitable enough relative to other similar investments, and thus, a capital shortfall may result. The standard measurement of return actually incorporates two types of returns. The first is the *normal return to capital*, which is what investors expect for the use of their capital. Investors would expect to make at the very least the risk free rate of return plus a risk premium reflecting the risk associated with the business within which the firm operates. If investors did not make this minimal level of return over the long-term, then they would be unwilling to invest future capital in the company. The second type of return is the *economic return*, which is the return over and above the normal rate of return expected by the investor. The prospects of economic returns are what really attract capital to a business for future investment and growth purposes.

The standard measure for economic return is the Economic Value Added (EVA) and it is what many top investors, financial analysts, and managers now use to evaluate the economic return to shareholders. Although, widespread acceptance of EVA throughout the financial industry has not occurred, it has gained acceptance with major investors, such as Warren Buffett.

Stern and Steward the originators of this measure of economic return describe EVA in the following fashion:

> To be successful, companies must essentially beat their respective capital competitors. They must earn returns on scarce capital that exceed the returns offered by its capital competitors who are also competing for scarce capital. Companies that succeed will add value to invested capital. The stock will then trade at premium to reflect this. Companies that don't succeed will essentially misallocate or misuse capital. The market will discount the stock accordingly...

A vivid demonstration of this principal is the calculations of a portfolio of all companies having positive EVAs in the TSE 300 and the subsequent year's investment returns on these companies. As illustrated in exhibit 11-5, this portfolio out performs the TSE 300 Index by a considerable margin. And although this performance can be attributed to a number of factors, it does provide some evidence of the EVA value as an indicator of potential performance.

exhibit 11-5   Performance of Positive EVA Portfolio of Companies (all companies in TSE 300* Index)

Fiscal Year	1996	1997	1998	1999
Companies identified	116	157	132	134
Total return for portfolio in subsequent year	24.7%	0.5%	29.1%	27.4%
Return for TSE300 Index for same period	13.0%	–3.9%	29.7%	6.2%

* Toronto Stock Exchange index of 300 companies.

Exhibit 11-6 is a sampling of several Canadian companies and their respective EVAs in 1999. This time period was economically very strong, yet many major companies had negative EVAs. A further analysis of all firms in the TSE 300 index (i.e., Toronto Stock Exchange 300 firm Index) indicated that 46 percent of the firms in this index had negative EVAs during this year.

exhibit 11-6   Economic Value Added Analysis for 1999 (in thousands of dollars)

Company	Net Income	Operating Capital Year End	Return on Operating Capital	Market Value Added	Cost of Capital	Economic Value Added
Nortel	4,323,382	34,865,987	12.4%	168,851,385	12.8%	(130,953)
BCE Inc.	911,821	33,771,145	2.7%	65,608,884	10.6%	(2,784,276)
Bombardier Inc.	1,379,556	9,715,180	14.2%	16,141,707	9.5%	340,059
TD Bank	2,120,855	10,765,760	19.7%	13,272,538	12.1%	724,270
Talisman Energy	457,622	7,040,344	6.5%	877,543	9.6%	(154,207)
Placer Dome	245,941	5,232,797	4.7%	701,647	10.3%	(201,066)
Nova Chemicals	317,740	5,385,416	5.9%	359,527	7.5%	(76,822)
FutureShop	54,033	415,635	13.0%	76,637	6.7%	27,162
Andres Wine	9,405	113,311	8.3%	(1,307)	7.1%	1,505
Magna Intl. Inc.	967,289	7,165,102	13.5%	(1,286,637)	7.9%	303,477
CP Ltd.	1,230,526	19,847,191	6.2%	(1,587,107)	8.3%	(399,028)

Calculating EVA

EVA is the difference between profits the company derives from its operation and the charge for capital incurred through the use of its "line of credit" that bears an "interest rate." It can be calculated in a number of different ways. Some of them are:

$$EVA = \text{operating profit adjusted for tax} - \text{cost of capital}$$

or

$$EVA = (\text{return on invested capital} - \text{cost of capital}) * \text{invested capital}$$

A more thorough analysis of how to assess or calculate EVAs can be found in many modern financial management textbooks or in one of the references at the end of this chapter.

EVA can aid managers in assessing the impact of a wide variety of managerial decisions. Some of the more important ones are:

● Assess the economic performance of the firm.
● Assess the capital structure (and costs of) for the firm.
● Identify operations and projects that are earning more than their cost of capital.
● Identify acquisition and joint ventures that have been or will potentially will provide a positive EVA.
● Identify the potential outcome of expanding in new markets.
● Identify the value of a business or business entity.

- Identify the different types of financial variables that influence EVA and use them to monitor managers and operations, teams, and individual tasks.
- Use EVA and the financial measures that influence it to motivate managers through tying the managers' remuneration incentives to these measures.

DISCOUNTED CASH FLOW

Discounted cash flow (DCF) is another method of estimating the economic return that a project will provide to the firm. DCF is normally used to estimate the economic return of future profits, while EVA is normally used for assessing economic returns of projects that have occurred.

DCF is the calculation of future free cash flow discounted using the cost of capital back to a specific point in time (often the present). Free cash flow is defined as Net Operating Profit plus Depreciation less Taxes less Investment in Fixed and Working Capital. Future cash flows are cash inflows and outflows that occur over different periods into the future. Again, the mechanics of this widely used calculation can be found in most financial management textbooks. Further, most financial calculators have functions that automatically calculate this complex mathematical expression.

Management decisions that require DCF calculations include essentially all future strategic alternatives and tactics. Examples of these are:

- Assessing the potential profitability of an acquisition, joint venture, or divestiture
- Assessing the potential profitability of building a new plant and/or buying new equipment
- Assessing the potential profitability of leasing versus acquiring
- Assessing the potential profitability of buying versus building parts for a manufacturing process

In reality, both the EVA and DCF methods of estimating economic return can be used interchangeably and for assessing similar types of strategic programs and projects. These methods have become the authoritative way in which managers justify strategic projects.

VALUING RISKY FUTURE STRATEGIC PROJECTS

Recently, a new approach has been employed to evaluate future strategic projects that have various risks associated with them that occur at different points in time. The approach taken is an option valuations approach, and it is similar to the DCF approach described earlier, but it incorporates the risk associated with different future outcomes and possible different chosen alternative project options as the project unfolds. In general, this approach requires the manager to perform the following steps:

- Complete a normal DCF analysis of the whole project
- Incorporate risk into the analysis through the use of an event tree that models the uncertainties
- Do DCF calculations for all of the various potential outcomes
- Identify the different decision points in the event tree so that the managers are aware when a specific decision must be taken regarding an alternative

This approach follows the *Black-Scholes option-pricing model* that is described in most financial management books.

EVALUATING NOT-FOR-PROFIT FIRMS' PERFORMANCE

In not-for-profit firms, estimating performance is much more complex because, usually, the not-for-profit firm has multiple objectives, which is unlike the for-profit sector that has the primary financial profit objective. For example, a Canadian hospital, which is subject to the Canada Health Act, has multiple primary objectives, including to provide the highest quality service available, treat as many patients as it possibly can, and keep its costs as low as possible. These objectives thus become the metric upon which the hospital must be evaluated. However, what makes it particularly difficult is that, at times, these objectives may be contradictory. For example, lowering costs is probably going to contradict the quality and quantity objectives, while quantity may contradict quality in certain instances. Thus, managing the number and priority of the objectives becomes a very important issue in not-for-profit firms.

Managing the number of objectives becomes important for a not-for-profit organization because, if there are many objectives, each requiring a specific performance metric, then the overall assessment of performance becomes very complex and difficult. Just as in a for-profit organization, it is helpful if the overall organization becomes focused on one or, at the most, several overall performance objectives. This helps managers keep the organization focused on a specific outcome, and it helps them coordinate, motivate and pull together the employees so that they are all working towards the same overall goal(s).

Managers of not-for-profit organization cannot use profit metrics for performance evaluation purposes. However, when the objectives have been clarified, management can develop means to evaluate the firm based upon these objectives. For example, in a hospital, managers may develop the following metrics for performance:

- Quantity—measure the number of patients treated, and this could even be categorized based upon the treatment provided to ensure that one is comparing apples to apples when comparisons with other time periods or institutions are done.

- Low Cost—measure the average cost of a treatment during a specific period. These costs could further be broken into direct and indirect, as well as fixed and variable costs. This activity based costing would enable the manager to examine detailed unit costs for the treatment. This break down would enable managers to study where and how their costs have moved from variance.

- Quality—this measure is the most controversial metric because it is necessarily somewhat subjective, yet, many consumers probably feel that it is the most important measure. Measures of this metric might involve examining the success rate as well as user satisfaction rates specific to various treatments and services.

All of these performance metrics will provide the hospital managers with metrics that they can compare against other time periods (e.g., are they getting better or worse?) and against other hospitals. They could also use these metrics to motivate staff to reach specific performance milestones.

A popular trend in not-for-profit firms is to attempt to select a key economic performance indicator, in a similar manner to that which was explained earlier in for-profit firms. Again, the key in developing such an indicator is to make it simple and relate it to a financial metric that is important in all not-for-profit firms. The measure relates to cash flow because of the importance in managing this particular aspect operationally relative to another key strategic variable. Therefore, to develop an indicator, management should think about the following question in the context of their strategy: *If management could select only one economic performance indicator—profit per X—to systematically strive for and increase over time, what X would have the greatest and most sustainable impact on performance?*

The Balanced Scorecard approach is also applicable to not-for-profit organizations. The top managers define strategic objectives for the firm and then the Balanced Scorecard methodology evolves down through the organization, identifying and developing measurement metrics for the key drivers that are necessary to attain these objectives.

Summary of Assessing Strategic Performance

Assessing performance in an organization is related to assessing the ultimate value creation in the organization for key stakeholders.

Measurement Metrics

Selecting a strategic measurement performance metric is related to understanding what the KSFs or important competitive advantages are in a firm.

Balanced Scorecard Measurement

The balanced scorecard approach to measuring performance is very effective because it ties performance at various levels in the organization together. Further, it is an excellent control mechanism to monitor performance throughout the organization on an ongoing basis.

Financial Performance Measures

Financial performance measures are very important for many firms. However, long-term financial performance must be the objective of any assessment because managers can easily distort short-term financial assessment.

Two important financial measures of performance are discounted cash flow (or net present value) and economic value added.

Additional Notes and Recommended Readings

Ampuero, Marcos et al., "Solving the Measurement Puzzle: How EVA and the Balance Scorecard Fit Together," *Perspectives on Business Innovations*, Ernest & Young (1998).

Armitage, H. and V. Jog, "Economic Value Creation: What Every Management Accountant Should Know," *CMA Magazine* (The Society of Management Accountants of Canada, October 1996): 21-24.

Bannister, R.J. and Jestuthasan, R., "Is Your Company Ready for Value-Based Management?" *Journal of Business Strategy* (March/April 1997): 12-15.

Kaplan, R. and Norton, D. "Putting the Balanced Scorecard to Work," *Harvard Business Review*, pp 147-155, 1993.

Kaplan, R. and Norton, D. *The Balanced Scorecard*, Harvard Business School Press, 1996

Readings

reading 1 Value-Building Growth: A Canadian Challenge

The clarion call to increase shareholder value—and the intense scrutiny of investors and analysts—has compelled many companies to focus on quarterly earnings to the point of obsession. Unfortunately, the temptation to downsize and cut costs can lull even the most astute managers into a profit trap that may generate respectable returns in the short run, but fail to exploit the company's potential to generate shareholder value over the long term. At the other extreme, unbridled growth cannot be viewed as the sole key to creating value.

In this article, we present ideas on growth and value that are based on an analysis of over 1,100 global companies, including three key sectors of the Canadian economy-retail, communications and financial services. We begin with an explanation of the true relationship between growth and shareholder value. We then describe the four types of companies that emerged from our analysis, and explain the fundamental drivers of value-building growth. Finally, we discuss the unique challenges and issues of growth for Canadian companies.

ANALYZING GROWTH ON A GLOBAL SCALE

An overriding issue for today's CEO is strategic balance. What is the correct balance between top-line and bottomline growth? What roles do growth and profitability play in the creation of shareholder value?

Recognizing this importance, A.T. Kearney launched a global initiative to investigate the characteristics of successful growth. We analyzed more than 1,100 companies (drawn from a database of more than 20,000 companies) worldwide over a 10-year period, covering 24 industries in 34 countries and including more than 80 in-depth case studies. In addition, our consultants interviewed more than 50 CEOs and senior executives of leading companies including Bayer, Ericsson, Federal Express, General Electric, Gehe, Mitsubishi Chemical, Norsk Hydro and Sprint (The Value Growers, A.T. Kearney, McGraw Hill, 2000).

Our final analysis challenges traditional thinking about the way top-line growth should be viewed and understood. In particular, it reveals an attractive kind of growth that we call value-building growth. The conscious pursuit of value-building growth has helped a select group of companies create levels of shareholder value above and beyond what conventional, complacent or bottom line-oriented companies in their industries generate. Between 1988 and 2000, these "value growers" significantly outperformed their peers in the growth of both revenue and shareholder value.

To claim that value growers merely emphasize growth over profit in their balance would oversimplify and misinterpret the point. We wanted more precise reasons: Why do value growers outperform other rapidly growing companies? Why do equity markets consistently prefer these companies to those that focus heavily on profit-oriented parameters, the so-called profit seekers? And what else does growth do for a company besides maximize shareholder returns?

CRACKING THE GROWTH CODE

For the purpose of this analysis, we define growth as each company's revenue performance relative to

Ivey Business Journal; London; Nov/Dec 2001; Dean Hillier; Tim MacDonald

industry averages. Four types of companies emerged when we compared companies according to relative performance in revenue growth against relative performance in shareholder value: value growers, profit seekers, simple growers and underperformers (see exhibit 1).

Value growers represent approximately 20 percent of the companies analyzed in each region (Asia Pacific, Europe and North America). Across all regions and industries, during the decade under study, they achieved average annual revenue growth of 18 percent and average annual growth in shareholder value of 21.5 percent.

A cluster of German conglomerates, for example (Bayer and Hoechst), sits among the profit seekers. These companies (19 percent of the companies studies) kept their sight on year-end results and grew only cautiously during the period studied, a strategy that resulted in below-average share price performance.

Korean chaebols may go down in history as the ultimate benchmark for simple growers. In an effort to push revenues ever higher, simple growers (14 percent of the companies) ran up relatively higher debt-to-equity ratios. The approach left them vulnerable to a whole range of financial and economic shocks-from the Asian currency crisis and the plunge in computer chip prices to the commoditization of plastic resins.

Finally, the underperformers quadrant is home base for a few Japanese carmakers and financial institutions. These companies did not necessarily fail to generate any revenue growth or shareholder value, but consistently lagged behind their peers in both areas and failed to break out into another growth quadrant.

In studying the characteristics and lessons learned from the companies in the four growth quadrants, we discovered that there are five fundamentals

of value-building growth. The five may offer some guidance for CEOs who want to pursue value-building growth and strike a balance between growth and profitability.

THE FIVE FUNDAMENTALS OF VALUE-BUILDING GROWTH

1. Innovation, geographic expansion and risk-taking fuel value-building growth. Value growers push themselves to explore opportunities through all these strategic options, continuously redefining their markets and reinventing themselves, whether growing internally or through mergers and acquisitions.

   Value growers focus on securing and stretching their core competencies. They stick to their knitting, avoiding wide-scale diversification and draw the bulk of their revenues and profits from building their core businesses. Furthermore, they do not divert funds from a successful business unit to bolster performance in other businesses.

   This does not mean that value growers are a one-product or niche business. In fact, it is just the opposite. They build a range of products and

exhibit 1   Value Growth Matrix (CAGR 1988-2000)

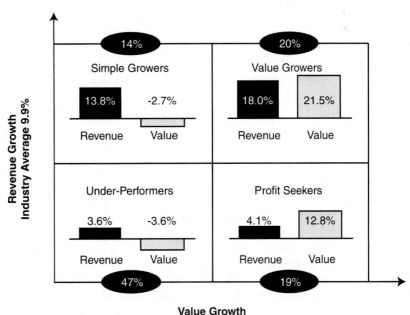

services that rely both on breakthrough innovations and incremental improvements. This explains why value growers do not cut back on R&D even in tough times, but move forward, keenly aware that innovation and product improvement are essential for future growth. This, along with an appetite and eye for innovation, leads value growers to invest (on average) four times as much in "white space" opportunities as companies in the other quadrants. ("White space" opportunities are new products/services that meet customers' latent needs or those needs that have yet to be identified.)

Value growers depend heavily on geographic reach for growth. Rather than focusing solely on exploiting growth in their home markets, value growers aggressively pursue geographic expansion. Over the past decade, they have been pioneers in realizing and capturing opportunities offered by globalization.

Value growers show no signs of preferring internal growth over growth through acquisitions. They do both well. What really matters is execution, which is where they excel. Put simply, value growers create opportunities and execute strategies that bottom line-oriented profit seekers and simple growers do not-and perhaps cannot-on a consistent basis.

2. Strong, stable growth is the decisive driver behind share price. This finding sheds new light on the importance of prevailing parameters such as year-end results, EVA (economic value added), EE (economic earnings) or CFROI (cash flow return on investment). We found a strong, longterm correlation across all companies in our database between revenue growth and growth in shareholder value. Although this may be the most compelling reason to shift the strategic balance, growth brings other tangible and intangible benefits to the company, including enhancing the firm's ability to attract and retain key talent through "excitement at workplace" and "upside in financial returns."

3. Strong, successful (value-building) growth is possible in any industry, in any region, and at any phase of a business cycle. A key fundamental of value-building growth is its universality. Companies in sluggish or smokestack industries often use these same labels as an excuse for below average growth, risk-averse behaviour and a sort of "sit on our hands" mentality.

Yet our findings show that value-building growth is applicable to any company in any industry. Every industry has a significant range of performance that allows value growers to emerge and differentiate themselves, even in mature industries such as precious metals (North America's Barrick Gold), construction (Ireland's CRH), and food processing and production (Denmark's Christian Hansen).

The flip side is also true. Contrary to the headlines generated by eBay and other dot-com pioneers, our research shows that entry into a "hot" sector, such as computer software, e-commerce or biotechnology, does not automatically bestow a licence on a company to print money for shareholders.

Value growers ride out economic downturns and the effects of other external influences, and do not claim to be immune to such developments. Instead, their balanced and conscious control over the process of value-building growth inoculates them, allowing them to respond more quickly and confidently to the effects of external developments.

4. Growth is spiral-shaped, and not linear. In viewing growth over time, most companies migrate among the different quadrants. Only nine percent managed to sustain value-building growth for more than five years. Even the best companies fall back to some point; however, value growers showed regular migration from quadrant to quadrant. We found that the growth is caused by consolidation periods.

In consolidation periods, value growers step back and view this downtime as an opportunity to realign their resources, establish a better understanding of market dynamics, and refine their strategies in preparation for the next wave of growth. Where do value growers go in the period of consolidation? Nearly 53 percent became simple growers, while less than 10 percent joined the profit seekers.

Value growers never slow their growth engine, even if it means sacrificing the bottom line for a certain period of time. They know that sinking into profit-seeker territory can make the eventual return to value growth both slower and more difficult. In fact, once the growth engine has been slowed, it takes twice as long to become a value grower again (three years) than it would from the simplegrower quadrant (1.5 years), where the growth momentum is still strong.

5. Value-building growth is highly linked to internal drivers. For example, value growers attribute nearly 90 percent of their growth to their ability to employ certain internal factors in a balanced way. Our study has revealed that there are eight major internal growth drivers across three broad categories of growth determination, stakeholder empathy, and an enabling business model. Exhibit 2 provides a closer look at these influencing factors.

A company that is not achieving value-building growth is prone to blaming external factors such as the economy or competition. In fact, the non-value-builders in our study attribute 44 percent of their revenue performance to external, environment factors. Many blamed a changing market. A value grower, in contrast, is more likely to "change" itself rather than blame the market. In other words, they believe that they control their own destiny.

THE CANADIAN CHALLENGE

Our analysis of 223 Canadian-owned companies revealed that the Canadian value-building growth profile is in line with our global findings; about 20 percent of the companies we analyzed in Canada are value-growers. Even more promising is that, on an aggregate level, Canada ranks among the value growers of the world economy (along with the U.S. the U.K. and others). Moreover, those Canadian companies skilled enough to manage themselves into the value-growers quadrant have raised the performance bar compared to the global averages. Canadian value growers showed 42 percent growth and 29.3 percent value growth against 18 percent and 21.5 percent, respectively, on a global basis.

But while many executives are prone to quoting today's difficult business climate and financial market jitters as compelling reasons for poor results, or study has demonstrated that value-building-growth is largely independent of external factors, such as an economic downturn, over the long term. There are no excuses for low growth; there are, however, challenges for achieving value-building growth in Canada.

In terms of the growth challenges, Canadian executives in the new millennium must face a new twist to the old question-"What business are we really in?" Certain Canadian companies are responding successfully to the global growth challenge in their industry sector. We look at three here: retail, communications and financial services.

RETAIL

From our sample of publicly traded retail companies in Canada, only Loblaws continues to demonstrate superior value-building growth characteristics. With a clear understanding of its core business-food retailing-Loblaws set out to become the best in one-stop shopping for everyday household needs including pharmacies, prepared foods, photo processing, dry cleaning, flower shops, travel and financial services. After first redefining the Canadian food industry through its launch of President's Choice private label in the mid-'80s, it began to produce a substantial portion of the extensive PC product line overseas. PC products are now being licensed in countries as far away as Hong Kong and the Caribbean. Loblaws's growth strategy has included the recent acquisitions of Provigo (Montreal) and Agora (Atlantic Canada) as well as numerous openings and dramatically new retail formats such as its Supercentres in Ontario. While Canadian department store retailers and do-it-yourselfers wage a costly battle for domestic market share with each other and formidable foreign foes such as Wal-Mart and Home Depot (also value growers), Loblaws continues to redefine itself on its own terms. Sobeys (a simple grower), the No.2 food retailer in Canada, also has growth high on its agenda. With a strong vision, a detailed growth plan and new leadership, it seems poised to move towards the value-grower quadrant.

On an international level, the value-building growers are clear leaders in geographic expansion, innovation and risk-taking. At the beginning of the 1990s, Home Depot rode out an economic downturn by undertaking an aggressive expansion. As competitors responded to Home Depot's re-definition of the market, the company responded in part through another wave of expansion, this time beyond U.S. borders to Canada and Europe.

Despite growth challenges in Europe and the United Kingdom, Wal-Mart continues to be a value-building grower because of its market

exhibit 2   Value-Building Growth Linked to Internal Growth Drivers

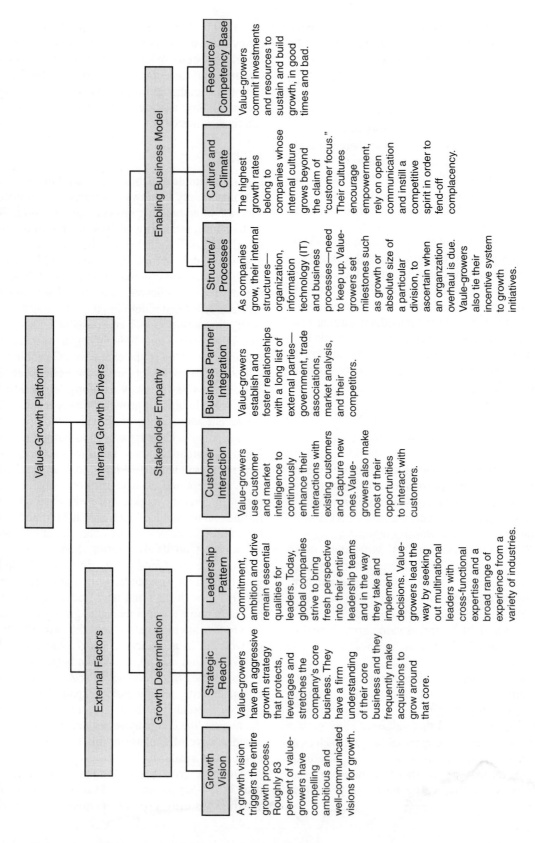

and innovation leadership. Ahold, the Dutch supermarket giant, continues to stretch its presence in the U.S. and globally, based on over 10 years of continuous yet patient growth through acquisition.

COMMUNICATIONS

Sample Canadian communications companies are not value growers. Despite having a comparative advantage in the plethora of new opportunities available in the sector itself, they have not taken advantage of these opportunities. Unlike some Canadian players, global value growers like Verizon and SBC have focused on significantly enhancing their consumer base through acquisitions. They have formed partnerships with other players to achieve market leadership, as demonstrated by Verizon and Vodafone's partnership to create the No. wireless operator in the United States. In another approach, Tele2, the pan-European telecom operator, provides fixed-line and mobile phone services, cable TV, data transactions, and Internet access to 12.9 million subscribers in 21 European countries. By focusing on the high-growth opportunity on their home turf,

Canadian companies have not participated in the opening up of the telecom sector globally.

In the domestic market, low penetration and new 2.5 and 3G technology present growth opportunities. To significantly grow value, however, Telus, Rogers AT&T and Bell Mobility will need to leverage their equity alliances to grow their respective subscriber bases. The lack of true scale in the Canadian market is an impediment to the growth of new services. The company that best leverages its global parmers will have the best opportunity to enter the value-wer quadrant.

FINANCIAL SERVICES

Based on our samples of the global financial services sector, Great-West Life is the only Canadian value grower. Our more traditional financial institutions have been relative underperformers compared to their global peers. These value growers have gained disproportionate global scale by focusing on product and market extension through cross-border mergers, acquisitions and alliances, so as to gain market share and pursue aggressive geographic expansion. Like

exhibit 3 Global Retail Sector

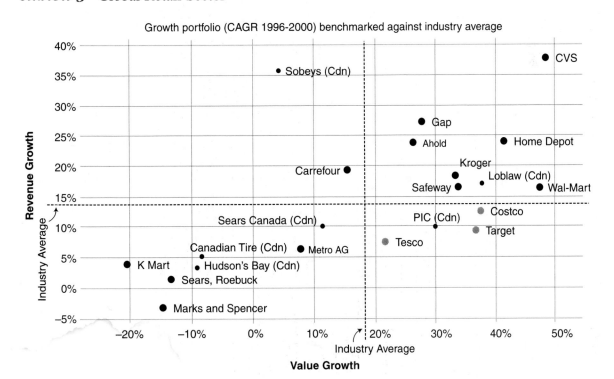

Growth portfolio (CAGR 1996-2000) benchmarked against industry average

these global value growers, Great-West Life has achieved a significant presence in Canada and the United States through large strategic acquisitions, especially London Insurance Group, and by strengthening its links with Power Financial, through Investors Group and the recently acquired Mackenzie Financial. Furthermore, it sold London Guarantee, the specialty property-liability insurance arm of London Life, as the business was not core to Great-West Life's operations, a reasoning that is followed by value growers globally.

While Canadian banks have historically limited themselves to growing market share, we have seen a rise in cross-border expansions that could boost long-term growth prospects and value creation. For example:

- Royal Bank executing a North American strategy with U.S. acquisitions in banking (SFNB, Centura), mortgages (Prism), insurance (liberty), and ealth management/investment banking Main Rauscher, Tucker Anthony Sutro)

- CIBC expanding into the U.S. with Amicus and its acquisition of Oppenheimer (investment banking)

- TD Bank acquiring Waterhouse and other discount brokerage operations globally

- Manulife's recent acquisition in Japan

SUMMARY

At the risk of generalizing too greatly, but with consideration for the 223 Canadian companies sampled as part of our global study, we believe there are three significant gaps in the growth strategies of Canadian non-value-building growth companies:

1. Too Canada-focused. Perhaps because of Canada's large territory, with its inherent and complex supply chain challenges and regional consumer preferences, Canadian companies are consumed with protecting their domestic markets. On the global stage, Canada is not a small market: 11th in the world based on 2000 GDP

exhibit 4   Global Communications Sector

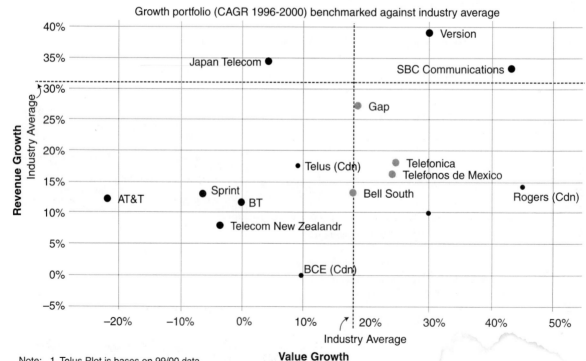

(between Mexico and Spain) and 10th based on 2000 GDP per capita (between Austria and Liechtenstein). But the gap in confidence that besets many Canadian companies can be based on the sheer magnitude of our neighbouring giant, the United States (first in total GDP and second in GDP per capita). Our research clearly shows that the markets reward those who pounce on market share and conquer new territories. Execution is critical. We must learn from our less-than-successful attempts of the past, the successes we have had, such as Bombardier's international expansion through acquisitions and alliances, as well as those of foreign companies (Royal Bank of Scotland's alliances with U.K. supermarket chains and Richard Branson's Virgin Group to offer personal banking).

One of the challenges facing Canadian business leaders who want to expand is that while the number of Canadian acquisitions of foreign companies still exceeds that of foreign companies buying Canadian companies, the gap is in fact narrowing. Furthermore, the transaction value of foreign acquisitions of Canadian companies has skyrocketed in the last two years and is now 2.2 times the average value of Canadian companies acquiring abroad. This makes Canadian growth through acquisition increasingly expensive for sectors prone to foreign investment, and so, increasingly, scale advantage is moving to foreign companies.

2. Innovation followers, not leaders. Value growers not only dominate markets, they dominate industry white space with new ideas that fuel their growth engines. Nonvalue-building growth companies seem to participate in their marketplaces rather than consciously redefine them. Value growers are leaders at stretching their core brand. For example, Loblaws defined the private-label market in food retailing and became an early adopter of extended service offerings for everyday use; CVS Corporation captured white-space opportunities in pharmacy services and managed care drug programs.

At the macro level, Canada ranked lowest among the G8 countries on competitiveness, far behind the leader, the United States. The follower mentality is clearly demonstrated by Canada's R&D expenditure. In 1998, Canada spent 1.6 percent of its GDP on R&D; the U.S. led the pack at 2.8 percent.

exhibit 5 Global Financial Services Sector

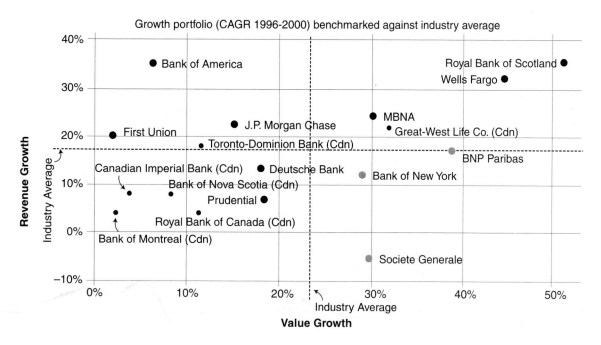

exhibit 6   Strategic Growth Gaps

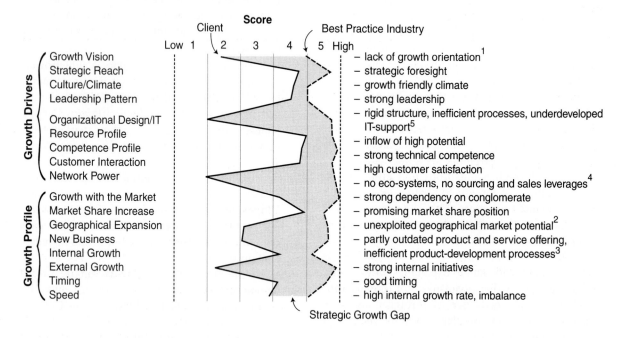

Strategic Growth Gap

3. Complacency with the status quo. Growth is an all encompassing passion that needs to flow through the bloodstream of an organization. It's not an initiative or q purely financial objective, it's the raison d'etre of a company, the strategic imperative. We often hear CEOs speak with conviction about "improving customer service," "squeezing additional cost savings" or "enhancing product profitability"-important tactics they wish their organizations would execute better, but which are hardly unique or strategic. Jack Welch even changed the now famous and very successful moniker for GE to emphasize growth as the new strategic paradigm: "Define your market in such a way that you have just 10 percent market share, then grow aggressively" Value growers must constantly pressure top performance, maintain investment stamina, redefine their businesses and markets, and consciously push the envelope.

Today, top-performing Canadian companies must strike a proper balance between the top and bottom lines, emphasizing revenue growth and profitable execution as the optimal path to superior shareholder value. CEOs who consistently achieve value-building growth do so by adhering to a strong growth strategy and promoting innovation, geographic expansion and risk-taking. They nurture and build their core businesses while stretching to capture the growth potential of white-space opportunities. Relying on lessons learned from the value growers, Canadian companies can better ensure that their underlying growth dynamics outstrip their global industry peers over the long term.

Dean Hillier is a vice-president and leader of the Canadian Consumer Products and Retail Practice. Tim MacDonald is president of A.T. Kearney Ltd. and co-leader of the North American Merger Integration Practice. Both work in the firm's Toronto office.

Reprint #9BOITFO7

reading 2   Ally or Acquire?

How Technology Leaders Decide

In their quest to develop profitable products, technology companies are constantly faced with the need to choose between alliances and acquisitions. Executives who understand where their products fit within the technology life cycle are more likely to make the right call.

Edward B. Roberts and Wenyun Kathy Liu

There are four phases in the life cycle of a technology, and for each there are appropriate ways of partnering with outsiders. Increasingly, the challenge for managers is to recognize which phase each of their products is in and decide what kinds of external partnerships are most likely to facilitate speedy development. Each product a company is juggling may be in a different phase, and because the partnerships developed for one phase of a given technology could serve a different purpose in another phase of another technology, partnerships must be handled with care. Despite the complexity that comes with the need to manage a variety of alliances, Microsoft Corp. and others are demonstrating that it can be done successfully.

The most dramatic change in global technological innovation—the movement toward externally oriented collaborative strategies that complement internal research-and-development investments—began more than a decade ago.[1] Today companies use alliances, joint ventures, licensing, equity investments, mergers and acquisitions to accomplish their technological and market goals over a technology's life cycle. How can companies decide when to use which form of partnership? In part, by understanding the externally focused technology-life-cycle model.[2]

THE TECHNOLOGY-LIFE-CYCLE MODEL OF ALLIANCES AND ACQUISITIONS

Understanding the role of alliances and acquisitions in the technology life cycle starts with understanding the cycle's four stages: the fluid phase, the transitional phase, the mature phase and the discontinuities phase.[3] The first three were identified in the 1970s by James M. Utterback. (See "The Utterback Model of the Technology Life Cycle.") He later added a fourth, discontinuities, stage. Each stage is shaped by changes in the character and frequency of innovations in technology-based products and processes and by market dynamics. (See "Characteristics of the Four Technology Phases.")

The Fluid Phase   In the fluid phase, the earliest pioneering products enter the market for that technology amid a high level of product and market uncertainty.[4] For example, CDs that use fluorescent technology are now entering the market for digital data storage, but it is too soon to tell if that technology will win out over DVDs—or other concepts. With the technology in flux, organizations seeking to increase data-storage capacity (say, the military or the movie industry) hesitate to place R&D bets on a single technology. (In an earlier time period, Exxon Enterprises found eight alternative computer-storage technologies equally attractive for investments during a fluid phase of emerging technology.)

The fluid stage also is characterized by a high rate of growth in market demand. Barriers to entry are low; companies with proprietary technologies can enter with ease. There is little brand loyalty; customers seek functionality and quality instead. Direct competition among existing companies is relatively low, so profit margins are high. The bargaining power of suppliers is low because the materials and equipment used to make the products are general in nature.

Today, as product life cycles in high-tech markets shrink, new technology needs quick acceptance. Hence managers of companies in the fluid stage should pursue aggressive outward-licensing strategies to promote their technologies. For example, after

Sun Microsystems introduced SPARC (scalable processor architecture) reduced-instruction-set computing (RISC) in 1989, the company licensed it to 21 hardware manufacturers and software developers, including IBM, Novell and Toshiba. And after introducing its Java technology in 1995, Sun made 32 Java licensing agreements in two years.

Startup companies often adopt variations of traditional licensing. For instance, open-source software creators make their source code available to independent programmers who then make compatible changes and share the results—an effective launch strategy for Linux and Apache, among other software products.

To enable a new product to reach customers quickly, high-tech companies in the fluid stage also form marketing alliances with key players in their supply chain. A difference from traditional marketing alliances is the current focus on speeding products to market. Business-to-business Internet companies such as Allaire, Ariba, BroadVision, ChannelWave Software, Veritas Software, Vignette and Webridge allied with key channel players: solutions providers, application-service providers (ASPs), systems integrators, Internet-service providers (ISPs) and consulting companies.

Among the new kinds of alliances, those organized to establish standards are increasingly important. Indeed, in 1999 and 2000, most prominent computer companies participated in one standards alliance or more. (See "Recent Standards Alliances in the Computer Industry.") Such alliances involve not only the promotion of the technology but also its further development—often among competitors. For example, in the high-profile Trusted Computing Platform Alliance (TCPA) of 1999, five competing giants joined forces to create standards for better security solutions.

During the fluid stage, well-established technology companies often acquire startups. The acquired companies get access to a wider range of resources, and the acquirer gains critical competitive technologies that would have been costly to develop in-house. Another attractive alternative is to form an R&D alliance with a startup while also making minority equity investments in it. Such strategic alliances allow established companies to keep pace with change while building high-level managerial connections and operational links that can lead to later acquisitions.

The Transitional Phase   The transitional phase of a technology life cycle starts with the emergence of a dominant design. As product and market uncertainty lessens and R&D efforts become focused on improving the dominant technology, design cycles shrink.

During the transitional phase, industry demand grows rapidly, customers require quality products and timely delivery, customers require quality products and timely delivery, and barriers to entry become even lower if the dominant design is easily accessible. Companies must realign themselves with the new standards and pursue an aggressive growth strategy.[5] To signal their commitment, they also should consider capital investment in production capacity. And to ensure product availability, they need supply and marketing agreements with customers. In the transitional phase, companies often collaborate to improve the dominant design and develop new technological extensions, features and applications

exhibit 1 The Utterback Model of the Technology Life Cycle

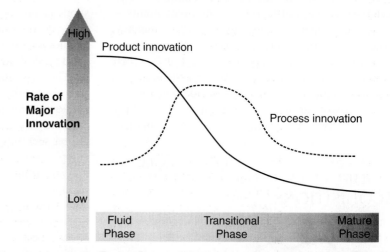

through joint R&D. Typically, once they possess sufficient technological capabilities, companies of similar size join forces.

For increased market share and revenue growth, companies need to move quickly to develop or adopt the dominant design. Those with the dominant design pursue their advantage and collect royalties (as Texas Instruments has done most effectively) by aggressively licensing the product to other enterprises. Organizations that have lost the standards battle should adopt the standards quickly by getting a license to use someone else's discovery or through internal R&D. The growth potential in the transitional phase makes entry particularly attractive for companies in mature technology markets. When the PC industry was in transition, Japanese electronics giants—Hitachi, NEC and Toshiba—invested heavily to enter the business. Mature companies seek to acquire businesses that either possess the dominant design or have the capabilities needed for quick adoption of the new standards.

Growing companies that possess the dominant technology may be able to make acquisitions of their own, thanks to the financial clout of their surging stock prices. Ideally, those acquisitions would have a strong strategic objective, and target companies would possess complementary technologies or an attractive customer base.

The Mature Phase   In the mature phase, products built around the dominant design proliferate. R&D emphasis shifts from product innovation toward process innovation.

Because process innovations are inherently time-consuming and expensive, many companies form R&D alliances to share the cost and risk. Last year's alliance between Fujitsu and Toshiba to codevelop one-gigabit DRAM (dynamic random-access memory) computer chips is a good example.

The high cost and risk of internal R&D make technology acquisitions attractive, too. In some respects, an acquisition is better than an alliance, in which partners are also competitors and have equal access to the new technology. Acquisitions give the acquirer exclusive rights to the proprietary technology. Between 1993 and 2000, Cisco Systems spent roughly $9 billion buying more than 50 companies.[6] Cisco's technology acquisitions freed up important resources for an internal focus on core competencies.

During the mature stage of a technology's cycle, the growth rate of market demand slows, but the total volume of demand expands. The once highly profitable market becomes commoditized, a direct result of cost reduction and excess capacity. There is a fierce price competition and pressure on profit margins. The need to bring down cost and grow volume increases. Given the technological and capital requirements, entry is harder for outsiders. The key to surviving the mature stage is strong commitment to organization wide improvement in efficiency. One way to reduce development cost is through cooperative alliances with suppliers—or even with competitors.

High-tech industries are notoriously cyclical, and companies that pursue manufacturing joint ventures in the mature stage have a better shot at controlling cost and guaranteeing availability and quality despite marketplace fluctuations. Marketing alliances are important, too, as competition intensifies and focusing on customers becomes critical. Marketing alliances help companies target the latent market, pursue competitors' customers and expand into new geographic markets.

In high-tech industries, horizontal mergers with complementary product lines are another popular method to reduce costs and obtain a stronger market position by offering more products and services. That was the apparent rationale when Compaq bought Digital Equipment Corp. in 1998. Compaq, facing a saturated PC market, saw DEC as its key to expanding into the then more lucrative high-end server and service markets.

In the mature stage, some companies divest non-core properties to alleviate pressures on earnings. In 1998, Texas Instruments, wishing to concentrate on its core digital-signal processing (DSP) business, sold its facilities for manufacturing DRAMs to Micron Technologies. This also is the phase during which technology companies have the highest propensity to make equity investments and acquisitions and to form alliances for R&D, marketing or manufacturing.

The Discontinuities Phase   The existing technology can be rendered obsolete by the introduction of next-generation technology (NGT), a more advanced technology or converging markets. During the discontinuities stage, the marketplace is volatile. A new market develops, taking demand away from the old

table 1   Characteristics of the Four Technology Phases

	Fluid Phase	Transitional Phase	Mature Phase	Discontinuities Phase
Dynamics of the Phase	• Uncertainty in products and markets • High rate of product innovation and high degree of process flexibility • Fast-growing demand; low total volume • Greater importance of product functionality than brand names • Little direct competition	• Appearance of dominant design • Increased clarity about customer needs • Incresed process innovation • Importance of complementary assets • Competition based on quality and availability	• Strong pressure on profit margin • More similarities than differences in final products • Convergence of product and process innovations	• Invasion of new technologies • Increasing obsolescence of incumbents' assets • Lowered barriers to entry; new competition • Convergence of some new technologies emerge
Priorities	• Development and preservation of technology (with a focus on product development and aggressive patenting) • Promotion of proprietary technology as industry standard	• Realignment of techno-logical capabilities with the dominant design • Continued exploration of technological opportunities • Pursuit of a growth stategy (through aggressive capacity building or by establishing a close relationship with suppliers and custmers)	• Cost control throughout the value chain • Strong customer focus • Lean and efficient organization	• A need for incumbents to identify new tech-nologies and realign core competencies • An option for incumbents to exit the market • Attackers' need to gain market recognition • Attackers' need to focus on product development
Strategic Alliances	• Formation of alliances to promote technology as the industry standard • Adoption of licensing strat-egies (say, open-source licensing or aggressive licensing to users) • Formation of marketing alliances (with key players of the supply chain or with one industry leader) • Formation of technology alliances with established companies, often coupled with equity investments	• Winners' aggressive licensing to customers and to companies that lost the dominant-design battle • Formation of joint R&D ventures with companies in the market • Formation of marketing alliances; signing of supply agreements to guarantee consistent quality, price and availability	• Formation of joint R&D ventures to share risks and costs of technology development • Formation of marketing alliances to attack latent markets or lure customers away from competitors • Manufacturing alliances to ensure availability of essential products • Open alliances with suppliers and customers	• Attackers' formation of marketing alliances to gain market recognition • Attacker agreements to supply technology leaders • Incumbents' acquisition of the disruptive technology through license agreements
Mergers and Acquisitions	• Acquisitions of starups by well-established technology companies from a more mature • Corporate equity investment by well-established high-tech companies	• Acquisitions of competitors by the winners of the dominant-technology battle • Acquisitions by established technology companiew entering the market	• Horozontal mergers between companies with complementary products and services • Divestiture of manufac-turing capabilities that are not essential • Acquisitions of technology startups making products that would be difficult to develop in-house	• Possible equity financing for attacker from establish-ed technology companies • Established companies' move into new markets through acquisition of niche technology companies • Established companies' acquisition of enterprises that have related product capabilities • Divesiture of companies as priorities shift with market convergence

market. As many previous barriers to entry (incumbents' specialized production facilities, their investments in R&D and their technology portfolios) lose their force, the likelihood of new entrants is high. The technology in the field gradually turns toward the fluid phase of a new technology life cycle. The process of technological evolution starts again.

Because technological discontinuities can render a company's competitive ability obsolete, companies must adjust business strategies. When next-generation technology increases system performance, it may either destroy or enhance company competencies.[7] If existing producers initiate the NGT (an uncommon scenario in high-tech industries), it is competence-enhancing to them. Even if the market conditions for their mainstream product deteriorate, the new technology may provide first-mover advantage. Companies that are first to increase capacity can capture near-monopoly rents. A one-month time-to-market advantage can dramatically increase the product's total profit margin. Marketing alliances and agreements to supply end users can accelerate the transition; they guarantee the new product's availability to high-end customers and alleviate the first mover's concern about uncertain market demand.

The definition of the technology's market becomes blurred as markets converge and horizontal mergers appear between attackers and incumbents. Companies with stronger financial bases become acquirers. For example, in an effort to stay ahead of the transition into IP (Internet-protocol) networks, telecommunications giant AT&T purchased cable, telecommunications, high-speed Internet and networking companies. At the same time, to focus on core competencies and avoid redundancy, AT&T made several divestitures. The company's joint R&D alliances and minority equity investments supported both capital and technology goals—without incurring the costs or risks of acquisitions. Such arrangements are popular between technology giants that have a need to collaborate. In May 1999, AT&T entered a critical alliance in which Microsoft put $5 billion into AT&T and supplied its Windows CE operating system to AT&T's set-top boxes. Similarly, Intel, having observed that networking and communications were displacing PCs as the opportunity for semiconductors, made 15 acquisitions in those fields during 1999 and 2000 alone.

COMPANIES' DECISIONS TO ALLY OR ACQUIRE

A decision to ally or acquire depends not only on company-specific competencies and needs but also on overall market development and the company's position relative to its competitors. (See "Propensity To Ally or Acquire.") Industry structure and critical success factors change as the underlying technology evolves over its life cycle and as competitive pressures vary. Companies are most inclined to form alliances as the technology becomes better defined and as competitive pressure increases. Then the number

table 2 Recent Standards Alliances in the Computer Industry

Date	Participants	Objective
Jan. 13, 1999	Adaptec, Compaq, Hewlett-Packard and IBM	To create a new input/output standard
April 26, 1999	Dictaphone, eDigital, IBM, Intel, Norcom Electronics, Olympus America and Philips Electronics	To develop a standard for the way voice commands and information are transmitted and received by mobile devices
Oct. 18, 1999	Compaq, Hewlett-Packard, IBM, Intel and Microsoft	To develop security standards for hardware used in e-commerce
Dec. 14, 1999	Akamai Technologies, Allaire, BroadVision, Exodus Communications, Finian Software, Network Appliance, Network Associates, Novell, Open Market and Oracle	To create a standard that connects multiple Web functions on any Internet-access device
Feb. 8, 2000	3Com, Cisco Systems, Extreme Networks, Intel, Nortel Networks, Sun Microsystems and World Wide Packets	To develop standards and technology for 10-gigabit Ethernet networks

Source: Techweb, http://www.techweb.com

of alliances declines in the discontinuities phase, when consolidation decreases the total number of companies in the industry. The number of M&As is often high during the transition stage because established companies acquire startups to enhance their technology portfolios. As the dominant design becomes clear and technology becomes more mature, companies increase acquisition efforts to stay ahead of the competition.[8]

MICROSOFT AND THE TECHNOLOGY LIFE CYCLE

Microsoft Corp. presents a good example of a company managing its external activities in sync with the underlying technological life cycle. (See "Microsoft and the Four Technology Phases.")

Microsoft's Fluid Phase (1975 to 1981)

When Microsoft was established in 1975 to provide software for the first personal computer, PC software was relatively new and crude; direct competition was minimal. Throughout the late 1970s, Microsoft focused on developing its PC-software products and technology portfolio. It built strategic relationships with domestic and foreign computer manufacturers, choosing licensing as its principal collaborative mechanism for attracting new customers. During its first six-year period, sales grew at an average annual rate of 165%; revenue reached $16 million by the end of 1981.[9]

Aggressive licensing of its own versions of generic software products such as Basic, Cobol, Fortran and Pascal helped Microsoft attract the attention of the most powerful mainframe-computer company, IBM. In 1980 Microsoft signed a contract to develop operating systems for IBM's first personal computer. The strategic partnership between the startup and the established manufacturer was key in making Microsoft's operating system technology (MS-DOS 1.0) part of the dominant design for PCs. IBM quickly triumphed in the personal computer

market, and as other computer manufacturers started to clone the IBM PC, they adopted Microsoft's operating system, too.

Microsoft's Transitional Phase (1982 to 1987)

By 1982 Microsoft's MS-DOS was the dominant operating system for the dominant IBM PC. While Microsoft continued to improve the functionality of its operating systems, it also enhanced its efforts to develop products for specific customer needs. It broadened its technology base by adding application-software programs to its portfolio. Its main objective was to create user-friendly operating systems and software programs for PC users. As the market for PC software grew, Microsoft continued its aggressive licensing strategy. In the first 16 months that MS-DOS was on the market, it was licensed to 50 hardware manufacturers.[10] By retaining distribution rights to DOS, Microsoft benefited from the PC boom. And the continuing IBM alliance helped establish Windows as the standard operating system after MS-DOS.

Microsoft's strong stock performance after its 1986 initial public offering enabled the company to make its first acquisition in 1987—of Forethought, the developer of Powerpoint.

Microsoft's Mature Phase (1988 to 1994)

By 1988 Microsoft had developed a complete technology portfolio. It surpassed Lotus Development Corp. as the world's top software vendor. In the mature stage

exhibit 2 Propensity to Ally or Acquire

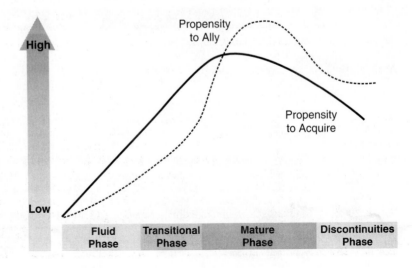

of its technology life cycle, Microsoft continued to develop and improve its operating systems and application software and to address PC users' needs for word processing, spreadsheets and multimedia software. Sales grew an average of 45% annually. The growth rate was significantly lower than during the fluid and transitional stages, but overall sales volume was larger.

To strengthen its dominance in the high-growth software market, Microsoft participated in strategic partnerships and made key acquisitions. From 1988 to 1994 Microsoft entered 36 joint ventures and alliances, 61% of which involved joint R&D agreements.[11] More important, because it had partnerships with all seven of the leading computer-hardware

companies (and because 21 out of 36 joint ventures were exclusive partnerships), Microsoft was able to develop more-functional, user-friendly software.

Microsoft's Discontinuities Phase (1995 to 1999) The Internet changed the industry's competitive landscape. Although it fueled the growth of the PC market, it also lowered the barriers to entry. Alternative devices appeared. From 1995 to 1999 Microsoft continued to improve the product lines that embodied its base technology. Meanwhile it began to develop Internet technologies to establish itself in the new growth market, introducing Internet Explorer 2.0 in 1995 in competition with leading

table 3 Microsoft and the Four Technology Phases

	Fluid Phase	Transitional Phase	Mature Phase	Discontinuities Phase
Dynamics of the Phase	• 165% growth rate • Poorly defined technology • Proliferation of products • Small niche market —the PC market • Limited competition	• 69% growth rate • Establishment of Microsoft's operating system as the industry standard • Competition from other application-software companies • Market growth as technology is better defined	• 45% growth rate • Enormous software sales • More competition in the application-software industry • Product upgrades and product development to meet customers' needs	• 32% growth rate • Slower growth of the current technology • Invasion of the Internet; converging markets • Market invasion by new companies with new Internet technologies • Need for incumbent to play technology catch-up
Priorities	• Rapid market recognition • Promotion of the technology as part of the dominant design for PCs	• Pursuit of growth strategy • Development of application software to run on Microsoft's operating system	• Easy-to-use application software programs • Keeping pace with technology developments	• Development of new technologies • Attempt to get established in the new technology area
Stategic	• Important strategic alliance with IBM • Aggressive licensing to commercial users and PC manufacturers	• Continued aggressive licensing to commercial users and PC manufacturers • Ongoing strategic alliance with IBM	• 36 joint ventures • Joint R&D ventures with PC-hardware companies • Joint marketing agreements • Continued focus on licensing	• High level of alliance activity • 35 alliances, including several that had more than one objective (46% for joint R&D; 52% for joint marketing; 17% for licensing)
Mergers and Acquisitions	• none	• Acquisition of Forethought, the developer of PowerPoint • No other M&A activity	• Two equity minority investments (one in competing OS, one in applicatiions) • Two technology acquisitions • Slightly more activity than during the transitional stage	• Much activity • 26 minority equity investments • Fifteen equity investments since 1999. all Internet-related • Fifteen companies bought, half Internet-related, half application-software technologies

Web browser Netscape Navigator. As it did with application software, Microsoft leveraged its effective operating-system monopoly, bundling Internet Explorer with Windows in the hope that people would use something preinstalled in their PCs.

Microsoft provides a textbook case of a company facing technological discontinuity. As the incumbent, the company possessed deep financial resources and a strong customer base. However, it neither pioneered the Internet nor reacted immediately to it—and consequently fell behind its attackers in the technology and product arenas. Once aware of the seriousness of the threat, Microsoft increased its alliance and acquisition efforts. From 1995 to 1999 alone, it participated in 35 joint ventures. Joint marketing agreements mounted as the market became more volatile and Microsoft strove to maintain a strong relationship with customers.

With the dawn of the Internet and mobile technologies, Microsoft bought 15 companies and, in four years, made 26 minority equity investments focusing on Internet-related technologies and application software.

THE RIGHT PARTNERSHIP ARRANGEMENT FOR THE RIGHT STAGE

Our life-cycle model indicates that during the fluid stage companies focus on improving product functionality and gaining quick market recognition. Because Microsoft established an important strategic relationship with IBM in that stage, its operating system became the industry standard and Microsoft could proceed to an aggressive licensing strategy.

In the transitional stage, high-tech companies generally form joint R&D ventures, pursue aggressive licensing strategies to realign their technology portfolio, and sign marketing and supply agreements to guarantee consistent quality, price and availability for their customers. Microsoft continued its licensing strategy, and its strategic alliance with IBM remained instrumental to growth.

In the mature stage of the technology life cycle, companies use numerous strategic alliances and acquisitions to share the risks and costs of technology development, ensure availability of essential products and expand into latent markets. Collaborating with leading hardware companies in 36 joint ventures and

alliances during its mature phase, Microsoft obtained access to the advanced technologies it needed.

The model anticipates that companies in the discontinuities stage will establish marketing and licensing agreements as well as joint R&D ventures. The phase also features a high level of product and market uncertainty, with technologies invading and markets merging. Thus, when the Internet changed the computer industry's competitive landscape, Microsoft turned increasingly to alliance efforts. Its 35 joint ventures helped maintain customer relationships and provide comprehensive solutions to clients. As of this writing, Microsoft also has made 26 minority investment and has acquired 15 companies to address the challenge.

Clearly, Microsoft exemplifies our model of the externally focused technology life cycle. Unpublished life-cycle case studies on Cisco and Compaq —plus statistical analyses of industry data—also lend support to our framework.[12] Nevertheless, additional empirical validation from many companies and industries is needed.

Ultimately, the model raises concerns for managers. It shows that a company should use, in a timely and appropriate way, every form of business development—alliances, joint ventures, licensing, equity investments, mergers and acquisitions—in order to perform optimally over its underlying technology life cycle. But doing so requires integrated technology and market and financial planning that may be beyond most companies.

Furthermore, few companies seem to excel, with either organizational or managerial processes, in implementing even a portion of what is needed in business development. A subjective search for benchmarks finds Texas Instruments remarkably capable of carrying out profitable outbound licensing. Cisco excels in acquisitions. Intel and 3M do different but comparably effective jobs of corporate venture-capital investing. Millennium Pharmaceuticals in Cambridge, Massachusetts, has rapidly built a multibillion-dollar enterprise from alliances and joint ventures. But no one company seems to be outstanding at more than one mode of business development. The challenge is not beyond companies' reach, but in order to rise to it, managers must understand the externally focused technology-life-cycle model, think about how it applies to their own situation—and learn to use partnerships that are targeted to a particular technology-life-cycle stage.

References

1 E.B. Roberts, "Benchmarking Global Strategic Management of Technology," *Research-Technology Management* 44 (March-April 2001): 25-36.

2 The authors appreciate the financial support of the global industrial sponsors of the MIT International Center for Research on the Management of Technology, as well as funding from the National Science Foundation to the MIT Center for Innovation in Product Development.

3 For a comprehensive literature review on different models of the technology life cycle, see P. Anderson and M.L. Tushman, "Technological Discontinuities and Dominant Designs: A Cyclical Model of Technological Change." *Administrative Science Quarterly* 35 (1990): 604-633. Further discussion of the model's evolution is provided by J.M. Utterback, "Mastering the Dynamics of Innovation" (Boston: Harvard Business School Press, 1994). Utterback's pioneering life-cycle work, begun in the 1970s, is best summarized by his book. Following Utterback, Tushman and Rosenkopf propose a similar technology-life-cycle model with four stages: eras of ferment, dominant designs, eras of incremental change, and technological discontinuities. See M.L. Tushman and L. Rosenkopf, "Organizational Determinants of Technological Change: Towards a Sociology of Technological Evolution," Research in Organizational Behavior 14 (1992): 311-347. See also R.R. Nelson and S.G. Winter, "Simulation of Schumpeterian Competition," *American Economic Review* 67 (1977): 271-276; R.R. Nelson and S.G. Winter, "The Schumpeterian Tradeoff Revisited," *American Economic Review 72* (1982): 114-132; G. Dosi, "Technological Paradigms and Technological Trajectories: A Suggested Interpretation of the Determinants and Directions of Technical Change," Research Policy 11 (1982): 147-162; N. Rosenberg, "Inside the Black Box: Technology and Economics" (Cambridge: Cambridge University Press, 1982); D.J. Teece, "Profiting From Technological Innovation: Implications for Integration, Collaboration, Licensing and Public Policy," Research Policy 15 (1986): 285-305; D.J. Teese, "Capturing Value From Technological Innovation: Integration, Strategic Partnering and Licensing Decisions," Interfaces 18 (1988): 46-61; and R.R. Nelson, "Recent Evolutionary Theorizing About Economic Change," *Journal of Economic Literature* 33 (1995): 48-90.

4 W.J. Abernathy and J.M. Utterback, "Patterns of Industrial Innovation," *Technology Review* 80 (1978): 40-47.

5 R.M. Henderson, "Underinvestment and Incompetence as Responses to Radical Innovation: Evidence From the Photolithographic Alignment Equipment," *Rand Journal of Economics* 24 (1993): 248-269.

6 http://www.cisco.com/warp/public/750/acquisition

7 M.L. Tushman and P. Anderson, "Technological Discontinuities and Organizational Environments," *Administrative Science Quarterly* 31 (1986): 439-465.

8 We define "propensity to ally" as the likelihood that a company will participate in joint ventures and alliances. Several ways for post hoc measurement of a company's propensity to ally seem plausible—for example, by examining its total number of alliances normalized by sales. We define "propensity to acquire" as the likelihood that a company will make an acquisition, perhaps measured similarly by the total number of acquisitions normalized by sales.

9 http://www.microsoft.com

10 Ibid.

11 Data from the Securities Data Company's (SCD) joint-venture data-base. Many joint ventures involve multiple agreements.

12 W. Liu, "Essays in Management of Technology: Collaborative Strategies for American Technology Industries" (Ph.D. diss., MIT Department of Political Science, 2000).

Edward B. Roberts is a professor of management of technology at the MIT Sloan School of Management. Wenyun Kathy Liu is an associate at Salomon Smith Barney in New York. Contac them at eroberts@mit.edu and wyliu@alum.mit.edu

Reprint 4312

reading 3   The Silent Killers of Strategy Implementation and Learning

Six silent killers of strategy implementation exist in most companies, but too many managers avoid confronting them. Leaders need to face these killers if they and their organizations are to learn and succeed.

Doctors call high cholesterol a "silent killer" because it blocks arteries with no outward symptoms. Companies, too, have silent killers working below the surface—mutually reinforcing barriers that block strategy implementation and organizational learning. The silent killers can overcome, but first leaders must engage people throughout their organizations in an honest conversation about the barriers and their underlying causes.

Companies have long known that, to be competitive, they must develop a good strategy and then appropriately realign structure, systems, leadership behavior, human resource policies, culture, values and management processes.[1] Easier said than done. Between the ideal of strategic alignment and the reality of implementation lie many difficulties.

For one think, senior managers get lulled into believing that a well-conceived strategy communicated to the organization equals implementation. For another, they approach change in a narrow, nonsystemic and programmatic manner that does not address root causes.

We began our research on strategy implementation when CEO Ray Gilmartin and chief strategy officer Ralph Biggadike of Becton Dickinson recognized that perfectly sound strategies were not easily implemented.[2] Nowhere was the challenge more evident than in their global strategy. As is often the case, good intentions embodied in a new structure were not sufficient to change behavior.[3] Teams created to enact strategies across several geographic regions couldn't seem to coordinate their research and development, manufacturing and marketing. A worldwide educational program created to demonstrate how the global organization should work failed to overcome barriers.[4] At the business-unit level, too, the lack of cross-functional systems blocked strategy implementation. Like other companies we know, Becton Dickinson bought in to the structures consultants recommended, but a gap appeared between knowing what to do and actually doing it.[5]

For a decade, we have conducted research focused on understanding the root causes of the difficulties that Becton Dickinson and other s encounter when responding to shifts in competitive strategy. Using an inquiry and action-learning method we call "Organizational Fitness Profiling (OFP)," we enlist a team of senior managers to serve as our co-investigators. The process provides a window for understanding deeply rooted barriers that are common to an array of companies. (See "Organizational Fitness Profiling.")[6]

The method starts with the top team of the business unit or corporation defining its strategy. Team members then commission a task force of either lower-level managers to collect data about perceived strengths as well as barriers to implementing the strategy. After the task force completes training, it interviews 100 people two or three levels below the top team—and some internal or external customers. In a three-day meeting, the managers and the researchers receive feedback from the task force, diagnose the root causes of the problems and identify and develop a plan to change the organization.

Of the profiles we conducted in 12 companies (consisting of more than 150 different units), we examined 12 profiles in depth from 4 companies—10 for business units and 2 for corporate entities. We facilitated each process from beginning to end and thus were able to obtain a deep understanding of the underlying organizational challenges the business faced.

OBVIOUS STRENGTHS, HIDDEN BARRIERS

What were the strengths in the companies in our sample? Feedback to the top team nearly always included "We have great people." Also, in many organizations, a function such as R&D or manufacturing was perceived as a strength.

ORGANIZATIONAL FITNESS PROFILING

A Way to Unearth the Root Causes of Strategy Blockers Step by Step

Organizational Fitness Profiling (OFP) is both an intervention method and a research approach. It unfolds over a series of meetings intended to promote an open and fact-based dialogue within the senior management team of an organizational unit, as well as between the top team and lower organizational levels. The process involves five steps.

1. **Create a statement about direction.** The senior management team develops a concise statement of strategic and organizational direction that articulates the links among the competitive environment, performance goals, business strategy and needed organizational and cultural changes. The statement will be used to communicate the strategy to the broader organization and to explain the logic behind it—and as a stimulus to collecting organizational information on barriers to implementation.

2. **Collect data on barriers and strengths.** A task force composed of a cross-section of well-regarded mangers, one or two levels below the top team, is appointed to conduct open-ended interviews inside and outside the organization about specific management practices and organizational arrangements that help or hinder the implementation of strategy. The task force selects the sample of individuals interviewed. The outside researchers conduct interviews with members of top management about their own views of barriers to strategy implementation and about their effectiveness as a team. The task force meets together to analyze the information collected from the interviews and identifies major themes.

3. **Develop an integrated plan for change.** In an intensive, three-day feedback and planning meeting, the top team receives a thorough and candid account from the task force on how the organization is functioning. Then, using a comprehensive analytic framework, the top team analyzes the underlying causes of the barriers to implementation and develops a broad vision for redesigning the organization. The team typically refines its own role, responsibilities, meetings and decision-making process. Senior managers also develop an implementation plan which integrates previous initiatives and adds supplements, if necessary. Work focuses on projects that directly improve business performance and that develop broader organizational capabilities, such as improved coordination, managerial competence and employee commitment. Projects are typically conducted by cross-functional teams and are periodically reviewed by the senior management team.

4. **Refine the plan.** The top team reviews and refines the proposed plan with the employee task force. The meeting serves as a reality check on the adequacy of the senior managements team's plan. It also furthers the development of a cross-level partnership for better managing strategy implementation and learning.

5. **Implement the plan.** Members of the task force are often asked to play leadership roles in implementing the plan. The overall process is championed as well as periodically reviewed by the senior team as a whole, and the task-force data-collection process is repeated, typically every year or two.

What were the barriers? The six silent killers listed below were most often mentioned, although structure, systems, management processes and human resource policies were sometimes identified.[7]

- Top-down or laissez-faire senior management style (9 of 12 cases)
- Unclear strategy and conflicting priorities (9 of 12 cases)
- An ineffective senior management team (12 of 12 cases)
- Poor vertical communication (10 of 12 cases)
- Poor coordination across functions, businesses or borders (9 of 12 cases)
- Inadequate down-the-line leadership skills and development (8 of 12 cases)

Employees saw the overall problem rooted in fundamental management issues of leadership, teamwork and strategic direction, not in the commitment of people or their functional competence. Successful implementation needs more than a leader,; it requires teamwork from a leadership group that, through dialogue and collaboration, stays connected to the knowledge embedded in lower levels.[8] The six barriers are silent killers because they are rarely publicly acknowledged or explicitly addressed. In fact, the core barrier, called "poor vertical communication," not only hinders strategy implementation, it also prevents discussion of the barriers themselves. The case of Santa Rosa Systems Division (SRSD), formerly of Hewlett Packard (HP) and now part of Agilent Technologies, illustrates the silent killers at work.[9]

SRSD was formed in 1992 from 14 product lines that came from five different divisions in HP's test-and-measurement organization. Its charter was to establish, in new and emerging markets, a beachhead for complex electronic systems capable of measuring and testing high frequencies emitted by equipment employed in communications, semiconductor manufacturing, aerospace and defense.

HP had competed successfully in the general-purpose instrument business, but customizing systems was a new enterprise. By 1994, general manager Scott Wright and his staff were experiencing difficulties implementing the strategy. Growth and profits lagged projections, and morale among employees was at an all-time low.

The performance gaps at SRSD were due, not just to a difficult competitive environment, but also to choices that Wright and the other leaders made about how they organized and managed SRSD, including how they operated as a team. They and others in the organization brought with them a no-longer-valid set of assumptions, values and skills formed in HP's traditional business. That business was built around standardized products—differentiated from competitors' by technical excellence, developed over a long cycle and sold to engineers. In contrast, success at SRSD involved speed, expensive integrated systems and customers who were often not engineers. The former HP managers were accustomed to the R&D function being the most powerful—with marketing, manufacturing and interfunctional cooperation of minor importance. In contrast, success at SRSD demanded interfunctional coordination and a greater voice for marketing and the manufacturing engineers who tailored systems to individual customers. An order no longer meant shipping a box. Cross-functional teamwork was required to customize and install systems on customers' sites.

Adding to the challenge was a strategic and resource-allocation trade-off unique to the systems business: whether to focus on building revenues through one-shot custom systems or to focus on developing standard systems platforms. The R&D function, headed by John Vink, had responsibility for long-term systems-platform development. It was up to the custom-systems group, located in Sam Scott's manufacturing group, to respond to current and highly variable customer requests for tailored systems. Custom-systems engineers, who managed to create a vibrant custom-systems business in just two years, also were expected to support long-term R&D: R&D engineers were needed to support the custom-systems business. Therein "lay the rub."

A cold war developed between the two groups. Competition for resources also appeared from the marketing function. Wright and his top team set up three cross functional teams to coordinated product and strategy development in three distinct product lines, but R&D section managers were assigned to run all three teams. Custom-systems engineers skipped meetings, complaining that no one paid attention to their business. Meanwhile R&D protested the custom-systems group's unwillingness to help develop new platforms. And the marketing group saw its resources dwindling in the struggle to serve both short- and long-term strategies. The approach that Wright and his team adopted to manage SRSD did not fit the competitive task at hand. The mismatch resulted in an organization plagued by the silent killers.

THE SILENT KILLERS

Silent killer one: top-down or laissez-faire senior management style. Aspects of Wright's leadership style exacerbated the tensions at SRSD. The aspects included a discomfort with conflict, frequent absences to manage an acquisition and use of the top team for administrative matters rather than focused strategic discussions. In addition, as one SRSD manager explained, "Scott is a very perceptive and intelligent manager. But he is also very opinionated. Whenever we sit down to discuss strategic issues, I have this nagging feeling that Scott's decision concerning that matter has already been prewired. Chances are that he has already had a closed-door meeting with one of the other functional managers to make the decision." Development of the necessary coordination to implement SRSD's strategy suffered; so did development of lower-level managers.

Silent killers two and five: conflicting priorities and the resulting poor coordination. Those barriers went hand in hand. As one employee explained, "We have two competing strategies that are battling each other for the same resources. The resulting factions around these two strategies are tearing this organization apart."

Silent killer three: ineffective senior management team. According to another manager, "The members of the top team operate within their own silos. They are like a group of fiefdoms that refuse to cooperate effectively for fear that they will lose power."

Silent killer four: poor vertical communication. As individuals, employees recognized the problems, but they feared the senior managers were not open to candid discussion. Employees suspected that the top team preferred to avoid potentially threatening and embarrassing issues and that people at lower levels would do better keeping their observations to themselves. Cynicism grew.

Silent killer six: inadequate down-the-line leadership skills and development. Lower-level managers were not developing skills through newly created opportunities to lead change, nor were they supported through leadership coaching or training. The situation cried out for open engagement with root causes.

HOW THE SIX BARRIERS INTERACT TO BLOCK STRATEGY IMPLEMENTATION AND LEARNING

Individually, the six barriers are troubling. Taken together, they created a vicious circle from which it is difficult to escape. To explain their interaction, we group them into three categories: quality of direction, quality of learning and quality of implementation. (See "How the Six Strategy Killers Interact.")

Quality of Direction

An ineffective top team, top-down or laissez-faire senior-management approach and unclear strategy are all related. The CEOs and general managers we observed often bypassed members of their senior team, getting information from and giving orders to those at lower levels—a surefire way to keep the leadership group from becoming an effective team. Laissez-faire managers, on the other hand, under-mined the team's potential by avoiding discussions that could cause conflicts or by not holding their subordinates accountable for coordinated decision making. It's a red flag if a leader manages members of the top team on a one-to-one basis and limits group discussions to nonthreatening administrative matters.

exhibit 1 How the Six Strategy Killers Interact

Three killers relate to ineffective leadership at the top, two to implementation. The sixth suggest that leaders and implementers are neither talking honestly about problems nor learning.

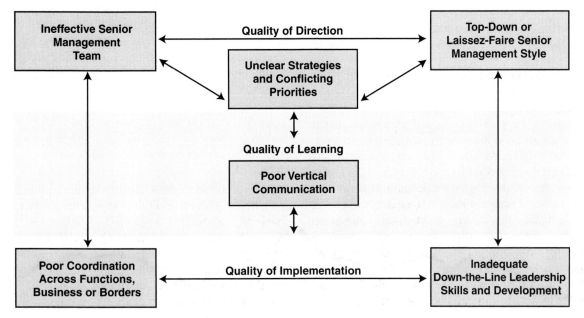

At SRSD, when members of the top team thought that important decisions had been made in a prior one-on-one with Wright, they were less motivated to address difficult but strategically important issues in the group. Wright admitted working one-on-one out of fear that he would be unable to resolve the conflict that might arise if decisions were put to the whole team. That kind of pattern has been shown to reduce trust, effective strategy reformulation and, ultimately, business performance, particularly in uncertain and dynamic business environments.[10]

The lack of a clear and compelling statement of the strategic direction deprives many top management groups of a common rallying cry that might help them coalesce as a team. Conversely, a team of managers unwilling to subordinate their individual functional interests to the needs of the overall business will never be able to develop a clear statement of priorities.

Effective business strategies are about making choices; deciding what not to do is as important as discussing what to do. The functional heads that make up the top management group each stand to gain or lose by the choices that are made. An emphasis on decreasing the product cost may tip the balance of power toward manufacturing: an emphasis on innovation will move power toward R&D. Vice presidents of quality push for increases in product reliability; vice presidents of sales want to increase market share.

A desire to help one's own department is not always a matter of self-interest. At Apple Computer, for example, Jean Louis Gasse had a sincere belief that the company's future lay in high-end computers. It was really CEO John Scully's unwillingness to engage his top team in constructive conflict that let Gasse, in effect, block Apple from responding properly to its competitive environment.[11] At SRSD, manufacturing's Sam Scott certainly cared about helping SRSD survive. But some of his assumptions needed to be challenged, and general manager Wright's aversion to conflict meant they never were.

Many top teams hide their differences rather than confront hard trade-offs directly. Some develop vague statements of strategic purpose. One division we studied articulated its overall strategic objective as "fortifying our quality, product cost and market share strengths, while also transforming the industry through expanded customer knowledge and product/service innovation." How was the organization to get direction from that? The goals are blameless, but which one is most important—and why?

Quality of Learning

Blocked vertical communication has a particularly pernicious effort on a business's ability to implement and refine its strategy—in short, to learn. In many of the organizations we examined, strategic-planning documents went into great detail on long-term technology trends, customer buying behavior and the competitive environment, but they failed to communicate downward a coherent story showing why the changing world outside the organization demanded new ways of working together.[12] Employees never heard how the strategy affected priorities nor received any guidelines showing the relative priorities of projects. How could employees decide on a day-to-day basis which of their activities would be most helpful in making the business successful?

Lack of strategic consensus and clarity undermines effective upward communication, too. Employees, unsure of where the business is supposed to be going, cannot help get it there, nor can they warn those at higher levels when the engine is "skipping the track." A top-down management style is often the main barrier to honest upward communication and organizational learning.

Apple Computer is again illustrative. Until 1990, senior managers did not seriously consider opening up the computer architecture, licensing the operating system or shifting from a high-end technical strategy to a middle- or low-end customer-driven strategy. All that despite the fact that Microsoft's development of Windows was known to be under way as early as 1984, and the likely impact of Windows on the cost of computing was fairly evident. Apple's difficulty lay in developing an open dialogue. One manager recounted his own frustration: "For two and a half years I wanted to do low-cost Macintoshes. I was always yelled at by senior managers that this was wrong." Not surprisingly, a 1990 survey revealed that many Apple employees saw senior managers as unconnected to what was going on at lower levels.[13]

If those charged with implementation cannot tell senior managers about problems, a company has no early warning system. Only after programs fail can corrective action be taken. Even then, most corrective action focuses on program content, not the silent killers. New goals, resources, technical programs and staff will not solve the root problems. As the vicious circle persists, lower levels become cynical.

They come to realize that their inability to communicate openly and directly with the leadership team about its role in blocking strategy implementation makes it highly unlikely that problems will be corrected. Frustrated, they adopt a passive stance. Lost is the commitment of employees to do everything in their power to make the business a success.

At quite a few of the organizations we studied, the new opportunity to speak candidly to senior managers reinvigorated employees. Task forces described long, emotional interviews. In one organization, task force members were besieged by unsolicited requests to be interviewed. At Hewlett Packard's SRSD, the task force that Wright and his top team members asked for permission to break with their role as reporters and speak for themselves about the need for change. Emotional releases show how much is suppressed when the silent killers cannot be addressed openly.

Quality of Implementation

The three silent killers associated with senior management make it very difficult to develop needed coordination at lower levels or to develop needed down-the-line leadership capabilities. Middle managers from different functions, businesses or country organizations cannot be expected to collaborate effectively when their leaders are pushing them in competing directions. Middle managers are not going to risk rejection by their own bosses or peers. At SRSD, the tensions between Sam Scott, to whom the custom-systems group reported, and John Vink, head of R&D, trickled down until each group was sure the other had the wrong priorities.

Understanding the strategic direction helps resolve differences of perspective and liberates the organization to be purposeful and tenacious. Lower-level managers are better able to exercise independent judgment if they know where the business is going and why. Otherwise, if an unexpected event occurs, their only recourse is to follow the rules or ask the boss. And the boss might be as confused about the strategy as they are. If the general manager is the only one who has the whole picture, all major decisions must be made at the top. That leads to the sixth barrier, inadequate leadership development down the line.

Senior managers who exercise top-down management fail to provide the opportunity for leadership development. Yet those same managers are often surprised to find a shortage of people to run cross-functional programs. Senior managers point to the paucity of management talent and conclude that lower-level managers can't handle increased responsibility. Another vicious circle.

In one organization we know, senior managers were about to invest resources in a management-education and succession-planning program when they decided to use OFP to uncover why the company had had difficulty developing managers in the first place. A task force of uppermiddle managers found that the first five silent killers were causing the sixth. According to employees, the CEO and his direct reports were an ineffective team. They operated in separate fiefdoms, unwilling to give up their best people to meet the needs of other business units—even though such developmental experiences are widely accepted as one of the best ways for an organization to develop future managers.[14] People were afraid to discuss barriers with senior managers, who were thus prevented from learning what was blocking management development. Task-force feedback showed that the company needed more than new human-resource systems and management education; it needed to attack the silent killers.

SIX CAPABILITIES REQUIRED FOR SUSTAINABLE COMPETITIVE SUCCESS

Why are the silent killers so pervasive? Probably because they represent critical organizational stress points where new capabilities are required to successfully transition to higher levels of performance, speed and responsiveness.

We challenged the senior executives at Becton Dickinson to describe the kind of organization needed to succeed in today's environment of ever more aggressive competitors and a dizzying pace of technological change. They spoke in terms of a virtual company—adaptive, agile, connected with a spider web of information, in touch with the environment. They also likened the company to a trauma unit: excellent people who are working, planning, innovating and making fast decisions together. Other analogies included antigens (representing outside opportunities) and the human immune system (a system that can respond in many different ways).

These images suggested an organization in which those with the most relevant expertise and information would be able to come together rapidly, across levels and locations, in response to threats and opportunities. The executives pictured such individuals and groups as having the authority and resources to take action. As Ray Gilmartin, now CEO of Merck, suggested, "a hierarchy of ideas replaces the hierarchy of position." [15]

Companies can become fast and agile only if the six silent killers are met head-on and transformed into the six core capabilities:

A leadership style that embraces the paradox of top-down direction and upward influence. The general manager advocates direction but learns from the feedback of those down the line.

Clear strategy, clear priorities. The top team formulates the strategy as a group and spends significantly amounts of time discussing it with lower levels.

An effective top team, whose members possess a general-management orientation. Through constructive conflict, the team arrives at a common voice and creates and maintains the organizational context needed to implement the strategy.

Open vertical communication. The top team and lower levels are engaged in an open dialogue about the organization's effectiveness.

Effective coordination. Effective teamwork integrates activities around customers, products or markets across diverse functions, localities and businesses.

Down-the-line leadership. Mid-level managers with the potential to develop leadership skills and a general-management perspective are given clear accountability and authority.

To develop such capabilities, hierarchical organizations must be managed in a nonauthoritarian manner.

Managers must use their authority both to set direction and to delegate authority to clearly accountable teams.[16] The dual approach requires lots of open communication about difficulties, including difficulties traceable to those in authority.[17]

SRSD struggled with, and ultimately succeeded in, managing the tension between the functional hierarchy that had worked so well in HP's traditional instrument business and the cross-functional business teams they created to develop and implement strategy.

Wright and the senior management team had a far more important role than oversight of details.

They needed to clarify the strategy and create an organization that would enable resource-allocation decisions to be made within cross-functional business teams close to the action. They, not the senior team, would decide how much focus to place on building current revenues through one-off custom systems vs. building future revenues through standard-systems-platform development. And given the dynamism of the systems business, good vertical communication between the business teams and Wright's senior team would enable the senior team to be abreast of progress and allocate resources between business teams accordingly.

WHAT CAN BE DONE?

We have observed three distinct responses to the silent killer—avoidance, managerial replacement and engagement. Although each response may prove successful in some circumstances, direct engagement of the barriers has the best chance of building long-term competitive capabilities.

Avoidance

It is not surprising that most CEOs and their senior management teams avoid engagement. Insecure managers are apt to view open discussion of the silent killers as a challenge to their authority. And whatever they are worried about hearing, down-the-line managers are worried about telling. What if the CEO acts threatened, embarrassed or defensive? Confrontation can be scary.

Using consultants is a popular way to avoid honest engagement. Consulting is a multibillion-dollar industry and growing, and our research suggests that a reason for the boom is tacit collusion between consultants and top management to avoid engaging the silent killers.[18]

One of our research sites was a highly regarded technology company we will call "Chipco." The CEO believed that the flagging pace of Chipco's product development (its key to success) was the reason that growth was beginning to plateau. Although he could see that a "silo mentality" was sabotaging cross-functional teamwork—particularly between marketing and the powerful R&D department—he did not address that problem directly. Instead, he called a consulting firm.

The consultants recommended a system that would be driven by cross-functional product-development teams and overseen by a committee of functional heads from R&D, manufacturing, marketing and finance.

After extensive interviews, discussions and education, Chipco charged ahead with the plan.

Two years later Chipco turned to OFP. The unsurprising discovery: Everyone thought that although the consultants' system had the potential to speed product development, the potential was undermined by the functional silos. In particular, the mighty R&D function undermined the marketing department.

Although the consultants' system called for a cross-functional review of all new projects for both technical and marketing viability, the review committee had difficulty saying no to anything the powerful R&D director supported. As a result, too many projects were chasing too few resources. Moreover, marketing's weakness was undermining new-product launches.

The leaders for approved projects expressed frustration that functional heads assigned people to the team who were "B" players or already overcommitted. Leaders complained that team members often skipped meetings because of functional responsibilities.

Team members (particularly from R&D), who functional heads were not ceding authority, had difficulty committing their departments to work on projects. Team leaders had to go directly to those functional heads.

Why did the consultants' new product-development system, with all its great potential, go astray? The answer: management by avoidance. Consultant- or staff-group-driven change efforts are successful mainly at helping managers avoid what cannot be avoided: the silent killers of strategy implementation.

Certainly, confrontation is scary. Chipco's CEO was loath to confront the powerful R&D vice president and the company's deeply engrained functional mindset. Although it is a normal human tendency to shrink from confronting one's own deficiencies, leaders do so at the peril of their business.

Consultants and staff groups have numerous incentives to maintain senior managers' dependence on them for change programs. But in failing to address root causes of problems, consultants and staff groups prevent organizations and managers from learning how to learn.

Managerial Replacement

When attempts to bypass the silent killers fail, the likelihood that the CEO or general manager will be replaced increases.[19] Managerial replacement can be an effective process for addressing the silent killers. New general managers are not directly implicated in the problems of the old regime and find it easier to surface hidden issues. Their mental models and relationships with key managers are not constrained by the past. They can—and often do—replace other managers and initiate a new direction.[20]

At first, the organization may be open to such change, but without ongoing identification and discussion of the silent killers, the honeymoon will end. The new leader will become closely identified with the new business direction and organizational arrangement, which in turn will run into difficulties as the business environment changes. Once again, employees at lower levels will be fearful of identifying the silent killers. If the new general manager's approach is to replace staff rather than engage in open discussion, senior and lower-level managers who want to speak up may worry that they will be shown the door. As upward communication falters, the organization's ability to self-correct will deteriorate. So although replacing the CEO can be an effective way of addressing the silent killers in the short term, it will not build the embedded organizational capabilities that prevent the barriers from recurring. Other costs include damage to morale and the loss of the manager's business-specific knowledge, experience and longstanding relationships.

Engagement

Our research points to engagement as the best alternative to avoidance and replacement of managers. If senior teams and lower-level staff together confront the silent killers and build up the organizational capabilities that are the barriers' opposites, companies can achieve sustainable competitive advantage.

Because the silent-killer syndrome represents deeply ingrained behavior, the cure necessitates large numbers of people acting in very different ways. Anyone who has tried to address unproductive but long-practices behaviors among family members or friends knows that behavioral change does not occur in a simple and linear manner. Progress requires all parties to engage in surfacing and discussing unproductive behaviors and to reflect and learn from their collective efforts to change.[21] Leaders must direct a learning process from which they also learn. Fortunately, for each silent killer there is an action principle that directly addresses the dysfunctional behavior and builds a corresponding organizational strength. (See "Attacking the Six Barriers to Strategy Implementation.")

THE PRINCIPLES OF EFFECTIVE MANAGEMENT

Effective leaders of organizational change intuitively follow the necessary action principles. Unfortunately, there's a shortage of such people.[22] And even if organizations have a natural leader, they lose the capabilities when the leader leaves. When new barriers arise, organizations will not have learned how to confront the strategy-blocking killers on their own. A disciplined and institutionalized learning process is required.

One of the few comprehensive organizational learning tools is General Electric's (GE) WorkOut process. Jack Welch used it to build organizational capabilities, and he fully expects it to be self-sustaining when he retires. OFP, with its strategic and systemic focus, offers another good way to attack silent killers.

Managers may find it helpful to observe how Scott Wright used profiling at Hewlett Packard's SRSD to tackle the six silent killers and turn them into capabilities.[23]

Principle 1: Turn Top-Down or Laissez-Faire Management Style Into Engaged Leadership

Wright and his senior team decided to use profiling after recognizing that the strategy was not being implemented and that morale was low. The cross-functional task force they appointed reported back on conflicts between functions and the widespread belief that decisions were being made off-line.

After receiving the feedback, Wright moved beyond his accustomed avoidance of conflict to directly engage his top team in frank discussions about the division's strategic and organizational problems. He had made a visible commitment to seeking the unvarnished truth, and the task force gave him a rich and comprehensive report that was difficult to ignore.

"I had known that there were some serious issues in the division that needed to be addressed," Wright said. "But when these problems were spelled out in detail to me and my staff by a group of employees, the situation took on a whole new light. Some of the

table 1   Attacking the Six Barriers to Strategy Implementation

Change starts with the leader

The Silent Killers	Principles for Engaging the Silent Killers
Top-down or laissez-faire senior management style	With the top team and lower levels, the CEO/general manger creates a partnership built around the development of a compelling business direction, the creation of an enabling organizational context and the delegation of authority to clearly accountable individual and teams.
Unclear strategy and conflicting priorities	The top team as a group develops a statement of strategy, and priorities are developed which members are willing to stand behind.
An ineffective senior Management team	The top team, as a group, is involved in all steps in the change process so that its effectiveness is tested and developed.
Poor vertical communication	An honest, fact-based dialogue is established with lower levels about the new strategy and the barriers to implementing it.
Poor coordination across functions, businesses or borders	A set of business-wide initiatives and new organizational roles and responsibilities are defined that require "the right people to work together on the right things in the right way" to implement the strategy.
Inadequate down-the-line leadership skills and development	Lower-level managers develop skills through newly created opportunities to lead change and to drive key business initiatives. They are supported with just-in-time coaching, training and targeted recruitment. Those who still are not able to make the grade must be replaced.

taskforce feedback directed at me and my staff was pretty hard to swallow. Frankly, I am not sure I would have taken it as seriously as I did if those remarks had been coming from a group of outside consultants."

Partnership with lower levels was solidified after Wright and his team asked the task force to evaluate the change plan the top team developed. After caucusing alone, the task force returned with some candid criticism. Wright experienced that feedback as the worst day in his HP career. But he made an important and courageous decision; he asked task force members to participate with senior team members in developing and evaluating alternatives. The result was an improved change plan that had the commitment of both the top team and the task force.

Many managers approach strategic change with the assumption that employees are barriers. Our research suggests the opposite; when properly involved, they become true partners.

Principle 2: Turn Unclear Strategy and Conflicting Priorities Into a Clear and Compelling Business Direction

To launch change at SRSD, Wright and his top team met off-site to discuss their own understanding of the strategy and to agree on a statement they could present to the organization. It was then that Wright learned that his views about the strategy—and the business teams created to enact it—were not shared. The top team had avoided strategic issues and the conflict inherent in them, so it had failed to develop agreement on priorities to guide resource allocation.[24]

The members of the top team were asked to write the strategy concisely and to develop and explanation about why it was important to achieve it. Later, when task-force members conducted interviews, they began with that story. SRSD employees said it was the first time they had been told about the strategy; many disagreed with aspects of it. Their feedback was vital in helping the top team clarify and refine the strategy.

Principle 3: Turn an Ineffective Senior Management Team Into an Effective One

With Wright and his senior team involved in every step of the change—including strategy development, organizational diagnosis, action planning, communicating the change and monitoring it—they had to work together.

They also underwent interviews with the authors. Our feedback, added to that of the task force, led to deep, searching team discussions of Wright's decision-making style, his aversion to conflict and his tolerance of the cold war between R&D and manufacturing/custom systems. At a critical moment, Sam Scott, the head of manufacturing, admitted: "I didn't know the problems I was causing." The sincerity of his tone startled everyone, and the trust needed for an open dialogue was created. The senior managers ended up completely redesigning the way they would work together.

Nevertheless, change takes time. As one task force member observed two years after the profile, "Our top team has taken some big strides in becoming more effective. Scott (Wright) looks to be taking more control of the reins and becoming the kind of leader the division needs. He and his staff will sit down as a group now and talk strategy, where before they would have only talked about administrative detail. But they are still not where they want to be as a team. They still seem to be having a tough time getting together and really coming to agreement over some tough and pressing issues. I think people in SRSD wanted an overnight change in the top team's behavior. But, realistically, most good teams are not made in a day."

There are no quick fixes. OFP is often a painful process, but after managers reveal the six silent killers, most are determined to take action.

Principle 4: Turn Poor Vertical Communication Into an Open Fact-Based Dialogue

Task force members at SRSD were energized by their charge to find the "unvarnished truth." Then top-team members refrained from defensiveness or retribution, trust and commitment revived throughout the organization.

As one member of the top team member recalls, "The task force feedback really served several important roles. Not only did it function as a powerful tool to communicate difficult issues, but it also showed that the top team cared about what the employees thought and that we could not institute a change process without asking for their input. Also, I believe, by asking for their 'unvarnished' opinions, the employees realized just how serious we were about improving SRSD's effectiveness. To Scott

(Wright)'s credit, he probably took the most amount of risk in initiating a process like this. He acted as a linchpin, and without his involvement, a process like this would have been spinning its wheels."

Truthful employee feedback relevant to strategy and business performance can give managers the needed push to manage change through open engagement.

Principle 5: Turn Poor Coordination Into Teamwork Through Realigning Roles, Responsibilities and Accountabilities With Strategy

Following feedback from the task force, Wright and his team engaged in a root-cause diagnosis. They concluded that many of their problems had their origins in the mismatch between HP's traditional approach to organizing and managing its instrument businesses and the demands of their current business. Over a two-day period, Wright and his team redesigned their organization. They chose to shift from functional silos overlaid with weak teams to a structure featuring strong cross-functional business teams accountable for profitability. The new matrix structure was quite alien to HP's tradition of organizing businesses into autonomous divisions, but SRSD needed an organization that fit its strategy.

One year later, a production manager commented, "What was really important was that we really understood what the process was trying to do—that is, align the different parts of the organization. I think that the alignment we now have after the reorganization is both accurate and necessary for us to become an effective organization. In the small systems business that we have, there is now way of getting around the matrix structure. In the past, there was no clear level of top-management responsibility and owner-ship for key decision making."

Principle 6: Turn Inadequate Down-the-Line Leadership Skills Into Strong Leadership With a General-Management Perspective

Increasingly the implementation of strategy requires more managers at lower levels who can lead teams that coordinate key strategic initiatives across functions, business units or geographic borders. The process SRSD followed enhanced leadership development. The task force produced eight people who had worked closely with the top team—a significant management-development experience that changed their own perspective and the perspective of the senior team about employee capabilities. A member of the top team remarked, "The work that the employee task force did was extremely impressive. They operated much like a professional consulting firm except, unlike consultants, they were a part of the organization and knew it inside and out. I think they worked so well together because they believed in what they were doing."

With increased confidence in lower-level managers, senior managers became more willing to delegate authority to them as members of business teams. Those teams, in turn, provided additional opportunities to develop down-the-line leadership skills and a general-management perspective.

CAN THE SILENT KILLERS BE OVERCOME?

The evidence from our research indicates that, when a top team follows the six principles for overcoming the silent killers, it has a good chance of developing an organization capable of both strategy implementation and learning. Ned Barnholdt—now CEO of HP's spinoff Agilent Technologies and formerly the HP executive with oversight responsibility for SRSD—praised SRSD's change efforts. "They have done a terrific job after a year or so of struggling to figure out what the business was and how to get it going. Today I see them as one of our star divisions. Compared to other divisions, it's probably the most dramatic improvement. Now they are one of the top divisions in terms of growth and profitability and return on assets, as well as customer satisfaction. Today SRSD represents best practices in a lot of areas. They have really turned weaknesses into strengths. This is not to say they don't have issues. They need to work on resource planning and being able to schedule resources and live up to commitments. But even in that area, they are doing better than our other division."

Can all organizations overcome the silent killers? Our research suggests not. Certain conditions and values must come together to motivate a manager to productively engage the barriers. There must be a compelling business need. The CEO must have some faith that building organizational capabilities is key to a high level of performance. He or she must be willing to learn and must believe in partnering with employees. It is easier for recently appointed CEOs or general managers to confront the root causes of blocked strategy implementation in their new organizations because they have fewer reasons to worry that they will be personally implicated. But when general managers of longer tenure, such as Scott Wright, summon the courage to directly confront the silent killers, their world view as well as their leadership style is likely to change. Wright gained a paradoxical and valuable insight: being vulnerable can be a source of strength and influence.

Additional Resources

Resources not mentioned in the footnotes but useful for interested readers include the 1996 book "Organizational Learning II: Theory, Method and Practice," by C. Argyris and D.A. Schon. An article in the November-December 1990 *Harvard Business Review*, "Why Change Programs Don't Produce Change," by M. Beer, R.A. Eisenstat and B. Spector, describes the fallacy of programmatic change and makes an argument for a deeper look at barriers. A spring 1995 *California Management Review* article by D. Hambrich, "Fragmentation and the Other Problems CEOs Have with Their Top Teams," relates directly to our own findings. K. Eisenhardt, K.M. Kahwajy and L.J. Bourgeois in "How Management Teams Can Have a Good Fight" in the July-August 1999 *Harvard Business Review* discuss problems of top teams and what to do about them. L. Hirschhorn and T. Gilmore's "The New Boundaries of the Boundaryless Company" in the May-June 1992 *Harvard Business Review* addresses the deeper issues that must be confronted when organizations transform into team-based, flexible organizations.

References

1 M. Beer, "Organization Change and Development" (Santa Monica, California: Goodyear Publishing, 1980); and N. Venkatraman and J.C. Camillus, "Exploring the Concept of 'Fit' in Strategic Management," *The Academy of Management Review*, Mississippi State, 9(July 1984): 513-526.

2 M. Beer and A. Williamson, "Becton Dickinson (A): Corporate Strategy and Culture," Harvard Business School case no. 9-491-151 (Boston: Harvard Business School Publishing Corporation, 1991).

3 M. Beer, R. Eisenstat and B. Spector, "The Critical Path to Corporate Revewal" (Boston: Harvard Business School Press, 1990); G. Hall, J. Rosenthal and J. Wade, "How to Make Reengineering Really Work," Harvard Business Review 71 (November-December 1993): 19; and R.H. Schaffer, "The Breakthrough Strategy: Using Short-Term Success To Build the High Performance Organization" (New York: Harper Business, 1990)

4 R. Biggadike, "Research in Managing the Multinational Company: A Practitioner's Experiences," in "Managing the Global Firm," needs. C. Bartlett, Y. Doz and G. Hedlund (London: Routledge, 1991)

5 J. Pfeffer and R.I. Sutton, "The Knowing Kdoing Gap" (Boston: Harvard Business School Press, 2000)

6 M. Beer and R.A. Eisenstat, "Developing an Organization Capable of Strategy Implementation and Learning," *Human Relations* (May 1996): 597-619.

7 M. Beer and R.A. Eisenstat, "The Silent Killers: Overcoming Barriers to Organizational Fitness," working paper, Harvard Business School, Boston, Massachusetts, 1996.

8 D. Hambrich, "Fragmentation and the Other Problems CEOs Have With Their Top Teams," *California Management Review* 37, no. 3(Spring 1995): 110; and K. Eisenhardt, K.M. Kahwajy and L.J. Bourgeois, "How Management Teams Can Have a Good Fight." *Harvard Business Review* 75, no. 4 (July-August 1999): 77-85.

9 M. Beer and G. Rogers, Hewlett Packard's Santa Rosa Systems Division (A): "The Trials and Tribulations of a Legacy," Harvard Business School case no. 9-498-011 (Boston: Harvard Business School Publishing, July 19, 1999).

10 Ibid.;Eisenhardt et al., "How Management Teams Can Have a Good Fight" (1999); and P. Lawrence and J. Lorsch, "Organization and Environment" (Boston: Harvard Business School Press, 1967).

11 M. Beer and M. Gibbs, "Apple Computer: Corporate Strategy and Culture," abridged Harvard Business School case no. 9-495-0441 (Boston: Harvard Business School Publishing Corporation, 1990)

12 S.W. Floyd and B. Woolridge, "Managing Strategic Consensus: The Foundations of Effective Implementation," Academy of Management Executive (November 1992): 27-39.

13 Beer and Gibbs, "Apple Computer," 1990.

14 M.W. McCall, "The Lessons of Experience: How Successful Executives Develop on the Job" (Lexington, Massachusetts: Lexington Books, 1988); and M.W. McCall, "High Flyers: Developing the Next Generation of Leaders" (Boston: Harvard Business School Press, 1998)

15 M. Beer, R.A. Eisenstat and B. Spector, "The Critical Path to Corporate Renewal" (Boston: Harvard Business School Press, 1990)

16 Beer, Eisenstat and Spector, "The Critical Path to Corporate Renewal," 1990.

17 D. Dunphy, "Embracing Paradox: Top Down vs. Participative Management of Organizational Change" and W. Bennis, "The Leadership of Change," in "Breaking the Code of Change," needs. M. Beer and N. Nohria (Boston: Harvard Business School Press, in press).

18 C. Argyris, "Good Communication That Blocks Learning," *Harvard Business Review* 72 (July-August, 1994): 77-85; and E. Shapiro, R.E. Eccles and T.L. Soske, "Consulting: Has the Solution Become Part of the Problem?" *Sloan Management Review* 34 (Summer 1993): 89-95.

19 Carol Hymowitz, "How To Tell When A CEO Is Toast," *The Wall Street Journal*, April 18, 2000, p.B1.

20 J. Gabarro, "The Dynamics of Taking Charge" (Boston: Harvard Business School Press, 1987); and B. Virany, M. Tushman and E. Romanelli, "Executive Succession and Organizational Outcomes in Turbulent Environments" An Organizational Learning Approach," *Organizational Science* 3 (February 1, 1992): 72-91.

21 P. Senge, "The Fifth Discipline" (New York: Doubleday, 1990).

22 John Kotter's research has documented the shortage of leaders in corporations and his recent book documents the errors managers make in leading change. See J. Kotter, "A Force for Change" (New York: Free Press, 1990).

23 See M. Beer and G. Rogers, "Hewlett Packard's Santa Rosa Systems Division (A1)(A2) (A3)(A4) and (B3)," Harvard Business School Publishing, 1997).

24 H. Mintzberg, "The Rise and Fall of Strategic Planning: Reconceiving Roles for Planning, Plans, Planners" (New York: Free Press, 1994).

Reprint 4142

Michael Beer is a professor of business administration at the Harvard Business School and chairman of the Center for Organizational Fitness. Russell A. Eisenstat is president of the Center for Organizational Fitness and a senior organizational fellow at McKinsey & Co. Contact them at mbeer@hbs.edu and reisenstat@orgfitness.com

reading 4   Building Competitive Advantage Through People

Most managers today understand the strategic implications of the information-based, knowledge-driven, service-intensive economy. They know what the new game requires: speed, flexibility and continuous self-renewal. They even are recognizing that skilled and motivated people are central to the operations of any company that wished to flourish in the new age.

And yet, a decade of organizational delayering, destaffing, restructuring and reengineering has produced employees who are more exhausted than empowered, more cynical than self-renewing. Worse still, in many companies only marginal managerial attention—if that—is focused on the problems of employee capability and motivation. Somewhere between theory and practice, precious human capital is being misused, wasted or lost.

Having studied more than 20 companies in the process of trying to transform themselves, we have concluded that although structure is undoubtedly an impediment to the process, an even bigger barrier is managers' outdated understanding of strategy. (See "The Evolving Focus of Strategy.") At the heart of the problem is a failure to recognize that although the past three decades have brought dramatic changes in both external strategic imperatives and internal strategic resources, many companies to have outmoded strategic perspectives.

In the competitive-strategy model in which many of today's leaders were trained, sophisticated strategic-planning systems were supposed to help senior managers decide which business to grow and which to harvest.[1] Unfortunately, all the planning and investment were unable to stop the competition from imitating or leapfrogging their carefully developed product-market positions.

In the late 1980s, the search for more dynamic, adaptive and sustainable advantage lead many to supplement their analysis of external competition with an internal-competency assessment. They recognized that development of resources and capabilities would be more difficult to imitate: The core-competency perspective focused attention on the importance of knowledge creation and building learning processes for competitive advantage.[2] But this approach, too, faced limits as companies recognized that their people were not equal to the new knowledge-intensive tasks. By definition, competency-based strategies are dependent on people: Scarce knowledge and expertise drive new-product development, and personal relationships with key clients are at the core of flexible market responsiveness. In short, people are the key strategic resource, and strategy must be built on a human-resource foundation. As more and more companies come to that conclusion, competition for scarce human resources heats up.

THE ROLE OF THE EXECUTIVE IN THE "WAR FOR TALENT" ERA

Senior managers at most traditional companies have been left gasping for air at the breadth and rapidity of change during the past two decades. Hierarchy has to be replaced by networks, bureaucratic systems transformed into flexible processes, and control-based management roles must evolve into relationships featuring empowerment and coaching. In observing companies going through such change, we have come to the conclusion that as difficult as the strategic challenges may be, they are acted on faster than the organizational transformation needed to sustain them. And however hard it is to change the organization, it is even harder to change the orientation and mind-set of its senior managers. Hence today's managers are trying to implement third-generation strategies through second-generation organizations with first-generation management.

In an earlier study we analyzed the evolution of CEO Jack Welch's thinking at General Electric Co. and the simultaneous adjustment of his leadership role during the company's two-decade transformation.[3] In many ways, however, Welch is an exception: Very few top executives have been able to transform themselves from being analytically driven strategy directors to people-oriented strategy framers. Yet for a traditional company to make the transition into the New Economy, that transformation is vital. In our ongoing research, we have identified three important changes the CEO must make.

A Changing View of Strategic Resources

The hardest mind-set to alter is the longstanding, deeply embedded belief that capital is the critical strategic resource to be managed and that senior managers' key responsibilities should center around its acquisition, allocation and effective use.

For the vast majority of companies, that assumption simply is no longer true. Without denying the need for prudent use of financial resources, we believe that, for most companies today, capital is not the resource that constrains growth. Global capital markets have opened up the supply side, while widespread excess industry capacity has reduced the demand side. The recent reversals in some sectors notwithstanding, most companies are awash in capital. Of them, many cannot even generate sufficient high quality capital-budget projects to use the available resources—and therefore go on merger-and-acquisition expeditions.

The stock market is telling managers what the scarce strategic resource is. Then it values a mature, capital-intensive company like GE at 10 times its book value, it is seeing something of greater worth than the physical assets recorded in financial accounts. Though the dot-com bubble burst, the exuberant and often irrational funding of technology-savvy entrepreneurs pointed to the same lesson: There is a surplus of capital chasing a scarcity of talented people and the knowledge they possess. In today's economy, that is the constraining—and therefore strategic—resource.

The implications for top management are profound. First, human-resources issues must move up near the top of the agenda in discussions of the company's strategic priorities. That means that a first-class human-resources executive must be at the CEO's right hand. Eventually, traditional strategic-planning processes will need to be overhauled and the financially calibrated measurement and reward systems will have to be redesigned to recognize the strategic importance of human as well as financial resources.

A Changing View of Value   Recognizing that the company's scarce resource is knowledgeable

table 1   The Evolving Focus of Strategy

	Competition for Products and Markets	Competition for Resources and Competencies	Competition for Talent and Dreams
Strategic	Defensible product-market positions	Sustainable competitive advantage	Continuous self-renewal
Major Tools, Perspectives	• Industry analysis; competitor analysis • Market segmentation and positioning	• Core competencies • Resource-based strategy • Networked organization	• Vision and values • Flexibility and innovation • Front-line entrepreneurship and experimentation
Key Strategic Resource	Financial capital	Organizational capability	Human and intellectual capital

people means a shift in the whole concept of value management within the corporation.

In the early 1980s, competitive strategy was seen as a zero-sum game. Michael E. Porter, for example, saw the company surrounded by its suppliers, customers, competitors and substitutes, engaged in a battle with them to capture the maximum economic value possible.

The subsequent interest in building and leveraging unique internal capabilities caused a gradual shift in emphasis from value appropriation to value creation. As information and knowledge came to provide competitive advantage, the game shifted. Unlike capital, knowledge actually increases when shared, thus eliminating the zero-sum game. Clearly, the focus on value creation demands a different approach than a focus on value appropriation.[4]

One of the most basic issues is how the value that the company creates should be distributed. Most companies operated under the assumption that shareholders, as contributors of capital, have the primary claim. But recruiting difficulties that large traditional companies face, employees' eroding sense of loyalty and cynicism over the growing gap between the compensation of those at the top and those on the front lines all indicate that value distribution must change. The rapid spread of stock options as a form of compensation shows that companies have begun to recognize that the owners of the scarce resources are no longer only the shareholders but also the employees.

The implications are profound. Top management must begin renegotiating both implicit and explicit contracts with key stakeholders, particularly with employees. Unless those who contribute their human and intellectual capital are given the opportunity to enjoy the fruits of the value creation they are driving, they will go where they have that opportunity—typically to newer, less tradition-bound companies.

A Changing View of Senior Managers' Roles

Unlike capital, scarce knowledge and expertise cannot be accumulated at the top of the company and distributed to those projects or programs in which it will yield the greatest strategic advantage. It resides in the heads of individuals at all levels and is embedded in the relationships of work groups—those closest to the customers, the competitors and the technology. Therefore, rather than allocate capital to competing projects (the zero-sum game), senior managers must nurture individual expertise and initiative, then leverage it through cross-unit sharing (the positive-sum game).

Already we have seen downsizing of corporate planning departments, simplification of strategic-planning and capital-budgeting processes, and massive overhauls of corporate structures and processes—all in an effort both to shift initiative to those deep in the organization who posses valued expertise and to break down the barriers to effective sharing of that expertise.

But senior managers also must rethink their role in shaping strategic direction. Their main contribution has shifted from deciding the strategic content to framing the organizational context. That means creating a sense of purpose that not only provides an integrating framework for bottom-up strategic initiatives, but also injects meaning into individual effort. It means articulating company values that not only align organizational effort with the overall enterprise objectives, but also define a community to which individuals want to belong. And it means developing organizational processes that not only get work done effectively, but also ensure the empowerment, development and commitment of all members of the organization. The philosophical shift requires executives to expand beyond strategy, structure and systems to a simultaneous focus on the company's purpose, process and people.

IMPLICATIONS FOR HR PROFESSIONALS

In many companies the transition process is becoming an important proving ground for the human-resources function, with many old-school HR executives finding that neither their training nor their experience has prepared them for a leading strategic role. In the 1980s era of competitive-strategy analysis, their function was typically supportive and administrative. Once line managers had translated top management's strategic objectives into specific operational priorities, the role of HR staff was to ensure that recruitment, training, benefits administration and the like supported the well-defined strategic and operational agenda.

When strategic priorities became more organizationally focused in the 1990s, human-resources managers increasingly were included in the strategic conversation, often to help define and develop the company's core competencies—and almost always to align the organizational design and management skills to support those strategic assets.

Now, as companies move into the war for talent and as individuals with specialized knowledge, skills and expertise are recognized as the scarce strategic resource, HR professionals must become key players in the design, development and delivery of a company's strategy. (See "The Evolving Role of Human Resources.")

Unfortunately, many top-level human-resources managers view the new task through old lenses. They continue to treat employees as raw materials to be acquired and then made useful through training and development, or at best they acknowledge employees to be valuable assets on whom expenditures in the form of development and generous compensation are worthwhile investments. In response to the demands resulting from the growing importance of human capital, they develop more-aggressive approaches to recruitment, create more-innovative training programs, and experiment with more-sophisticated compensation packages. The problem is

twofold: They are tackling a strategic task with old, functional tools, and they are trying to bring about major systemic change with incremental, programmatic solutions. Human-resources managers must see employees as "talent investors," to be treated as partners and rewarded the way other investors are.

We have identified three core tasks that align the human resources function with the strategic challenge of developing the company's human capital for sustainable competitive advantage: building, linking and bonding.

The Building Challenge   Many companies claim that their people are their most important asset, but few have built the human resources systems, processes or cultures that can even offset, let alone challenge, the deeply embedded bias toward financial assets. For example, in almost any company, decisions relating to capital expenditures are subjected to well-documented capital-budgeting procedures. Typically, guidelines define approval levels (for example, division presidents may approve expenditures up to $1 million, the CEO up the $5 million, and the board above that level), require clear evaluation processes (for example, positive discounted-cash-flow returns above the weighted cost of capital) and set specific benchmarks (for example, payback on new equipment in three years).

When it comes to hiring a district sales manager or a shift foreman, however, decisions are routinely made by front-line managers who choose the best available among three or four marginal applicants to address a short-term difficulty. Yet that is at least a $2 million decision if one calculates recruiting costs, training costs and a discounted cash flow of the expected future stream of salary and benefits payments over the average tenure of such employees. But by recruiting a merely average individual, the company loses the opportunity to gain competitive advantage through a hiring decision. If the company were to make the decision strategic, it would have to set standards, monitor activities and measure recruiting outcomes in a way that made the decision as precise and rigorous as those guiding capital allocation.

Converting recruitment into a strategic task means making an ongoing commitment to locating and attracting the best of the best at every level and from every source. Microsoft Corp. is unusually thorough in its recruitment process, annually scanning the entire pool of 25,000 U.S. computer-science

table 2　The Evolving Role of Human Resources

	Competition for Products and Markets	Competition for Resources and Competencies	Competition for Talent and Dreams
Perspective on Employees	People viewed as factors of production	People viewed as valuable resources	People viewed as "talent investors"
HR's Role in Strategy	Implementation, support	Contributory	Central
Key HR Activity	Administering of recruitment, training and benefits	Aligning resources and capabilities to achieve strategic intent	Building human capital as a core source of competitive advantage

graduates in order to identify the 8,000 in whom it has an interest. After further screening, it targets 2,6000 for on-campus interviews and invites just 800 of those to visit the company's Redmond, Washington, headquarters. Of them, 500 receive offers, and 400—the top 2% of that year's graduates—typically accept. Yet that massive college-recruiting effort provides less than 20% of the company's new-people needs. To locate the rest, the company maintains a team of more than 300 recruiting experts whose full-time job is to locate the best and brightest in the industry. That strike force builds a relationship with literally thousands of the most capable systems designers, software engineers and program managers, often courting them for years. In the late 1990s, the effort resulted in more

than 2,000 of the most talented people in the industry joining Microsoft annually.

After a company has acquired top talent, the building challenge also requires the human-resources function to lead company efforts in constantly developing those talented individuals. That requires more than traditional training programs provide. Today development must be embedded in the company's bloodstream, with all managers responsible for giving their team members ongoing feedback and coaching. That is something McKinsey does unusually well, which helps to explain why M.B.A.s worldwide are more likely to seek employment there than at any other employer. (See "One Company's Way of Valuing People.")

ONE COMPANY'S WAY OF VALUING PEOPLE

The global management-consulting firm McKinsey & Co. is an example of a company that truly values its employees, as it demonstrates through its commitment to their development. Although formal training plays an important role, by far the most critical development tools are intensive individual feedback and coaching.

Such activities absorb 15% to 20% of the average partner's time. Every consultant receives a formal performance review from his or her office's partner group twice a year, with the individual's designated development director offering detailed feedback, counseling and career advice. The input for that biannual review comes from reports prepared by

each of the client-engagement managers, senior-level consultants who are responsible for the day-to-day management of the team to which the individual belongs and who have supervised the individual's work. The engagement managers also provide the consultant with feedback, evaluation and development advice after each of the four or five engagements that span a typical year's assignment. During each engagement, the consultant also has dozens of additional one-on-one feedback and coaching sessions with the more senior people managing and directing the project. In total, each consultant receives scores of specific, detailed coaching sessions per year. The company maintains that its in-depth approach to development is one of the main reasons why people join McKinsey—and why they stay.

There is one other aspect of building human capital that is grossly undermanaged at most companies. As any good gardener knows, to promote healthy growth, in addition to fertilizing and watering you also must prune and weed. That is a metaphor Jack Welch used often in describing the performance-ranking process he introduced to cull chronic underperformers at GE. Yet in most companies, the human-resources department focuses considerable effort on planting, staking, watering and fertilizing—and practically none on cutting out deadwood or growth-inhibiting underbrush.

Culling is no longer confined to hard-driving U.S. industrial companies. South Korea's LG, traditionally a cradle-to-grave employer, uses a "vitality index" as a critical performance measure. All managers have to rank their direct reports on a 1-to-5 scale (with 1 equal to the bottom 10% and 5 representing the top 10%). The vitality index is the ratio of new recruits who are ranked at 4 or 5 to employees of rank 1 or 2, who are counseled to move on.

The Linking Task Just as there is value in attracting and developing individuals who hold specialized knowledge, there is a value in the social networks that enable sharing of that knowledge. Indeed, unless a company actively links, leverages and embeds the pockets of individual-based knowledge and expertise, it risks underutilizing it or, worse, losing it. As companies seek the best ways to convert individual expertise into embedded intellectual capital, the classic response is to give the task to the chief information officer—along with the faddish title of chief knowledge officer.

Not surprisingly, people with information-systems background immediately focus on the task of mapping, modeling and codifying knowledge. Under their leadership, companies have developed databases, expert systems and intranets to help capture and make accessible the company's most valuable information. Yet in many companies, managers do not take full advantage of those elegant new knowledge-management systems.

At the heart of the problem is a widespread failure to recognize that although knowledge management can be supported by an efficient technical infrastructure, it is operated through a social network. Information technologists may help in organizing data and making it accessible, but they must be teamed up with—and operate in support of—those who understand human motivation and social interaction. Only then can individual roles and organizational processes be designed to ensure the delicate conversion from available information to embedded knowledge.

Thus, the second core strategic role of the top HR executive is to take the lead in developing the social networks that are vital to the capture and transfer of knowledge. Because that requires an understanding of organization design, process management, interpersonal relationships and trust-based culture, it calls for leadership from sophisticated human-resources professionals who also have a strong understanding of the business.

The most obvious challenge is to build on the process reengineering that most companies implemented during the 1990s to break down bureaucracy and unlock core competencies. The reengineered processes (whether at a micro level, as in order entry, or a macro level, as in new-product development) had two major objectives: breaking down hierarchical barriers to rapid decision making, and opening up new horizontal channels and forum for cross-unit communication and collaboration. Those activities are precisely what will link isolated individuals and organizational units into dynamic social networks.

In the early 1990s, British Petroleum built such networks under the leadership of John Browne, who at the time was overseeing the development of BP's prototype knowledge-management and organizational-learning program as head of BP Exploration. Transferring the approach to the whole company when he became CEO in 1995, Browne avoided installing a new set of information systems, focusing instead on a practice he described as "peer assists." The assist was a small-scale project that encouraged those on the front line in one business unit (operators on a drilling platform in the North Sea, for example) to contact other BP operations (offshore drillers in the Gulf of Mexico, for instance) that had the expertise to help solve particular problems. Cutting through formal layers and complex procedures, the process became an accepted way of doing business, and managers soon recognized that it was not acceptable to refuse a request for help.

The process was supplemented by "peer groups" of business units engaged in similar activities at similar stages of their life cycle (for example, all start-up oil fields, all mature oil fields or all declining-yield oil fields) and facing similar strategic and technical challenges. The idea was to create a way that managers of BP's newly decentralized operations could compare experiences and share ideas. In recent years "peer assist" has been expanded into "peer challenge," in which peers not only review one another's goals and business plans, but the best performers are formally made responsible for improving the performance of the worst performers.

In a third major element of the program, technology was introduced—but only as the transmission pipeline and storage system for ideas that were already flowing. Rejecting the notion of trying to capture and encode the company's knowledge, the virtual teams built networks to give those with problems access to those with expertise.

Although the initiative involved a major investment in hardware and software, including multimedia e-mail, document scanners, videoclip encoders, desktop videoconferencing and chat rooms with chalkboards, the IT function took responsibility only for installing the equipment. The project was driven by the Virtual Teamwork group and its subteams. About one-third of the Virtual Teamwork budget was allocated for coaches to help managers use the new tools to achieve their business objectives. In the end, it was the ability to change individual behavior and to shape group interaction using the powerful IT tools that allowed BP's process change to succeed.

BP has created processes and a supportive culture to link and leverage the expertise of individual employees, embedding knowledge within the organization. Its social networking is strategic because it drives innovation, responsiveness and flexibility yet is extremely difficult for competitors to imitate.

The Bonding Process   The third major strategic task HR must undertake is to help management develop the engaging, motivating and bonding culture necessary to attract and keep talented employees. In such a culture, the potential in competent individuals and fully functioning networks can be converted into engaged, committed action. Companies must reject the notion that loyalty among today's employees is dead and accept the challenge of creating an environment that will attract and energize people so that they commit to the organization. Such advice flies in the face of conventional wisdom, which maintains loyalty has been replaced by a free-agent talent market that requires companies to convert their long-term trust-based relationships

with employees to short-term contracts. Higher employee turnover, the use of temporary help and the expansion of outsourcing are all part of the envisioned future.

But if a company can outsource services or hire temporary expertise, so can its competitors. Such actions, therefore, are unlikely to lead to any competitive advantage. And if recruitment and retention are based primarily on the compensation package, the person lured by a big offer will almost certainly leave for a bigger one.

Consider SAS Institute, a billion-dollar software company based in Cary, North Carolina, which rejects the use of contract programmers and other outsourcing yet still attracts people to work without stock options and maintains turnover below 5%. How is that possible? CEO Jim Goodnight explains that what has consistently given his company a prominent place in Fortune's survey of the best U.S. companies to work for is not stock-option programs, which he calls Ponzi schemes, but rather, competitive salaries and generous bonuses based on the company's performance and the individual's contribution.

In an industry featuring high pressure and burnout as the norm, SAS Institute has created an island of common sense. Actions and decisions are based on four simple principles: to treat everyone equally and fairly to trust people to do a good job, to think long term and to practice bottom-up decision making. Then there are the hours. The software-industry joke may be generally apt (flex time means the company doesn't care which 15 hours you work each day), but company policy at SAS Institute is to work 35 hours per week. Exceptional benefits also reflect the value SAS puts on its people: There is a free, on-site medical facility for employees and family members, a subsidized on-site day-care facility, a gymnasium free to employees and their families, subsidized restaurants and cafes, and so on. That environment makes employees feel like valued members of a community, not replaceable gunslingers for hire. And for these self-selected individuals, that is reason enough to want to spend their career at SAS.

But the bonding process involves more than creating a sense of identity and belonging. It also must lead to an engaging and energizing feeling of commitment to the organization and its goals. But the visioning exercises and values cards many companies have developed in response to that need often fall short. The role of the HR professional is to get senior managers to move beyond hollow, slogan-driven communications, which are more likely to lead to detached cynicism than to engaged motivation, and to help them develop a clear personal commitment to an organizational purpose. Commitment implies a strongly held set of beliefs that not only are articulated in clear human terms, but also are reflected in managers' daily actions and decisions.

Henri Termeer, CEO of Genzyme, a biotechnology firm based in Cambridge, Massachusetts, regularly meets with people suffering from the diseases on which his researchers are working. He wants to feel angry about the pain and loss the disease is causing and passionate about the need to help. And he wants to transmit that passion to those working at Genzyme. Equally important, Termeer backs his words with actions. Because the company focuses on therapies for rare diseases, the cost of treatment is high. But the company refuses to let economics get in the way of its commitment to treat the afflicted and literally searches them out in Third World countries to provide free treatment. By acting on the company's beliefs, Termeer stirs the passion and engages the energy of Genzyme's employees.

The bonding process can succeed only when senior management realizes that the company is more than a mere economic entity; it is also a social institution through which people acting together can achieve meaningful purpose. In the war for talent, organizations are engaged in what one senior executive describes as "a competition for dreams."

THE HEART OF STRATEGY

The arrival of the information-based, knowledge-intensive, service-driven economy has forced massive change on companies worldwide, most dramatically in the way they must redefine their relationship with their employees. The shift in strategic imperatives over the past 25 years has necessitated new battle plans. The competition remains intense for strategic market positions and for scarce organizational resources and capabilities, but the war for talent has shifted the locus of the battle front. Today managers must compete not just for product markets or technical expertise, but for the hearts and minds of talented and capable people. And after persuading them to

join the enterprise, management also must ensure that those valuable individuals become engaged in the organization's ongoing learning processes and stay committed to the company's aspirations.

It was this recognition that led McKinsey's partners to reexamine their long-established mission "to serve clients superbly well." After much debate, the partners decided that the changes occurring in the world of business were significant enough for them to reconsider the core purpose of their firm. Now McKinsey has a dual mission: "to help our clients make distinctive, substantial and lasting improvements in their performance and to attract, develop, excite and retain exceptional people." McKinsey and other organizations making the change have found new meaning in the term competitive strategy as they compete for the hearts, minds and dreams of exceptional people.

References

1 For a review of such approaches, see C. Hofer and Dan Schendel, "Strategy Formulation: Analytical Concepts" (St. Paul, Minnesots: West Publishing, 1978), 69-100.

2 The core-competence model is elaborated in G. Hamel and C.K. Prahalad, "Competing for the Future" (Boston: Harvard Business School Press, 1994)

3 S. Ghoshal and C.A. Bartlett, "The Individualized Corporation" (New York: HarperCollins, 1997), 243-270. An overview of GE's transformation is also contained in our article "Rebuilding Behavioral Context: A Blueprint for Corporate Renewal," *Sloan Management Review* 34 (winter 1996): 11-23.

4 For a richer elaboration of that argument, see S. Ghoshal, C.A. Bartlett and P. Moran, "A New Manifesto for Management" in "Strategic Thinking for the Next Economy," ed. M.A. Cusumano and C.C. Markides (San Francisco: Jossey-Bass, 2001), 9-32.

Reprint 4323

Christopher A. Bartlett is a professor of business administration at Harvard Business School, and Sumantra Ghoshal is a professor of strategic leadership at London Business School. Contact them at cbartlett@hbs.edu and sghoshal@london.edu

reading 5   The Strategy Concept I: Five Ps for Strategy

Henry Mintzberg

Human nature insists on a definition for every concept. The field of strategic management cannot afford to rely on a single definition of strategy, indeed the word has long been used implicitly in different ways even if it has traditionally been defined formally in only one. Explicit recognition of multiple definitions can help practitioners and researchers alike to maneuver through this difficult field. Accordingly, this article presents five definitions of strategy—as plan, ploy, pattern, position, and perspective—and considers some of their interrelationships.

STRATEGY AS PLAN

To almost anyone you care to ask, strategy is a plan—some sort of consciously intended course of action, a guideline (or set of guidelines) to deal with a situation. A kid has a "strategy" to get over a fence, a corporation has one to capture a market. By this definition, strategies have two essential characteristics: they are made in advance of the actions to which they apply, and they are developed consciously and purposefully. (They may, in addition, be stated explicitly, sometimes in formal documents known as "plans," although it need not be taken here as a necessary condition for "strategy as plan.") To Drucker, strategy is "purposeful action"[1]; to Moore "design for action," in essence, "conception preceding action."[2] A host of definitions in a variety of fields reinforce this view. For example:

- in the military: Strategy is concerned with "draft[ing] the plan of war ... shap[ing] the individual campaigns and within these, decid[ing] on the individual engagements."[3]
- in Game Theory: Strategy is a "a complete plan: a plan which specifies what choices [the player] will make in every possible situation."[4]
- in management: "Strategy is a unified, comprehensive, and integrated plan ... designed to ensure that the basic objectives of the enterprise are achieved."[5]
- and in the dictionary: strategy is (among other things) "a plan, method, or series of maneuvers or stratagems for obtaining a specific goal or result."[6]

As plans, strategies may be general or they can be specific. There is one use of the word in the specific sense that should be identified here. As plan, a strategy can be a ploy, too, really just a specific "maneuver" intended to outwit an opponent or competitor. The kid may use the fence as a ploy to draw a bully into his yard, where his Doberman Pinscher awaits intruders. Likewise, a corporation may threaten to expand plant capacity to discourage a competitor from building a new plant. Here the real strategy (as plan, that is, the real intention) is the threat, not the expansion itself, and as such is a ploy.

In fact, there is a growing literature in the field of strategic management, as well as on the general process of bargaining, that views strategy in this way and so focusses attention on its most dynamic and competitive aspects. For example, in his popular book, Competitive Strategy, Porter devotes one chapter to "Market Signals" (including discussion of the effects of announcing moves, the use of "the fighting brand," and the use of threats of private antitrust suits) and another to "Competitive Moves" (including actions to preempt competitive response).[7] Likewise in his subsequent book, Competitive Advantage, there is a chapter on "Defensive Strategy" that discusses a variety of ploys for reducing the probability of competitor retaliation (or increasing his perception of your own).[8] And Schelling devotes much of his famous book, The Strategy of Conflict, to the topic of ploys to outwit rivals in a competitive or bargaining situation.[9]

STRATEGY AS PATTERN

But if strategies can be intended (whether as general plans or specific ploys), surely they can also be realized. In other words, defining strategy as a plan is not sufficient: we also need a definition that encompasses the resulting behavior. Thus a third definition is proposed: strategy is a pattern—specifically, a pattern in a stream of actions.[10] By this definition, when Picasso painted blue for a time, that was a strategy, just as was the behavior of the Ford Motor Company when Henry Ford offered his Model T only in black.

In other words, by this definition, strategy is consistency in behavior, whether or not intended.

This may sound like a strange definition for a word that has been so bound up with free will ("strategos" in Greek, the art of the army general[11]). But the fact of the matter is that while hardly anyone defines strategy in this way,[12] many people seem at one time or another to so use it. Consider this quotation from a business executive:

> Gradually the successful approaches merge into a pattern of action that becomes our strategy. We certainly don't have an overall strategy on this.[13]

This comment is inconsistent only if we restrict ourselves to one definition of strategy: what this man seems to be saying is that his firm has strategy as pattern, but not as plan. Or consider this comment in Business Week on a joint venture between General Motors and Toyota:

> The tentative Toyota deal may be most significant because it is another example of how GM's strategy boils down to doing a little bit of everything until the market decides where it is going.[14]

A journalist has inferred a pattern in the behavior of a corporation, and labelled it strategy.

The point is that every time a journalist imputes a strategy to a corporation or to a government, and every time a manager does the same thing to a competitor or even to the senior management of his own firm, they are implicitly defining strategy as pattern in action—that is, inferring consistency in behavior and labelling it strategy. They may, of course, go further and impute intention to that consistency—that is, assume there is a plan behind the pattern. But that is an assumption, which may prove false.

Thus, the definitions of strategy as plan and pattern can be quite independent of each other: plans may go unrealized, while patterns may appear without preconception. To paraphrase Hume, strategies may result from human actions but not human designs.[15] If we label the first definition intended strategy and the second realized strategy, as shown in Figure 1, then we can distinguish deliberate strategies, where intentions that existed previously were realized, from emergent strategies, where patterns developed in the absence of intentions, or despite them (which went unrealized).

Strategies About What? Labelling strategies as plans or patterns still begs one basic question: strategies about what? Many writers respond by discussing the deployment of resources (e.g., Chandler, in one of the best known definitions[16]), but the question remains: which resources and for what purposes? An army may plan to reduce the number of nails in its shoes, or a corporation may realize a pattern of marketing only products painted black, but these hardly meet the lofty label "strategy." Or do they?

As the word has been handed down from the military, "strategy" refers to the important things, "tactics" to the details (more formally, "tactics teaches the use of armed forces in the engagement, strategy the use of engagements for the object of the war"[17]). Nails in shoes, colors of cars: these are certainly details. The problem is that in retrospect details can

figure 1 Deliberate and Emergent Strategies

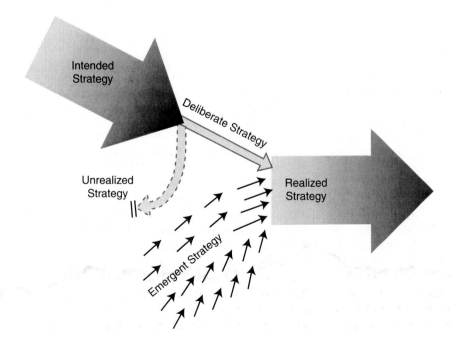

sometimes prove "strategic." Even in the military: "For want of a Nail, the Shoe was lost: for want of a Shoe the Horse was lost ..." and so on through the rider and general to the battle, "all for want of Care about a Horseshoe Nail."[18] Indeed one of the reasons Henry Ford lost his war with General Motors was that he refused to paint his cars anything but black.

Rumelt notes that "one person's strategies are another's tactics—that what is strategic depends on where you sit."[19] It also depends on when you sit: what seems tactical today may prove strategic tomorrow. The point is that these sorts of distinctions can be arbitrary and misleading, that labels should not be used to imply that some issues are inevitably more important than others. There are times when it pays to manage the details and let the strategies emerge for themselves. Thus there is good reason to drop the word "tactics" altogether and simply refer to issues as more or less "strategic," in other words, more or less "important" in some context, whether as intended before acting or as realized after it.[20] Accordingly, the answer to the question, strategy about what, is: potentially about anything. About products and processes, customers and citizens, social responsibilities and self interests, control and color.

Two aspects of the content of strategies must, however, be singled out because they are of particular importance and, accordingly, play major roles in the literature.

STRATEGY AS POSITION

The fourth definition is that strategy is a position—specifically, a means of locating an organization in what organization theorists like to call an "environment." By this definition, strategy becomes the mediating force—or "match," according to Hofer and Schendel[21]—between organization and environment, that is, between the internal and the external context. In ecological terms, strategy becomes a "niche"; in economic terms, a place that generates "rent" (that is "returns to [being] in a 'unique' place"[22]); in management terms, formally, a product-market "domain,"[23] the place in the environment where resources are concentrated (leading McNichols to call this "root strategy"[24]).

Note that this definition of strategy can be compatible with either (or all) of the preceding ones: a position can be preselected and aspired to through a plan (or ploy) and/or it can be reached, perhaps even found, through a pattern of behavior ("the concept of strategy need not be tied to rational planning or even

conscious decision-making assumptions. Strategy is essentially a descriptive idea that includes an organization's choice of niche and its primary decision rules ... for coping with that niche")[25].

In military and game theory views of strategy, it is generally used in the context of what is called a "two-person game," better known in business as head-on competition (where ploys are especially common). The definition of strategy as position, however, implicitly allows us to open up the concept, to so-called n-person games (that is, many players), and beyond. In other words, while position can always be defined with respect to a single competitor (literally so in the military, where position becomes the site of battle), it can also be considered in the context of a number of competitors or simply with respect to markets or an environment at large.[26] Since head-on competition is not the usual case in business, management theorists have generally focussed on the n-person situation, although they have tended to retain the notion of economic competition.[27] But strategy as position can extend beyond competition too, economic and otherwise. Indeed, what is the meaning of the word "niche" but a position that is occupied to avoid competition.

Thus, we can move from the definition employed by General Ulysses Grant in the 1860s, "Strategy [is] the deployment of one's resources in a manner which is most likely to defeat the enemy," to that of Professor Rumelt in the 1980s. "Strategy is creating situations for economic rents and finding ways to sustain them,[28] that is, any viable position, whether or not directly competitive.

Astley and Fombrun, in fact, take the next logical step by introducing the notion of "collective" strategy, that is, strategy pursued to promote cooperation between organization, even would-be competitors (equivalent in biology to animals herding together for protection).[29] Such strategies can range "from informal arrangements and discussion to formal devices such as interlocking directorates, joint ventures, and mergers."[30] In fact, considered from a slightly different angle, these can sometimes be described as political strategies, that is strategies to subvert the legitimate forces of competition.

STRATEGY AS PERSPECTIVE

While the fourth definition of strategy looks out, seeking to locate the organization in the external environment, the fifth looks inside the organization, indeed inside the heads of the collective strategist. Here, strategy is a perspective, its content consisting not just of a chosen position, but of an ingrained way of perceiving the world. Some organizations, for example, are aggressive pacesetters, creating new technologies and exploiting new markets; others perceive the world as set and stable, and so sit back in long established markets and build protective shells around themselves, relying more on political influence than economic efficiency. There are organizations that favor marketing and build a whole ideology around that (an IBM); others treat engineering in this way (a Hewlett-Packard); and then there are those that concentrate on sheer productive efficiency (a McDonald's).

Strategy in this respect is to the organization what personality is to the individual. Indeed, one of the earliest and most influential writers on strategy (at least as his ideas have been reflected in more popular writings) was Philip Selznick, who wrote about the "character" of an organization—distinct and integrated "commitments to ways of acting and responding" that are built right into it.[31] A variety of concepts from other fields also capture this notion: psychologists refer to an individual's mental frame, cognitive structure, and a variety of other expressions for "relatively fixed patterns for experiencing [the] world"[32]; anthropologists refer to the "culture" of a society and sociologists to its "ideology"; military theorists write of the "grand strategy" of armies; while management theorists have used terms such as the "theory of the business"[33] and its "driving force"[34]; behavioral scientists who have read Kuhn[35] on the philosophy of science refer to the "paradigm" of a community of scholars; and Germans perhaps capture it best with their word "Weltanschauung," literally "worldview," meaning collective intuition about how the world works.

This fifth definition suggests above all that strategy is a concept. This has one important implication, namely, that all strategies are abstractions which exist only in the minds of interested parties—those who pursue them, are influenced by that pursuit, or care to observe others doing so. It is important to remember that no-one has ever seen a strategy or touched one; every strategy is an invention, a figment of someone's imagination, whether conceived of as intentions to regulate behavior before it takes place or inferred as patterns to describe behavior that has already occurred.

What is of key importance about this fifth definition, however, is that the perspective is shared. As implied in the words Weltanschauung, culture, and ideology (with respect to a society) or paradigm (with respect to a community of scholars), but not the word personality, strategy is a perspective shared by the members of an organization, through their intentions and/or by their actions. In effect, when we are talking of strategy in this context, we are entering the realm of the collective mind—individuals united by common thinking and/or behavior. A major issue in the study of strategy formation becomes, therefore, how to read that collective mind—to understand how intentions diffuse through the system called organization to become shared and how actions come to be exercised on a collective yet consistent basis.

INTERRELATING THE PS

As suggested above, strategy as both position and perspective can be compatible with strategy as plan and/or pattern. But, in fact, the relationships between these different definitions can be more involved than that. For example, while some consider perspective to be a plan (Lapierre writes of strategies as "dreams in search of reality"[36]; Summer, more prosaically, as "a comprehensive, holistic, gestalt, logical vision of some future alignment"[37]), others describe it as giving rise to plans (for example, as positions and/or patterns in some kind of implicit hierarchy). This is shown in figure 2a. Thus, Majone writes of "basic principles, commitments, and norms" that form the "policy core," while "plans, programs, and decisions" serve as the "protective belt."[38] Likewise, Hedberg and Jonsson claim that strategies, by which they mean "more or less well integrated sets of ideas and constructs" (in our terms, perspectives) are "the causes that mold streams of decisions into patterns."[39] This is similar to Tregoe and Zimmerman who define strategy as "vision directed"—"the framework which guides those choices that determine the nature and direction of an organization."[40] Note in the second and third of these quotations that, strictly speaking, the hierarchy can skip a step, with perspective dictating pattern, not necessarily through formally intended plans.

Consider the example of the Honda Company, which has been described in one highly publicized consulting report[41] as parlaying a particular perspective (being a low cost producer, seeking to attack new markets in aggressive ways) into a plan, in the form of an intended position (to capture the traditional motorcycle market in the United States and create a new one for small family motorcycles), which was in turn realized through an integrated set of patterns (lining up distributorships, developing the appropriate advertising campaign of "You meet the nicest people on a Honda," etc.) All of this matches the conventional prescriptive view of how strategies are supposed to get made.[42]

But a closer look at Honda's actual behavior suggests a very different story: it did not go to America with the main intention of selling small, family motorcycles at all; rather, the company seemed to fall into that market almost inadvertently.[43] But once it was clear to the Honda executives that they had wandered into such a lucrative strategic position, that presumably became their plan. In other words, their strategy emerged, step by step, but once recognized, was made deliberate. Honda, if you like, developed its intentions through its actions, another way of saying that pattern evoked plan. This is shown in figure 2b.

Of course, an overall strategic perspective (Honda's way of doing things) seems to have underlaid all this, as shown in the figure as well. But we may still ask how that perspective arose in the first place. The answer seems to be that it did so in a similar way, through earlier experiences: the organization tried various things in its formative years and gradually consolidated a perspective around what worked.[44] In other words, organizations would appear to develop "character"—much as people develop personality —by interacting with the world as they find it through the use of their innate skills and natural propensities. Thus pattern can give rise to perspective too, as shown in figure 2c. And so can position. Witness Perrow's discussion of the "wool men" and "silk men" of the textile trade, people who developed an almost religious dedication to the fibers they produced.[45]

No matter how they appear, however, there is reason to believe that while plans and positions may be dispensable, perspectives are immutable.[46] In other words, once they are established, perspectives become difficult to change. Indeed, a perspective may become so deeply ingrained in the behavior of an organization that the associated beliefs can become subconscious in the minds of its members. When that happens, perspective can come to look more like pattern than like plan—in other words, it can be found more in the consistency of behaviors than in the articulation of intentions.

Of course, if perspective is immutable, then change in plan and position is difficult unless compatible with

figure 2   Some Possible Relationships Between Strategy as Plan, Pattern, Position, Perspective

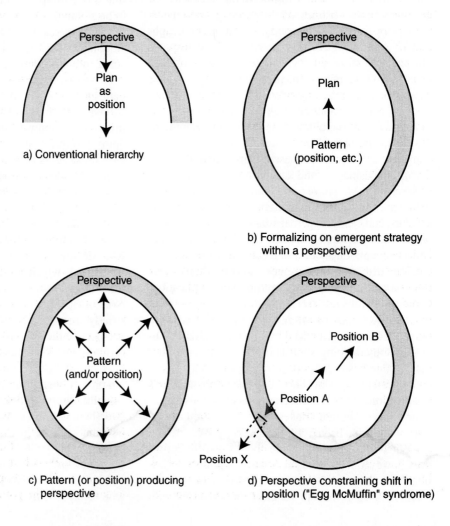

a) Conventional hierarchy

b) Formalizing on emergent strategy within a perspective

c) Pattern (or position) producing perspective

d) Perspective constraining shift in position ("Egg McMuffin" syndrome)

the existing perspective. As shown in figure 2d, the organization can shift easily from Position A to Position B but not to Position X. In this regard, it is interesting to take up the case of Egg McMuffin. Was this product when new—the American breakfast in a bun—a strategic change for the McDonald's fast food chain? Posed in MBA classes, this earth-shattering (or at least stomach-shattering) question inevitably evokes heated debate. Proponents (usually people sympathetic to fast food) argue that of course it was: it brought McDonald's into a new market, the breakfast one, extending the use of existing facilities. Opponents retort that this is nonsense, nothing changed but a few ingredients: this was the same old pap in a new package. Both sides are, or course, right—and wrong. It simply depends on how you define strategy. Position changed; perspective remained the same. Indeed—and this is the point—the position could be changed so easily because it was compatible with the existing perspective. Egg McMuffin is pure McDonald's, not only in product and package, but also in production and propagation. But imagine a change of position at McDonald's that would require a change of perspective—say, to introduce candlelight dining with personal service (your McDuckling à l'orange cooked to order) to capture the late evening market. We needn't say more, except perhaps to label this the "Egg McMuffin syndrome."

THE NEED FOR ECLECTICISM IN DEFINITION

While various relationships exist among the different definitions, no one relationship, nor any single definition for that matter, takes precedence over the others. In some ways, these definitions compete (in that they can substitute for each other), but in perhaps more important ways, they complement. Not all plans become patterns nor are all patterns that develop planned; some ploys are less than positions; while other strategies are more than positions yet less than perspectives. Each definition adds important elements to our understanding of strategy, indeed encourages us to address fundamental questions about organizations in general.

As plan, strategy deals with how leaders try to establish direction for organizations, to set them on predetermined courses of action. Strategy as plan also raises the fundamental issue of cognition—how intentions are conceived in the human brain in the first place, indeed, what intentions really mean. Are

we, for example, to take statements of intentions at face value? Do people always say what they mean, or mean what they say? Ostensible strategies as ploys can be stated just to fool competitors; sometimes, however, those who state them fool themselves. Thus, the road to hell in this field can be paved with those who take all stated intentions at face value. In studying strategy as plan, we must somehow get into the mind of the strategist, to find out what is really intended.

As ploy, strategy takes us into the realm of direct competition, where threats and feints and various other maneuvers are employed to gain advantage. This places the process of strategy formation in its most dynamic setting, with moves provoking countermoves and so on. Yet ironically, strategy itself is a concept rooted not in change but in stability—in set plans and established patterns. How then to reconcile the dynamic notions of strategy as ploy with the static ones of strategy as pattern and other forms of plan?

As pattern, strategy focusses on action, reminding us that the concept is an empty one if it does not take behavior into account. Strategy as pattern also introduces another important phenomenon in organizations, that of convergence, the achievement of consistency in behavior. How does this consistency form, where does it come from? Realized strategy is an important means of conceiving and describing the direction actually pursued by organizations, and when considered alongside strategy as plan, encourages us to consider the notion that strategies can emerge as well as be deliberately imposed.

As position, strategy encourages us to look at organizations in context, specifically in their competitive environments—how they find their positions and protect them in order to meet competition, avoid it, or subvert it. This enables us to think of organizations in ecological terms, as organisms in niches that struggle for survival in a world of hostility and uncertainty as well as symbiosis. How much choice do organizations have, how much room for maneuver?

And finally as perspective, strategy raises intriguing questions about intention and behavior in a collective context. If we define organization as collective action in the pursuit of common mission (a fancy way of saying that a group of people under a common label—whether an IBM or a United Nations or a Luigi's Body Shop—somehow find the means to cooperate in the production of specific goods and services), then strategy as perspective focusses our attention on the reflections and actions of the collectivity—how intentions diffuse through a group of people to become shared as norms and values, and how patterns of behavior become deeply ingrained in the group. Ultimately, it is this view of strategy that offers us the best hope of coming to grips with the most fascinating issue of all, that of the "organizational mind."

Thus, strategy is not just a notion of how to deal with an enemy or a set of competitors or a market, as it is treated in so much of the literature and in its popular usage. It also draws us into some of the most fundamental issues about organizations as instruments for collective perception and action.

To conclude, a good deal of the confusion in this field stems from contradictory and ill-defined uses of the term strategy, as we saw in the Egg McMuffin syndrome. By explicating and using five definitions, we may be able to remove some of this confusion, and thereby enrich our ability to understand and manage the processes by which strategies form.

References

1 P. F. Drucker, *Management: Tasks, Responsibilities, Practices* (New York, NY: Harper & Row, 1974), p. 104.

2 Moore, in fact, prefers not to associate the word strategy with the word plan per se: "The term plan is much too static for our purposes unless qualified. There is not enough of the idea of scheming or calculation with an end in view in it to satisfy us. Plans are used to build ships. Strategies are used to achieve ends among people. You simply do not deal strategically with inanimate objects." But Moore certainly supports the characteristics of intentionality. D. G. Moore, "Managerial strategies," in W. L. Warner and N. H. Martin, needs., *Industrial Man: Businessmen and Business Organizations* (New York, NY: Harper & Row, 1959), pp. 220, 226.

3 C. Von Clausewitz, *On War*, translated by M. Howard and P. Paret (Princeton, NJ: Princeton University Press, 1976), p. 177.

4 J. Von Newmann and O. Morgenstern, *Theory of Games and Economic Behavior* (Princeton, NJ: Princeton University Press, 1944), p. 79.

5 W. F. Glueck, *Business Policy and Strategic Management*, 3rd Edition (New York, NY: McGraw-Hill, 1980), p. 9.

6 *Random House Dictionary*.

7 M. F. Porter, *Competitive Strategy: Techniques for Analyzing Industries and Competitors* (New York, NY: The Free Press, 1980).

8 M. E. Porter, *Competitive Advantage: Creating and Sustaining Superior Performance* (New York, NY: The Free Press, 1985).

9 T. C. Schelling, *The Strategy of Conflict*, 2nd Edition (Cambridge, MA: Harvard University Press, 1980).

10 H. Mintzberg, "Research on strategy-making," *Proceedings After the 32nd Annual Meeting of the Academy of Management*, Minneapolis, 1972, pp. 90–94; M. Mintzberg, "Patterns in strategy formation," *Management Science*, 24/9 (1978):934–948; H. Mintzberg and J. A. Waters, "Of strategies, deliberate and emergent," *Strategic Management Journal*, 6/3 (1985): 257–272.

11 Evered discusses the Greek origins of the word and traces its entry into contemporary Western vocabulary through the military. R. Evered, "So what is strategy," *Long Range Planning*, 16/3 (1983):57–72.

12 As suggested in the results of a questionnaire by Ragab and Paterson; M. Ragab and W. E. Paterson, "An exploratory study of the strategy construct," proceedings of the Administrative Sciences Association of Canada Conference, 1981. Two notable exceptions are Herbert Simon and Jerome Bruner and his colleagues; H. A. Simon, *Administrative Behavior*, 2nd Edition (New York, NY: Macmillan, 1957); J. S. Bruner, J. J. Goodnow, and G. A. Austin, *A Study of Thinking* (New York, NY: Wiley, 1956), pp. 54–55.

13 Quoted in J. B. Quinn, *Strategies for Change: Logical Incrementalism* (Homewood, IL: Richard D. Irwin, 1980), p. 35.

14 *Business Week*, October 31, 1983.

15 Via G. Majone, "The uses of policy analysis," in *The Future and the Past: Essays on Programs, Russell Sage Foundation Annual Report*, 1976–1977, pp. 201–220.

16 A. D. Chandler, *Strategy and Structure: Chapters in the History of the Industrial Enterprise* (Cambridge, MA: M.I.T. Press, 1962), p. 13.

17 Von Clausewitz, op. cit., p. 128.

18 B. Franklin, *Poor Richard's Almanac* (New York, NY: Ballantine Books, 1977), p. 280.

19 R. P. Rumelt, "Evaluation of strategy: theory and models," in D. E. Schendel and C. W. Hofer, needs., *Strategic Management: A New View of Business Policy and Planning* (Boston, MA: Little Brown, 1979), pp. 196–212.

20 We might note a similar problem with "policy," a word whose usage is terribly confused. In the military, the word has traditionally served one notch in the hierarchy above

strategy, in business one notch below, and in public administration in general as a substitute. In the military, policy deals with the purposes for which wars are fought, which is supposed to be the responsibility of the politicians. In other words, the politicians make policy; the generals, strategy. But modern warfare has confused this usage (see Summers), so that today strategy in the military context has somehow come to be associated with the acquisition of nuclear weapons and their use against non-military targets. In business, while "policy" has been the label for the entire field of study of general management (at least until "strategic management" gained currency in the 1970s), its technical use was as a general rule to dictate decisions in a specific case, usually a standard and recurring situation, as in "Our policy is to require long-range forecasts every four months." Accordingly, management planning theorists, such as George Steiner, describe policies as deriving from strategies although some textbook writers (such as Leontiades, Chang and Campo-Flores, and Peter Drucker) have used the two words in exactly the opposite way, as in the military. This reflects the fact that "policy" was the common word in the management literature before "strategy" replaced it in the 1960s (see, for example, Jamison, and Gross and Gross). But in the public sector today, the words "policy" and "policymaking" correspond roughly to "strategy" and "strategy making." H. G. Summers, On Strategy: The Vietnam War in Context (Carlisle Barracks, PA: Strategic Studies Institute, U.S. Army War College, 1981); G. A. Steiner, *Top Management Planning* (New York, NY: Macmillan, 1969), p. 264 ff; M. Leontiades, *Management Policy, Strategy and Plans* (Boston, MA: Little Brown, 1982), p. 4; Y.N.A. Chang and F. Campo-Flores, *Business Policy and Strategy* (Goodyear, 1980), p. 7; Drucker, op. cit., p. 104; C. L. Jamison, *Business Policy* (Englewood Cliffs, NJ: Prentice-Hall, 1953); A. Gross and W. Gross, needs., *Business Policy: Selected Readings and Editorial Commentaries* (New York, NY: Ronald Press, 1967).

21 C. W. Hofer and D. Schendel, *Strategy Formulation: Analytical Concepts* (St. Paul, MN: West Publishing, 1978), p. 4.

22 E. H. Bowman, "Epistomology, corporate strategy, and academe," *Sloan Management Review*, 15/2 (1974):47.

23 J. D. Thompson, *Organizations in Action* (New York, NY: McGraw-Hill, 1967).

24 T. J. McNichols, *Policy-Making and Executive Action* (New York, NY: McGraw-Hill, 1983), p. 257.

25 Rumelt, op. cit., p. 4.

26 R. P. Rumelt, "The evaluation of business strategy," in W. F. Glueck, *Business Policy and Strategic Management*, 3rd Edition (New York, NY: McGraw-Hill, 1980), p. 361.

27 E.g., Porter, op. cit. (1980, 1985), except for his chapters noted earlier, which tend to have a 2-person competitive focus.

28 Expressed at the Strategic Management Society Conference, Paris, October 1982.

29 W. G. Astley and C. J. Fombrun, "Collective strategy: social ecology of organizational environments," *Academy of Management Review*, 8/4 (1983):576–587.

30 Ibid., p. 577.

31 P. Selznick, Leadership in Administration: A Sociological Interpretation (New York, NY: Harper & Row, 1957), p. 47. A subsequent paper by the author (in process) on the "design school" of strategy formation shows the link of Selznick's early work to the writings of Kenneth Andrews in the Harvard policy textbook. K. R. Andrews, *The Concept of Corporate Strategy*, Revised Edition (Homewood, IL: Dow Jones-Irwin, 1987).

32 J. Bieri, "Cognitive structures in personality," in H. M. Schroder and P. Suedfeld, needs., *Personality: Theory and Information Processing* (New York, NY: Ronald Press, 1971), p. 178. By the same token, Bieri (p. 179) uses the word "strategy" in the context of psychology.

33 Drucker, op. cit.

34 B. B. Tregoe and J. W. Zimmerman, *Top Management Strategy* (New York, NY: Simon & Schuster, 1980).

35 T. S. Kuhn, *The Structure of Scientific Revolution, 2nd Edition* (Chicago, IL: University of Chicago Press, 1970).

36 My own translation of "un rêve ou un bouquet de rêves en quête de réalité." L. Lapierre, "Le changement stratégique: Un rêve en quête de réel," Ph.D. Management Policy course paper, McGill University, Canada, 1980.

37 Summer, op. cit., p. 18.

38 G. Majone, op. cit.

39 B. Hedberg and S.A. Jonsson, "Strategy formulation as a discontinuous process," *International Studies of Management and Organization*, 7/2 (1977):90.

40 Tregoe and Zimmerman, op. cit., p. 17.

41 Boston Consulting Group, *Strategy Alternatives for the British Motorcycle Industry* (London: Her Majesty's Stationery Office, 1975).

42 E.g., H. I. Ansoff, Corporate Strategy (New York, NY: McGraw-Hill, 1965); Andrews. op. cit.; Steiner, op. cit.; D. E. Schendel and C. H. Hofer, needs., *Strategic Management: A New View of Business Policy and Planning* (Boston, MA: Little Brown, 1979), p. 15.

43 R. T. Pascale, "Perspectives on strategy: the real story behind Honda's success," *California Management Review*, 26/3 (Spring 1984):47–72.

44 J. B. Quinn, "Honda Motor Company case," in J. B. Quinn, H. Mintzberg, and B. G. James, *The Strategy Process: Concepts, Contexts, Cases* (Englewood Cliffs, NJ: Prentice-Hall, 1988).

45 C. Perrow, *Organizational Analysis: A Sociological View* (Belmont, CA: Wadsorth, 1970), p. 161.

46 E.g., N. Brunsson, "The irrationality of action and action rationality: decisions, ideologies, and organizational actions," *Journal of Management Studies*, 19/1 (1982): 29–44.